# Surfing the South

# Surfing the South

## The Search for Waves and the People Who Ride Them

**Steve Estes**

THE UNIVERSITY OF NORTH CAROLINA PRESS

*Chapel Hill*

*This book was published with the assistance of the
Fred W. Morrison Fund of the University of North Carolina Press.*

Designed by Jamison Cockerham
Set in Scala and Cooper
by codeMantra

Cover illustration: Man with surfboard in Outer Banks,
NC © Margaret619 / Dreamstime.com.

*Manufactured in the United States of America*

The University of North Carolina Press has been a
member of the Green Press Initiative since 2003.

LIBRARY OF CONGRESS CATALOGING-IN-PUBLICATION DATA
Names: Estes, Steve, 1972– author.
Title: Surfing the South : the search for waves and
the people who ride them / Steve Estes.
Description: Chapel Hill : The University of North
Carolina Press, [2022] | Includes bibliographical
references and index.
Identifiers: LCCN 2021049356 |
ISBN 9781469667775 (paperback) |
ISBN 9781469667782 (ebook)
Subjects: LCSH: Surfing—Southern States. |
Surfing—Social aspects—Southern States.
Classification: LCC GV839.5.S9 E77 2022 |
DDC 797.3/20975—dc23/eng/20211020
LC record available at https://lccn.loc.gov/2021049356

*For Carol and Zinnia*

My object in living is to unite

My avocation and my vocation

As my two eyes make one in sight.

Only where love and need are one,

And the work is play for mortal stakes,

Is the deed ever really done

For Heaven and the future's sakes.


*Robert Frost, "Two Tramps in Mud Time"*

# Contents

# Illustrations

# Surfing
# the South

# *Introduction*
# **Dawn Patrol**

Glenn Tanner works at the paper mill north of Charleston, South Carolina. This week, he will have six twelve-hour shifts in as many days. He grumbles that the company would rather pay existing workers overtime than hire new ones and pay more benefits. Even though the hours are tough, Glenn is sticking it out. He is closing in on retirement and can see the light at the end of the tunnel. Only, in Glenn's case, it's sunlight illuminating the opening of a head-high, glassy tube as the Atlantic Ocean barrels into the Carolina coast.

Glenn was the second surfer I interviewed for a project on surfing in the American South. The interview took place 200 yards from the ocean after a dawn patrol surf session at the Folly Beach pier in South Carolina. Glenn insisted that we meet in the water. A storm brewed. Lightning forked menacingly a few miles offshore. None of that mattered to Glenn. He was most comfortable in the ocean, and perhaps he wanted to test me.

We surfed waist-high, choppy waves that morning, mostly lefts, breaking haphazardly southward away from the pier. Like many mediocre sessions on the Carolina coast, the waves that morning didn't peel cleanly down the line like those at point breaks in California or reef breaks in Hawaii. Folly is a beach break. Most of the surf is produced by winds close to the Atlantic seaboard, driving ocean water over shallow, shifting sandbars. Although these wind swells can occasionally pulse in long, clean lines, they often produce short, chopped-up sections of waves that require skill to link together lengthy rides.

Decades of surfing Folly and other southern breaks gave Glenn Tanner an uncanny surfing vision. Glenn spied oncoming waves long before anyone else. A novice might see nothing but windswept chaos on the surface of the ocean. An intermediate surfer might watch the rise and fall of swell on the pilings at the end pier to anticipate a set of breaking waves. An expert like Glenn could scan the horizon, reading subtle shifts in the ocean to distinguish between unrideable wind chop and a roller that might form into a wall with more potential. At one point, Glenn hooted me into what looked like a weak, tiny bump on the ocean's surface, I turned toward the beach in anticipation, but pulled back, judging the wave unworthy of the effort. Of course, the small bump grew into a beautiful little left that could have been my best ride of the day. Glenn had known. I should have listened.

Glenn had a sixth sense of how to navigate short sections of the Carolina beach break with well-timed turns. Masterful cutbacks allowed him to weave far down the beach from where he initially took off. He made Folly look like Malibu on his old Hansen longboard, cross-stepping back and forth to accelerate down the line or maneuver back toward the breaking whitewater. The sixty-one-year-old waterman could curl his toes over the nose or stomp on the tail to turn nimbly as if he were a much younger man on a much shorter board. After each ride, he'd paddle back out to the line-up with a grin. This wasn't a look of self-satisfaction, the not-so-subtle claim of pride flashed by many surfers after particularly good rides. Glenn's smile said simply, "This is where I am meant to be."

A few hours later, as I laid my recorder on Glenn's antique longboard, he was circumspect about his millwork, but when I asked him about the ocean, his answers stretched out in long, swooping arcs that mirrored his classic surf style. He spoke proudly about winning the U.S. Surfing Championship on the Outer Banks in 1982. At that moment, he was no longer some guy that worked at the paper mill. He was a savvy competitive surfer, one who held his own against some of the best wave riders in the country.

Perhaps I should come clean. Compared to folks like Glenn Tanner, I am a kook. After more than thirty years of surfing, it's hard to acknowledge this. For non-surfers, a kook is basically someone like you—a novice who takes a surfboard out into the ocean and flails around where the waves break. If veterans like Glenn always seem to be in the right place at the right time to catch waves, kooks have a similarly uncanny ability to find themselves in the perfect spot to sabotage the rides of better surfers. As in any sport, surfing ability exists along a spectrum. Who you deem to be a kook depends on your level of experience, where you have surfed, and for how long.

There are many folks like Glenn Tanner who hail from the southern coast of the United States and who are naturals, born to ride. They surf big waves well and small waves even better. Some southern surfers rank among the best in the world. Some travel the globe to charge monstrous waves that break above razor sharp reefs and fearsome rocks. Many of these people have been surfing for more than half a century. They are decidedly not kooks. If I wanted to learn about the South and surfing, I needed to talk to them. More important, I needed to listen.

The tales I heard came from a cast of characters stranger and more wonderful than fiction. The retired Mississippi riverboat captain and alligator hunter who was one of the first people to surf the Gulf Coast of Louisiana. The sheet-metal worker from Pensacola who ran the China Beach Surf Club while he was stationed in Vietnam. The Daytona Beach swimsuit model who shot the curl in the 1966 World Surfing Championships before circumnavigating the globe in search of waves and adventure. The Virginia Beach entrepreneur who bought half of a surf shop for less than $1,000 in the 1970s and became a millionaire when he sold his stake in what became an international surf brand. These stories chronicle not only the history of southern surfing but, in a sense, the modern South. They reflect many of the major trends that shaped the region and nation since World War II: Cold War militarization, civil rights, the counterculture, the women's movement, environmentalism, and coastal development.

Over two summers, I traveled along the Gulf Coast and then up the Atlantic Seaboard to ride waves and chat with longtime surfers at breaks along the way. In a journey that stretched nearly 2,500 miles, I interviewed over forty surfers from all walks of life. Invariably, the conversations extended far beyond riding waves. We talked about life in and out of the water. The common perception of southern swells is that they pale in comparison to their California cousins and Hawaiian elders. This is mostly true, but, as I found out from my trip to surf in the American South, anywhere with waves can produce wild surf and even wilder surfers.

As a native southerner, I am used to reading books on the region by outsiders who caricature the place. These authors find the most exotic locales and freakiest folk to provide local color, but their works often seem to paint by numbers, reinforcing stereotypes. On the other hand, I have no patience for "defense of Dixie" accounts that turn a blind eye to the problems of the

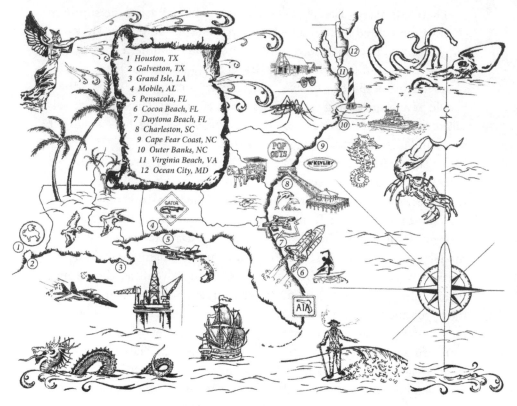

A southern surf odyssey.
*By Philip Estes.*

The map legend reads:

1 Houston, TX
2 Galveston, TX
3 Grand Isle, LA
4 Mobile, AL
5 Pensacola, FL
6 Cocoa Beach, FL
7 Daytona Beach, FL
8 Charleston, SC
9 Cape Fear Coast, NC
10 Outer Banks, NC
11 Virginia Beach, VA
12 Ocean City, MD

region. Instead, I sought a balance between the inherent sympathies of a native southerner and the critical objectivity of a California outsider. I realized that I was both part of the "we" and the "y'all" of the story.

My twelve-year-old daughter, Zinnia, accompanied me on the journey. Born in California, she had little firsthand knowledge of the South other than brief visits to see relatives in South Carolina and Florida. The trip became a way to connect Zinnia to our southern roots, to reveal the world that shaped us. I hoped that she would connect to my southern heritage and that this connection, in turn, would help us to bond just as she was entering her rebellious teenage years.

When I set out to explore the history of southern surfing and my own southern heritage, I understood that this was a near-impossible task—not too dissimilar from learning to surf at the aptly named Folly Beach in South Carolina. Surf sagas mix history, memory, and myth. This book blends all three in a quest to find and ride the southern swell.

# 1

# *A Fool's Errand*
## Houston, Texas

Even under the best of circumstances, surf trips result in epic failures as often as they yield great waves. I *designed* this trip to be a failure, at least on the wave front. This was not going to be your average surf trip. It was going to be far below average. Not surprisingly, when I asked surf buddies to join me, most had other plans. Bald friends had to wash their hair. Folks living in concrete jungles had to mow their lawns. Only my daughter, Zinnia, agreed to come along. We headed to the Gulf Coast in the early summer, before hurricane season pumped beautiful groundswells toward the southern coasts and after the winter storms kicked up rugged, ridable surf. In other words, the waves were probably going to suck. Despite all evidence to the contrary, I told Zinnia that the surf would be fun.

Surfers are the best liars. We lie to ourselves to motivate trips to the water even when the forecast, report, and beach cameras provide solid evidence that we are wrong. Once we've lied to ourselves, we can, in all sincerity, lie to our buddies. We now believe that the .00001 percent chance of good surf has suddenly become a fifty-fifty proposition. That probability nearly doubles if we can convince just one more sucker to join us. The sucker in this case was my own flesh and blood. Like the dutiful daughter that she is, Zinnia said, "Let's go!"

It's the Cardinal Rule of surfing that the waves were always better just before you arrived at any beach. With a shake of their heads, locals taunt the traveler: "You should've been here yesterday . . . or last week . . . or last month!" As I made advance calls to plan interviews on the Gulf Coast before the trip, surfers and surf shop owners told me that I was missing an epic swell. A storm in the southern Gulf had coincided with light offshore winds at a number of beaches from Texas through the Florida panhandle.

It was overhead and glassy for a few days. Never fear. That swell would be long gone by the time Zinnia and I arrived.

We flew from San Francisco to Houston, landing with plenty of time to interview one of the pioneers of the surf industry in Texas. Before I left California, folks had told me that if I came through Houston, I had to track down BJ Williamson. BJ was as close as the Gulf Coast came to a surf mogul in the 1960s and '70s. He owned nine different surf shops in Texas and Louisiana over the years, making him a resident expert on the industry.

I got in touch with BJ not long after we landed and rented an SUV for our trip. He was just finishing up lunch at Buffalo Wild Wings in the Houston suburb of Katy. We could meet him there. This was far out of the way, and a sports bar is probably the worst place to record an interview, but I was sure it would all work out. I figured that we'd race to Katy, do the interview, and then get back on the 610 Loop before what I seemed to recall was the mildly annoying rush hour traffic of the Houston metro area.

If you have not been to Buffalo Wild Wings, how can you call yourself an American or say that you have really lived? The nondescript suburban sports bar's tagline should be "We're Hooters . . . without the hooters." BJ met us at the door and escorted us past the lightly populated, spacious restaurant to the absolutely empty, cavernous bar. About twenty-five to thirty flat-screen TVs hung on the walls. There may have been a cricket match in the remote mountains of Pakistan at that moment that was not visible, but no American or European sporting event seemed beyond the reach and remote control of the Buffalo Wild Wings bartender. At BJ's request, the bartender kindly reduced the deafening cacophony of play-by-play and commentary to mere earsplitting levels.

It soon became apparent that Buffalo Wild Wings was not just BJ's favorite sports bar, but also his office. He had a computer *and* printer set up on one of the bar tables along the wall by a bank of arcade games. My daughter noticed during the interview that BJ's name dominated the leaderboard on a nearby Golden Tee arcade game. I was immediately suspicious when I saw the computer/printer setup and the easy familiarity with which BJ interacted with the Buffalo Wild Wings staff. Then, I realized that this wasn't too different from the hip coffeehouse work spaces of high-flying tech coders in San Francisco. Just substitute an inexpensive pint of beer for an overpriced shot of espresso, and you've got the twenty-first-century Houston office cubicle. The volume of the TVs might have been a bit high, but BJ's overhead remained low.

The former surf shop mogul who greeted us wore the weathered skin of a lifelong surfer and shaper. I knew from talking to him on the phone that he was a little manic, speaking in long, passionate monologues about a sport and business that had consumed his life in more ways than one. I barely had time to order Zinnia some boneless wings and turn on my recorder before BJ launched into his surfing history.

~~~~~~~~~~~~~~~~~~~~~~~~~~~~~~~~~~~~~~~~~~~~~~~~~~~~~~~~~~~~~~~~~

BJ Williamson caught his first wave in 1960, the same year that legendary Texas shaper Henry Fry began crafting the first generation of home-brewed Gulf Coast boards. BJ wasn't riding a Fry. He rented mass-produced boards on family trips to Galveston until he scraped together the money to buy his own. When friends started asking BJ if he could get them boards, the budding entrepreneur found the contact information for California board makers in the back of surfing magazines and asked if he could become their official Texas dealer. BJ founded his business while still in high school, hawking T-shirts, decals, and stickers of major surf brands from his childhood home. Starting in 1964, he sold boards by California luminaries like Hobie Alter, Greg Noll, and Dewey Weber.

Like many of the early southern surf shops, BJ's started out with a tiny budget as a subsidiary to another business. In BJ's case, he sold boards out of his mom's paint store. By the early 1960s, beach communities in California and Hawaii had enough surfers to support full-fledged shops, dedicated solely to the sport. Southern surfers had to find boards wherever they could get them—a dive shop in Alabama or department store in Florida. In Folly Beach, South Carolina, Dennis McKevlin started selling boards out of the back of a bowling alley. BJ's shoestring operation in suburban Houston had good company.

BJ's shops capitalized on the growing popularity of surfing throughout the 1960s, but also on the exploding population of Houston and the Gulf Coast. Houston wasn't even ranked among the top ten cities in the nation in 1950, when just over half a million people called the city home. By 1970 the population had more than doubled to over 1.2 million people in what was by then the sixth largest city in the United States. When I arrived in the city for college in 1990, Houston staked its claim as the fourth largest city in the country, a position it holds to this day.

People moved to Houston because of jobs in oil, aerospace, medicine, real estate, finance, and education. Just about any economic sector you can name grew by leaps and bounds. This growth defined the Sun Belt boom that started in the 1960s. Cities from Los Angeles to Houston, San Diego to Miami threw shade on the old centers of American industry in the Midwest and Northeast. Surfing became both a metaphor and a product of these dramatic changes.

The Sun Belt seemed a perfect incubator for a young surf shop. Still, BJ and other entrepreneurs needed potential customers to walk through the doors. The baby boom that began right after World War II fueled demand for surfboards and other products. Teenagers coming of age in the late 1950s and early 1960s sought ways to separate themselves from their parents, to carve out new identities. The sleek lines of longboards epitomized modern design while also harkening back to an ancient Hawaiian tradition. This combination felt exciting and authentic even after countless Beach Boys hits and *Beach Party* movies diluted the coolness of surf culture. People associate surfing in this period with southern California, but BJ and southern shop owners like him knew a secret. Most southern kids couldn't make it to the West Coast, but they could buy a piece of the California dream from the local surf shop.

In the mid-1960s, as surf fever swept eastward from California across the Texas Gulf Coast, BJ's shops became the number one dealers of Dewey Weber boards in the country. A fair number of the folks I talked to in Texas learned on a Weber Performer in the 1960s, and many of those boards came from one of BJ's nine surf shops. His motto: "Have a nice wave!"

The nice wave of surfing popularity in Texas crested in the late 1960s and then began to ebb. Some shops did fine in the 1970s. Texas oil booms brought buyers into stores with cash to burn, but as anyone with a cursory knowledge of the oil business knows, booms inevitably go bust. One Texas shop owner explained the cycle to me this way: "I was having these guys that were head engineers and CEOs of these companies coming in and spending wads of dough. Next thing I know, they're driving up in their trucks trying to sell me everything back. It was awful, dude, awful. They all lost their jobs. A few of them asked me for jobs, dude, to work at the surf shop for fucking minimum wage. It just broke my heart." Even with the occasional boost from oil booms, the Texas surf industry doldrums of the 1970s were a far cry from the golden era of the previous decade. BJ's shops limped along until he shuttered the last one in 1977.

After closing up shop, BJ worked various jobs in the oil industry and construction. He shaped boards with Henry Fry for a time and always maintained some connection to the surf industry. Recessions and a disastrous fire destroyed BJ's businesses, but they didn't crush his stoke. When we met at Buffalo Wild Wings, BJ was admittedly at a low point, but he was already dreaming of his next big entrepreneurial enterprise. Just chatting idly, he said he had been experimenting with ways to resuscitate delaminated boards, making them good as new. As Zinnia and I escaped the over-air-conditioned bar into the warm sunshine of the Texas afternoon, I really hoped that BJ's next big idea worked out.

~~~~~~~~~~~~~~~~~~~~~~~~~~~~~~~~~~~

During our brief stop in Houston, Zinnia and I had some time to kill, so I decided to take her on a tour of my old stomping grounds around Rice University. When I started thinking about where to apply for college in the late 1980s, I wanted to get far away from South Carolina but, ideally, stay close to the ocean. One high school surfer friend of mine went to Pepperdine, a stone's throw from the legendary break at Malibu. Another buddy chose North Carolina State, within striking distance of the Outer Banks. For reasons that defy logic, I went to college in Houston. Like thousands of other Houston surfers before me, trips to Galveston (with fingers crossed for swell) defined and limited my surfing life in college. When I chose Rice, my priorities were clearly screwed up. Still, I wanted to show Zinnia my alma mater, so off we went.

At eleven, my daughter, Zinnia, had just started exhibiting the first signs of a behavior pattern dreaded by all parents—teenage ennui. I know "ennui" sounds pretentious, but only the French could come up with a word to cover the crushing weight of feigned boredom that oppresses teenagers. Ennui also divides teens from their endlessly embarrassing parents. As a friend advised me when I was trying to decide whether to take Zinnia along on this trip, "You better do it now before she really starts to hate you." I may not have made it in time.

Oblivious to the few college students on campus for summer classes, I gestured wildly and spoke too loudly to Zinnia, pointing out the significant landmarks that punctuate any college tour. "Over there, you can see the bushes where your dad puked on his Adidas Sambas after a raging party called 'Night of Decadence'. And here's where your dad broke into the organ recital hall to experience the insane resonance of his Les Paul guitar." With such highlights, the tour proved mortifying for a disinterested daughter. I made Zinnia pose for a picture in front of the university founder's statue, where I had "played in lots of cool drum circles." As if to underscore the point that there are *no* cool drum circles, Zinnia flashed me a withering glare from beneath the flat bill of her baseball cap and then threw a gang sign at the camera.

~~~~~~~~~~~~~~~~~~~~~~~~~~~~~~~~~~~~

The last item on the agenda for Houston was to track down a used surfboard. Surely, somewhere in the greater megalopolis, an old log lay gathering dust in some garage or attic with my name on it. I had planned to buy one of a number of longboards that I had seen on Craigslist in the weeks leading up to the trip. This "plan" turned out to be a fool's errand.

Buying a board on Craigslist in the best of circumstances is a sketchy proposition. Sellers flake. They promise to meet you at the most inconvenient time in a distant location maddeningly lost in the 1 percent of North America that Google has yet to map. More often than not, they sell the board twenty minutes before you arrive to some dude for five dollars more than you were offering. Or maybe they give you the old bait and switch. The beautiful pictures of the pristine, hand-shaped board that you thought you were buying catfish into a dinged-up beater, MacGyvered with duct tape and chewing gum back in 1987. If those are the normal problems of local Craigslist commerce, imagine the complications of buying online from 1,500 miles away. Several boards I made offers on fell through. Still, there were two possibilities near Houston.

One of the Craigslist prospects was a beautiful nine-foot, six-inch longboard made by a reputable Florida shaper. There were a few red flags. The guy selling the board lived forty miles northwest of Houston, the opposite side of town from the beach. More ominously, he would take cash for the board, but he preferred to trade it for a four-wheeler, welding equipment, or guns. Perhaps you are hearing the banjo line from *Deliverance*. Or maybe you're the person in the horror movie audience that screams out "No, don't do it!" right before a likable character volunteers to investigate strange noises in the basement of a rented lake house. Look, I survived in Texas for four years. I wasn't too worried about buying a board from an adrenaline-fueled hobby welder and gun collector. Then again, I had my daughter with me. It might not be the smartest move to drive to a nondescript Houston suburb with hundreds of dollars in cash to haggle with Rando Rambo. Luckily, the guy didn't return my calls. He later explained via text that he had slept through our meeting. The board (bait?) was still listed on Craigslist two months later.

I had really been hoping to get the first board, even if I did have to trade some guns to get it. The second option looked much less appealing. Both boards measured nine feet six inches, but the similarity ended there. The first prospect had been shaped with care for performance—relatively narrow and thin with a nice bit of rocker. If that board had been a naval ship, it would have been a destroyer, large and fearsome, but still maneuverable. The inspiration for the second board—wide, thick, and flat for ease of paddling—must have been an aircraft carrier. Actually, this is unfair to carriers. A better comparison would be to a school bus . . . if a school bus could float. To make matters worse, this board was painted the same exact color as a school bus. That obnoxious yellow paintjob supposedly makes buses safer for their passengers. This board seemed to be painted for the safety of anyone unlucky enough to be surfing nearby.

The board had been made at Bingo's, a surf shop and café on the Gulf Coast not known especially for quality boards or food. One online review suggested that better eats and gear could be had down the street at a place called Kook's, which has since closed. Bingo's soldiers on.

With all of this advance research, I had low expectations for the Bingo Board. Part of me secretly hoped that the owner would continue my perfect record of Craigslist failures. Just when I had resigned myself to buying a used board from a shop in Galveston, my phone buzzed with an incoming text. It was about the Bingo Board. The text read, "I should be home by 5:00 P.M. and am happy to show it to you. Would you like to set a location in order to try and counter my potential ambush murder or just come by the house?"

I figured a crazed Craigslist murderer probably wouldn't lead with that, so we agreed to meet at his house in Friendswood, southeast of Houston. Friendswood is such a vanilla suburb that Kirk, the seller, warned me not to speed unless I "look like Flanders" from *The Simpsons*. Coincidentally, the older I get, the more I resemble Ned Flanders, minus the awesome paintbrush mustache. My daughter and I sped through Friendswood in our rented SUV. No cops even gave us a second glance.

Kirk turned out to be a former military guy about my age with tons of surf experience not only on the Gulf Coast, but around the world. In his garage, Kirk had an impressive quiver of boards. There was a bagged eight-foot fun-shape in the front of the rack. I wanted it sight unseen. Nope, that was his favorite board, not for sale. Sadly, I watched Kirk move a series of nice boards out of the way until he unearthed the Bingo Board from its shameful place at the back of the rack. The Bingo belonged to his brother. Its leash had snapped during an ill-fated session, sending the board careening toward some rocks. The boulders beat on the Bingo Board like a gang of mobsters in matching tracksuits, leaving the board pockmarked with dings. These boulders clearly knew what they were doing. Kirk patched the worst one of the dings, a gash on the right rail, and threw it up on Craigslist, hoping some fool would buy it.

The fool told Kirk about his crazy plans for the southern surf odyssey. Kirk nodded noncommittally. He exhibited the practiced poker face of a pro with a sucker on the line. We made small talk about the breaks in Texas. The best waves, he said were a six-hour drive the opposite direction from where I was headed. Of course, I had just missed a solid swell a few days earlier. The small talk wound down. I had a decision to make about the Bingo Board.

At this point, I was pretty desperate to buy the board despite all of its obvious flaws and blemishes. If I didn't close this deal, I was going to have to pay a shop hundreds more dollars for a similarly suspect log. My only real concern about the Bingo Board was that it didn't come with fins, a leash, or a bag, all of which were going to eat away at my already tiny budget. I voiced these concerns, and Kirk magically produced three bottom-of-the-barrel fins and a calf leash with a rusted swivel. Then, in a moment of charity or pity, he actually haggled me *down* in price for the board, fins, and leash. This was too easy. Was the Bingo Board a cursed artifact that could only be passed voluntarily to its next victim? Was that creepy old doll in the dark corner of Kirk's garage really tracking me with its googly eyes?

I came to the conclusion that this was a win-win transaction. Kirk was getting rid of a white elephant—or rather a school-bus-yellow one. I was acquiring a board that, while not exactly a work of art, would catch even the smallest ripple in the Gulf or Atlantic. Given that ripples constituted a best-case scenario for this trip, the Bingo Board made sense. After strapping the Craigslist miracle on the truck, a California kid and a mustacheless Ned Flanders raced toward a date with the wild waves of Galveston, Texas.

# 2

# If Everybody
# Had an Ocean
## Galveston, Texas

Before the advent of webcams and swell forecasts, surfers checked a series of beaches to make sure the waves weren't breaking better just down the road. The Tour de Galveston often began at the Sixty-First Street pier and then proceeded east along the seawall past the rock jetties (called "groins") at Fifty-Third, Fifty-First, and Thirty-Seventh Streets before getting to the Flagship Pier, now known as the Pleasure Pier. Depending on wind and swell direction, any one of these breaks or other "secret" spots might be going off.

More likely, however, none were. Surfers on the Gulf Coast, like those throughout the South, take pride in their local breaks, but they are not blind to the primary downfall of the region's surf: inconsistency. If absence (of swell) makes the heart grow fonder, Gulf Coast surfers got downright romantic talking about good days. "When Old Man Gulf and Lady Luck come arm-in-arm to the beach party," a local once wrote in the *Houston Chronicle*, "Lone Star surfers have reason to celebrate." Mixing in the obligatory gunslinger metaphor, he explained that infrequent swells forced Gulf Coast surfers to be "quick-draw artists," ready to pull the trigger on surf trips at a moment's notice.

This is not just true in Texas. Surfers the world over are notorious for dropping everything—missing meetings, office hours, doctor appointments, work shifts, church, birthdays, and anniversaries—when there is swell in the water. Surf first. Ask permission later. I like to think this philosophy makes surfers endearingly unpredictable. My family begs to differ.

An archipelago of surf shops dots the southern coast from South Padre Island through Virginia Beach. The 1960s saw an explosion of such enterprises. Copeland's and Down South Surf Shop anchored the scene in Corpus Christi. Bay Surf Shop had locations from South Padre to Galveston, and of course, Houstonian BJ Williamson reigned over his small retail empire. From the 1960s through the '70s, these shops and many others along the Texas coast gathered the tribe by sponsoring teams, contests, film screenings, even occasionally, fashion shows.

As important as contests and fashion shows were to the scene, nothing brought local surfers together like films shown by the shops in the 1960s. *Barefoot Adventure*, *The Endless Summer*, and *The Fantastic Plastic Machine* became instant classics. Some even crossed over to popular, non-surfing audiences. But most American moviegoers with less discriminating tastes lapped up Hollywood swill like *Beach Blanket Bingo* and *How to Stuff a Wild Bikini*. Even Elvis Presley, perhaps the most famous southerner of this period, dipped his toe in the water with *Blue Hawaii*. Sixties surfers grudgingly admitted to watching these corny rom-coms set against backdrops of sand and sea, but mostly, they claimed, on dates with non-surfers. By contrast, a real surf film, like the ones made by Bruce Brown, brought the sunburned locals pouring into the high school gymnasium with beer and popcorn. Hoots and howls punctuated particularly gnarly waves or impressive footwork. As much as surf shops enjoyed building camaraderie with the films, they also understood that they were creating demand for their products and a loyal customer base that helped them ride out winter business lulls.

With the advent of videocassettes in the 1980s and then the internet in the 2000s, the importance of surf movie screenings declined, but shops continued to form the nucleus of local surf communities. Each shop, including, I'm sure, Bingo's Surf and Skate, has at least a few locals who stand around the counter and talk story with the staff, particularly in winter months. In this way, surf shops are like neighborhood bars, and the owners are the trusty bartenders. When I was fixin' to start the Texas leg of my journey, I called up a couple of the shops in Galveston to chat with the owners and get their recommendations of old-timers to interview.

The first Galveston shop owner I called was William "Boog" Cram, proprietor of Ohana Surf and Skate. Although Boog was too young to be a surf pioneer in the 1950s and early '60s, a babysitter blessed him with his suitably sixties nickname. Big Kahuna, Moon Doggie, and Wingnut were already taken, so the shortened form of "little booger" somehow stuck. Luckily, Boog stumbled into one of the few professions where a funny nickname actually helped his career.

As a kid, Boog didn't go to sleep dreaming about the glamourous life of surf shop ownership. His grandfather, father, and most of the men in the Cram family worked in commercial fishing. A great uncle tragically fell overboard and drowned in rough seas before Boog was born. Much of Boog's early childhood revolved around the water and the Catholic Church. The annual blessing of the fleet ceremony in Galveston brought these worlds together. Boog and other fishermen's kids made papier-mâché decorations for the boats each year to bring a safe and bountiful season.

Boog realized that commercial fishing might not be his calling during his first day on the shrimp boat. The alarm clock woke him at 3:30 A.M., and things got worse from there. Out on the Gulf, Boog and the other deckhands stood in the bow of the boat, peering bleary-eyed into the darkness. The romantic idea that Boog might soon take his place in a long line of family fishermen lost its appeal minute by minute.

As a surfer, Boog wasn't unfamiliar with dawn patrol sessions. Getting out on the water early could yield a glassy ocean surface untroubled by even the hint of wind. Without regular ground swells, wind was the southern surfer's best friend and worst enemy. Storms and low-pressure systems kicked up good waves, but the same weather patterns that produced sizable surf also left it disorganized. A windless dawn patrol after several days of stormy seas could produce nirvana-like perfection. You stroked out into the Gulf, mesmerized by the ripples racing across a shimmering surface of quicksilver. Dawn patrol sessions winnowed out the weekend warriors from Houston and local kooks. Early risers could surf the best sandbar, jetty, or pier with a small crew of friends.

Waking up hours before first light to work on a shrimp boat bore little resemblance to dawn patrol surfing other than the ungodly time of day. Boog and the rest of the deckhands motored out onto the Gulf and then labored for hours under an increasingly sweltering Texas sun. They separated trash fish from shrimp or other marketable seafood. At the end of the brutal shift, Boog had had enough. His first day on the trawler was also his last. There had to be better ways to make money from the water.

Boog started surfing in 1969 when his cousin—a "Gidget of Galveston"— let him borrow her nine-foot, six-inch Dewey Weber Performer. He fell in love with the sport. By the mid-seventies, Boog was working summers in local shops and skating just as much as he surfed. Irregular Gulf Coast swells couldn't compete with the permanent waves of streets curbs, pools, and halfpipes. Injuries landlocked Boog for good in the 2000s. He found his stoke on the retail side of surfing. The gig may not have been glamorous, but opening the air-conditioned shop at the civilized hour of 10:00 A.M. every day sure beat trawling the Gulf Coast to fill the plates at Red Lobster or Bubba Gump.

~~~~~~~~~~~~~~~~~~~~~~

When Zinnia and I pulled into Galveston, we drove by a beautiful beachfront resort called Casa del Mar. "Is that where we are staying?" Zinnia asked, eyes wide as she saw the swanky pools and porches overlooking the ocean. She should have known better. "No, we're staying at *that* place," I corrected her, pointing to the nondescript hotel behind the resort. "Why?" she whined. "Because it's almost two hundred dollars cheaper per night, and we can still walk to the beach." "Yeah, but, but, but," she sputtered, craning her neck as we drove past the resort pools.

Our Galveston digs were a step up from a Motel 6. Okay, maybe a half step. I appreciated the clean albeit generic decor of our room. Zinnia, still smarting from the pool not taken, crinkled her nose in disgust. "It smells like rotten eggs in here, Dad." It wasn't that bad until we opened the door to the porch. There was barely room for a single chair outside the second-story room. There was, however, an excellent view of a field filled with wildflowers and abandoned shipping containers. Clearly, there was also a gas leak somewhere close by. The longer we stayed out on the porch straining to see an ocean view, the more beautiful the wildflowers and shipping containers became. Feeling lightheaded, I realized that my grip on the guardrail was loosening. We retreated back inside to get some fresh air.

We arrived in town so late that our only dining option was a Waffle House within walking distance from the hotel. We strolled through the parking lot and past the diner's dumpsters. Some might argue that there is no *good* way to approach a Waffle House, but this was undoubtedly the worst. The place needs a little upscale rebranding. Taking a page from the nearby resort, I suggest using Spanish to bring a little class. Casa de Gofres has a nice ring to it.

The next morning, we remedied our Casa de Gofres hangover with a little hair of the dog that bit us, breakfasting on hotel waffles shaped like the

*If Everybody Had an Ocean*

Lone Star state. The waffles gurgled in our stomachs as we threw on rash guards and bathing suits for our first Gulf Coast surf mission.

The two-to-three-foot wind chop broke with consistent mediocrity up and down the length of the Galveston seawall, so we just walked from the hotel to the beach at the Sixty-First Street fishing pier. We shook off our flip-flops in the sand, tucked the Bingo Board under our arms, and jumped in.

After fifteen years of surfing in Northern California, I am always pleasantly surprised by the bathtub warmth of southern seas in the summer months. I'd guess the water temperature was in the upper 70s in Galveston—a stark contrast to the mid-50s of the Pacific, where wetsuits are advisable year-round. The moment our toes touched the Gulf, we both laughed and relaxed.

Before she had time to get scared, Zinnia surfed two waves. I was still pushing her into most rides, but she was starting to get the feel for catching waves solo. Paddling into your own wave constitutes a crucial skill for surfers. That's how the sport's addiction really sinks its teeth into you. Sure, the feel of riding the wave is paramount, but the ability to harness the ocean's power . . . that's the real trick. Zinnia did paddle into her own wave that first day, and I beamed with pride. After she started getting tired and overthinking the takeoffs, she began to wipe out and get frustrated. Fatigue brought out her preteen surliness. She said that I was ashamed of her. Nothing could have been further from the truth. Watching her paddle into a wave, pop up into a crouch for stability, stand shakily, right herself, and then throw her arms into the air with joy as the wave carried her toward shore . . . that's what being a surfing dad is all about.

I took a turn with the Bingo Board. It proved just as unwieldy as I expected, but also just as much of a wave magnet as I had hoped. The board stretched out so wide and long, with so much foam, I felt like I could ride any ripple that came my way. Catching waves was going to be easy, turning on them, not so much. Angling the Bingo Board down the line (parallel to the beach to maintain speed on the wave), required a few seconds of forethought. It felt like turning a long hook-and-ladder fire engine around a street corner, except these trucks often have steering wheels in both the front and back. The Bingo Board had no steering wheel at all.

When I first started riding the nine-foot, six-inch beast, it seemed to turn (or more often, not turn) with a mind of its own. Accustomed to shorter, more maneuverable boards, I would lean into a move and then face plant into the water as the Bingo continued along on its merry way directly toward the beach. I could almost hear the board laughing at me. Come to think of it, that may have been the fishermen on the Sixty-First Street pier. No other surfers joined us that the afternoon. For any surfer on the beach contemplating a paddle out, the bright yellow of the Bingo Board bouncing dangerously around the impact zone would have convinced them that another break, any other break, was a better option.

Famished after surfing, I took Zinnia to a Salvadoran restaurant on the bay side of the island's East End. Rivera's actually offers a mix of Mexican and Salvadoran cuisine, a nod to Texas tastes. As hungry as we were, the Casa de Gofres might have rated a Michelin star in our book, but the *platanos fritos* and beef tacos at Rivera's were a welcome change from our all-waffle diet.

Before my trip, I reached out to Galveston legend Dewayne Munoz on Boog Cram's recommendation. I called Dewayne around 10:30 A.M. San Francisco time. It was early afternoon in Galveston. But when Dewayne answered he sounded surprisingly groggy. "Could we talk in about thirty minutes?" he asked. "I have to eat breakfast and wake up a little." I took this as a bad sign. Other than bouncers, rock stars, and folks who work the graveyard shift, most people have breakfast before noon. When I called him back a half hour later, I inquired about Dewayne's curious breakfast schedule just to make conversation. Laughing, he explained that I caught him on the North Shore of Oahu, where it was three hours earlier than California.

The North Shore is the mecca of surfing, with some of the biggest, most beautiful waves on the planet. Pipeline, Sunset Beach, and Waimea Bay are just the most famous and fearsome breaks on the North Shore. A surfer could live there for several lifetimes and never master the infinite complexities of the waves on that mythical stretch of coastline. If Dewayne surfed there even recreationally, he must have been damn good. Dewayne split his time between the North Shore and the American South, one of several folks I would meet on my journey to do so.

When Dewayne gave me directions to his Galveston home, he told me that I'd get to see where real locals live on the island. The house stood on the West End, closer to the bay than the beach. The East End—especially the beachfront along Seawall Boulevard—was heavily developed. Most tourists come to stay and play there. I had never even ventured west of Sixty-First Street—the island's dividing line.

As Zinnia and I drove toward Dewayne's place, the thicket of condos and hotels gave way to single-family homes and then vacant lots broken up by inlets and small ponds. A horse grazed lazily just off the road. We saw more seagrass than sunglasses shops, a pleasant surprise in a beach community an hour from Houston. The inlets and lakes suggested one reason for this. The West End (particularly the bay side) stands just above sea level. The landscape there reflects the dangerous potential of flooding from frequent hurricanes that rake across barrier islands.

Centuries of storms have scarred Galveston's history, but none devastated the island like the Great Hurricane of 1900. In the late nineteenth century, Galveston seemed destined to become the most important port in Texas and one of the Lone Star state's leading cities. Although storms lashed the coast with high winds and waves every few years, Galveston residents and investors remained confident that their city could handle anything Mother Nature threw at them. Isaac Cline, the leading meteorologist for the U.S. Weather Service on the island in the 1890s, confidently assured his neighbors that a seawall was unnecessary to protect a city that stood less than nine feet above the Gulf.

The storm that struck Galveston on September 8, 1900, proved Cline wrong and exacted a heavy toll both on the meteorologist and the city. Throughout that day, the approaching storm pushed increasing swells toward the island. Barometers dropped so low that some observers thought the instruments must be broken. Cline realized too late that they were not and that a deadly storm was bearing down on his city. Leaving his office that afternoon, he waded two miles through waist-deep water to get back to his family. "My wife and three little girls were in our home, surrounded by the rapidly rising water, which already covered the island from the Gulf to the Bay," Cline later remembered. "In reality there was no Island, just the ocean with houses standing out of the waves which rolled between them."

That night, Cline opened his home, which had been built to withstand hurricane force winds and flooding, to dozens of other Galveston residents. The house held firm against the onslaught through the early evening. But then the waves ripped a railroad trestle from its foundations and drove it against the Cline residence "like a battering ram." The building shuddered violently and disintegrated into shards of timber and plaster. Bricks tumbled down from the home's three chimneys in an avalanche. The walls collapsed. The Gulf rushed in. Dragged deep under water, Cline gave up and lost consciousness. Miraculously, he came to, floating on debris not far from his youngest daughter. He saw his other daughters and his brother clinging to wood in the water nearby. His wife, however, was gone.

The fifteen-foot storm surge that swept in from the Gulf with the hurricane killed Cline's wife along with an estimated 6,000 to 12,000 additional people—one in five of Galveston's residents. The Great Hurricane obliterated the city, reducing most buildings to unrecognizable stacks of debris. In the wake of the storm, engineers brought in barges of sand to raise the elevation of the city by more than fifteen feet. They also built the first section of a seventeen-foot-high sea wall that now armors the shoreline.

Just over a century later in 2008, Hurricane Ike followed nearly the same path as the Great Hurricane. A Category 4 storm, Ike's eye passed directly over the East End of Galveston. The storm destroyed or damaged nearly three-quarters of the buildings on the island, including the iconic Flagship Pier. Yet, as devastating as Ike was, the hurricane took the lives of only a few dozen residents. The lessons that Cline and other American meteorologists had learned in the Great Hurricane saved thousands of residents on the Texas Gulf Coast.

In recognition of the potential for both danger and beauty on Galveston's West End, Dewayne Munoz's house stands on stilts high above sea level. A former union carpenter, Dewayne built an impressive two-story, wooden deck on the house, crowned by a lanai with gorgeous views of both the Gulf and Bay. The "backyard" is a lagoon, perfect for paddle boarding and kayaking.

When Dewayne met us at the door, he welcomed us with a friendly handshake and warm smile. The solidly-built, soft-spoken Texan still had the arms and shoulders of someone who could paddle to distant reef breaks or through thick shore pound. He wore a T-shirt advertising Doug Surfboards—a once influential but long defunct Galveston shop. Dewayne had ridden on Doug Pruns's team in the early 1970s. A faded photo from that era suggests that long, shaggy locks were an essential component of the team uniform. Nearly half a century later, Dewayne had lost the long hair, but not the jaunty, informal style of the younger man from the team picture.

When Dewayne Munoz started surfing in the mid-1960s, he couldn't have known that a revolution was about to rock youth culture. In Galveston,

The author *(l)*, Zinnia Estes, and Dewayne Munoz
outside Dewayne's house in Galveston, Texas.
*Courtesy of the author.*

there were jocks, nerds, and surfers. For Dewayne, the choice was clear from the start. He was a surfer.

Even though surf contests sponsored by the Gulf Coast Surfing Association and various local shops weren't as vital to Texas culture as the Friday night lights of high school football, the contests did provide an avenue for young Texans, particularly boys, to prove themselves. In this way, surfing was not nearly as rebellious a sport as has often been depicted in popular culture. Dewayne was no rebel in high school. He just pursued a different athletic passion.

Yet this unorthodox hobby did expose Dewayne and other Galveston locals to the counterculture that began to infuse surfing communities in the late 1960s. Almost overnight, it seemed, corduroy replaced khaki, huarache sandals eclipsed Weejun loafers, and T-shirts muscled aside Madras button downs. "The hair got long and the boards got short," surfers from this era like to say, reflecting on the experimentation in new surfboard designs that coincided with the cultural experimentation of the hippie movement. Texas surfers embraced the new trends.

By the time he graduated from high school in the early 1970s, Dewayne had gone all-in on surfing and the counterculture lifestyle. He managed Island Surf Shop on Sixty-First Street, which allowed him to surf most mornings before work. In the winter, when business was slow, Dewayne and his buddies just hung around the otherwise empty shop all day. Maybe they'd play cards or listen to the radio. Jimi Hendrix's epic guitar solos spooled out of the speakers, creating a psychedelic soundtrack as the cold, gray afternoons faded into nights of partying.

In other words, Dewayne explained, they'd just "do what surfers did back in the early seventies." He added a subtle wink and punctuated the gesture with, "You know what I mean?" The implied reference to drug use was meant to protect the ears of my daughter, Zinnia, who sat just to my right, quietly drawing throughout this interview and many others on the trip. In hindsight, the decision to bring Zinnia along on interviews clearly tamed some of the wilder stories of the surfers that I interviewed. Then again, as a San Francisco native, Zinnia can already distinguish between Pepé Le Pew and Purple Skunk. She probably caught more than a whiff of Dewayne's meaning about his wild youth. Still, I appreciated his restraint.

Dewayne's reticence was not simply driven by politeness, but also a bit of regret. He left the surf shop to become a carpenter, got hitched, and continued to surf and party with abandon. He was, as he said, "living the dream." But something felt missing. "People were searching; they were doing drugs," Dewayne said by way of explanation. "This Jesus movement swept across the country." He started to read the Bible. It changed his life.

What some call the "Fourth Great Awakening" of evangelical Christian fervor rolled through American society in the 1970s. Jesus Christ became a superstar, not just in the Bible Belt, but on Broadway. Jimmy Carter became the first born-again president. Chuck Smith, the founder of Calvary Chapel in Southern California, reached across the cultural divide to hippies, surfers, and other folks who felt disconnected from traditional religious institutions. Dewayne Munoz heard this call.

"Surfing was my god at one point," Dewayne told me. "When I came to the Lord, I said, 'That's never going to fill the need in my life.' I kept surfing, but now I look at surfing as more of a gift instead of the end all, be all of everything."

Surfers across the South had similar epiphanies. Les Stinson, a surf shop owner on the Alabama coast, and Yancy Spencer on the Florida Panhandle, also came to Jesus. Yancy even named his Pensacola shop Innerlight in honor of his newfound faith and devotion. Christian Surfers, founded in the 1970s in Australia, became the largest organization of devout wave riders, with chapters across the United States. Many smaller groups and congregations sprang up, connecting surfers' devotion to God and the ocean.

Even the most hardened atheists or skeptical agnostics have to acknowledge that there is something spiritual about communing with nature in the water. I've never attended services in a house of worship more beautiful than the ocean. The ceiling of the Sistine Chapel can't hold a candle to the coastal sky, painted in infinite variations of white cirrus brushstrokes and deep hues of blue. Surfers talk about the faces of waves as walls, but the real walls of the ocean curve upward in magnificent arcs from all points of the horizon. As the sun rises in the early morning, it sends shafts of light through the clouds glimmering off the surface of the ocean in a spectrum of colors more varied than the prism of the most masterfully carved stained glass.

"No synonym for God is so perfect as Beauty," the naturalist John Muir wrote in his journals. "Whether as seen carving the lines of mountains with glaciers, or gathering matter into stars, or planning the movements of water . . . still, all is Beauty!" Muir found God while hiking the slopes of his beloved Sierras. Surfers touch the divine with every stroke.

Aside from the worshipful setting, surfing requires, perhaps more than any other sport, that the participants get in tune with the rhythms of the natural world. That act is a certain form of sacrament. Whether this sacrament is tied to a traditional religious belief system or not, it often conjures up the awe associated with a belief in God or some higher power.

~~~~~~~~~~~~~~~~~~~~~~~~~~~~~~~~~~~~~~~~

I first experienced the spiritual side of surfing in high school. It started, like most things with my generation, as a joke. My friend Alexander Krings and I learned to surf together in South Carolina. Our morning sessions often began before first light. Arriving at the beach in the dark, we would literally pray for surf. With far too much time on our hands, we dreamed up a wacky cosmology that centered on Bogo, the god of surf. As dawn spread westward from the Atlantic horizon, we would dance around like maniacs chanting, "Bogo, Bogo, Bogo," until we were loopy from breathlessness. Whether or not Bogo brought us great surf, our silly ritual did warm up our extremities on cold mornings.

Alexander and I did not begin our surfing career on a spiritual quest. We were looking for girls. Alexander's family had recently relocated from Germany to the United States when we started surfing in the mid-1980s. Too young to drive, we had to beg for rides from our parents. They dropped us off far from the good breaks on Folly Beach. Veteran surfers went to the Washout near the northeast end of the island. We went the opposite direction. We didn't want competition for the girls that would be flocking to us with our dayglow board shorts and puff-paint T-shirts.

Truth be told, girls rarely showed up and even more rarely gave us the time of day, so almost despite ourselves, we actually learned to surf. The waves at Folly average about knee-to-waist high in the summer months. At first, Alexander and I stood in shallow water and launched ourselves shoreward as waves passed beneath us. After the 964th belly ride, one of us actually stood up. I'm not sure who gets that honor, but given that Alexander was far more athletic, I'm guessing it was him. We headed straight toward the shore on waves that had already broken, riding the weak, frothy whitewater. By the end of that first summer, we finally started to realize that the rides would be longer, faster, and more controlled if we turned the boards sideways and tried to ride along the unbroken face of the waves parallel to the beach.

What we lacked in skills and wave quality, we made up for in unbridled enthusiasm. Hooting and yelling punctuated even the shortest of rides. Despite Alexander's usual quiet reserve, he learned how to yell like a true Carolina rebel when he saw me taking off on a thunderous two-foot tall bomb. I did the same for him—minus the German accent. To this day, I still yell "Yeehaw" for friends and strangers alike in northern California.

Alexander and I took many failed surf trips together, but the worst one by far took us to Corpus Christi the spring of our first year in college. Alexander drove twenty hours straight from Raleigh to Houston for a spring break of surfing. My other Rice friends were headed to South Padre for poolside keg parties. Hindsight suggests that would have been the wiser itinerary. Instead, Alexander and I threw our boards on the top of his car, a mud-brown, egg-shaped Honda Civic nicknamed "Bertha," and headed to the beach. We hadn't looked at either the surf forecast or weather report. We just knew it would be good. Bogo had foreordained it.

We prayed to the wrong god. Our first night in Corpus Christi, a violent storm hit the beach right as we set up our tent. If we had not gotten inside immediately, the tent would have blown away. As it was, the wind ripped our tiny, steel stakes from the sand and whipped them around like karate nunchucks. We tried to get out and repair the damage, only to watch the tent collapse on itself and our belongings. Sharp needles of windblown sand and rain blinded us as we grabbed our stuff, rolled up the tent (now more like a sandbag), and ran to the car. We spent the night alternating between futile attempts to sleep and even more futile attempts to jam with our acoustic guitars. I have no other memories of the trip. No epic waves. Not even mediocre waves. Just a storm of biblical proportions, humbling two lost souls on the Texas coast.

The soulful or spiritual side of surfing crystallized for me during a frigid dawn patrol at Folly Beach on Thanksgiving Day in 1989. On cold mornings at the beach, the sun doesn't so much shine with yellow warmth as glow with cool, white luminescence. It's almost as if the winter sun reflects the moon's light instead of the other way around. That Thanksgiving morning, the sun rose like a white pearl from the ocean. The air had to be in the 30s and the water felt like the lower 50s. The temperature didn't matter. We had prayed to Bogo, and he had delivered. The coincidence of chest-high glassy surf and a school holiday easily persuaded us to brave the freezing air temperature for a two-hour session.

At the end, we could barely wiggle our fingers, much less use them. I was not a religious kid, and my hands were still too frozen to fold into prayer. Nonetheless, I gave thanks that morning, feeling closer to God than I ever had before. I had never really understood the spiritual side of Thanksgiving until that day. Before, it just meant turkey and dressing, football and family. Every Thanksgiving since that day, especially ones where I find myself lucky enough to surf, I try to take a minute or two to pray to a higher power that could create a universe where such mornings are possible.

On our last morning in Galveston, Dewayne Munoz had invited Zinnia and me to a church picnic at the beach. We politely declined, opting to squeeze in one last surf at Sixty-First Street. Jaywalking across Seawall Boulevard on a Saturday morning is no joke. Texas trucks and family minivans speed this way and that to stake claims on prime, sandy real estate. I told Zinnia that it felt like a live-action version of an old video game called *Frogger*. "No, Dad, it's like that app *Crossy Road*," she corrected me. Whatever, whippersnapper. Your post-millennial technobabble means nothing to me!

The wind died down overnight, but a modest swell remained. It was still two to three feet with occasional four-foot sets. No one would have called that morning epic. Still, it was going to be a nice, mellow longboard session. There were four or five other surfers out already. More joined the party throughout the morning. Music pumped from fishermen's radios on the pier. That day's playlist included Parliament's "Flashlight," giving the session a decidedly funky groove.

I hadn't dialed in the Bingo Board yet, but I didn't eat it as much on the take-offs. Once up and riding, I started to walk it a bit. This increased comfort with moving the board backward and forward under my feet made turns easier. The slightly longer lines of the clean morning swell didn't hurt. Zinnia struggled a bit more to stay up. With the sun shining and fish jumping around us, she still had fun, especially when I stopped making her try to catch waves by herself. Eventually, we just took belly rides together.

Belly rides were my original strategy to get Zinnia over her fear of the ocean and part of a torturously long process of teaching her to swim. Some kids seem to be born with gills. They are swimming at age three or four and surfing by age seven. I've seen these kids on the internet with their smug, smiling parents. I hate them. Zinnia was not this kind of water baby. She demanded goggles in the bathtub. Our first big fights took place at a public pool.

As a former lifeguard and water safety instructor, I figured it'd be easy to teach Zinnia how to swim. I was definitely not going to make the mistake my grandmother had made. She took my brother and me to Clearwater, Florida, near her Tampa home and hired a gruff World War II navy veteran, whose idea of "teaching" kids how to swim amounted to throwing us in the

*If Everybody Had an Ocean*

deep end and screaming, "Quit crying, you babies!" This particular baby cried his eyes out after he stopped coughing up chlorine.

In contrast to Coach Crackerjack, I was going to be patient, kind, and follow all of the Red Cross guidelines. This sounded good in theory, until the tenth Daddy swim lesson, during which Zinnia once again refused to release her white-knuckle death-grip on the pool gutter. I dribbled water on Zinnia's head to acclimate her. She recoiled as if I had washed her hair with battery acid. The retired navy guy's teaching strategy started looking better and better.

Zinnia learned to swim, but she remained hesitant around the ocean until we started to take rides at Kiawah Island, South Carolina. The gentle rollers at Kiawah rarely reach waist high. We found an almost indestructible canvas raft and rode together on our bellies every morning. By the time that raft gave up the ghost, its red, ripped cover trailing behind us like a super hero cape, Zinnia was hooked. Near the end of our last surf in Galveston, Zinnia asked me if I remembered the canvas raft and the Kiawah belly rides. How could I forget? That was the moment I witnessed the magical alchemy of surfing transform fear of the ocean into love.

On the way out of Galveston, we dropped by Ohana Surf and Skate, where Boog Cram manned the counter despite being sick as a dog that day. Earlier, I had wondered aloud about the name of the shop. Zinnia informed me that *ohana* means "family" in Hawaiian, and family means "nobody gets left behind." She learned this from the Disney movie *Lilo and Stitch*. I can imagine no more authoritative source on Hawaiian language and culture than the Walt Disney Company, but just in case, I looked the word up. Sure enough, "ohana" does mean family, but that doesn't quite capture the full power of the word. A better definition would be "extended family" or maybe even "community." I didn't ask Boog about this, both because it would have embarrassed Zinnia and also because I didn't really have to ask. As Boog told us more about his shop and the surf camp that he ran, I saw kids coming in to sign up and others stopping by to rent boards for the weekend. Here was the next generation of Texas surfers. The ohana continued to grow.

# 3
## *Atlantis on the Gulf*
### Grand Isle, Louisiana

We left Galveston via a ferry to the Bolivar Peninsula. The cars of local beachgoers mixed with the RVs of retirees crisscrossing country. We found ourselves somewhere in between, the only car with a surfboard on the roof heading east toward the famously good parties and notoriously bad surf of Louisiana.

My experience in Louisiana before this trip began and ended with New Orleans. I'd collected beads and hangovers at Mardi Gras, sweated it out with the Soul Rebels brass band at Le Bon Temps Roule, and even crashed in a Catholic church for a weekend (long story). But as a surfer, I always wondered whether any waves lay south of the French Quarter. I pondered the possibilities at the end of the mighty Mississippi, inspired by Mark Twain.

Though Twain cut his teeth as a waterman on the Big Muddy, he actually tried surfing during a trip to Hawaii (known to Twain as the Sandwich Islands). The Missouri writer admired Hawaiians' abilities to ride "prodigious billows" of waves on boards faster than an express train for hundreds of yards. He decided to give it a go. "I tried surf-bathing once, subsequently, but made a failure of it," Twain admitted. "I got the board placed right, and at the right moment, too; but missed the connection myself. The board struck the shore in three-quarters of a second, without any cargo, and I struck the bottom about the same time, with a couple of barrels of water in me."

Instead of an interactive map of surfing locations, the Louisiana page of one forecasting website includes a photo of gators lazing on a sunny riverbank captioned by the above Mark Twain quote. The message is clear: no map needed, no surf here. Silt from the Mississippi River tamps down all but the hardiest approaching swells from the Gulf of Mexico. Yet videos of surfers at Grand Isle and Port Fourchon suggested that there are occasionally ridable waves in the Pelican State. Zinnia and I aimed to find them.

I steered the car off the interstate southward onto Louisiana 1, which drives through the heart of Acadiana, or Cajun Country. Locals call Louisiana 1 the "longest Main Street in America." *Guinness World Records* has not corroborated this claim. The road parallels Bayou Lafourche, once a large tributary of the Mississippi River and now home to shrimp boats and fishing vessels with names like *Capn. Jimmy* and *Miss Anna*. Zinnia and I whiled away the time on this longest of Main Streets, coming up with ludicrous origin stories for the boat names. A sordid tale of intrigue worthy of a soap opera climaxed in a shootout between Capn. Jimmy and Miss Anna, resulting in the untimely deaths of both parties followed by immortalization in two broke-down fishing boats.

Near its southern terminus at the Gulf of Mexico, Louisiana 1 launches skyward onto a causeway that soars more than twenty feet above the bayou and wetlands below. Driving on the causeway at dusk felt like flying down the Mississippi River—although the main channel of the river flowed dozens of miles to the east. The vast vistas took our breath away. They felt like glimpses of the end of the world. Small shoals and marshy islands breached the surface of placid water, appearing ready to submerge at any moment. Ghost trees stood on bigger islands, bony fingers pointing at the sky. The trees that had once sunk their roots into fertile delta soil had been strangled of nutrients by salt poisoning or stripped of their foliage by hurricanes. Pelicans flew in formation. Smaller sea birds wheeled in widening circles, sharp eyes peeled in the hunt for fish. As we drove toward the Gulf, old-school funk crackled over the airwaves from a college radio station in New Orleans two hours to the north—a strange soundtrack to a surreal landscape. Waterscape was more like it.

From the vantage point of the causeway, you can't help but notice the old path of Louisiana 1 and the nearby town of Leeville, both partly flooded by the rising waters that worry climate scientists. According to the U.S. Geological Survey, since the 1930s Louisiana has lost almost 2,000 square miles of land—an area the size of Delaware—to the Gulf. The National Oceanic and Atmospheric Administration (NOAA) offers two reasons: subsidence (sinking of the land) and a rise in sea level due to global warming. The land is sinking at a rate of three-quarters of an inch per year. Silt that once replenished the wetlands has been channeled offshore by levies and jetties. Canals and pipelines crisscross the marshland altering the flow of water and sediment as well, interrupting the process of wetland nourishment. Relative sea levels in the area are rising approximately one foot every thirty years. At the end of the Louisiana 1 causeway, Fourchon and Grand Isle are perfect places for scientists to study these phenomena. They are also the best places in Louisiana to surf.

~~~~~~~~~~~~~~~~~~~~~~~~

Billy Hingle could count on one hand the number of Louisiana surfers when he started at Grand Isle in the mid-1960s. Others suggest that he might have been the first surfer in the state, but Billy's too humble for such a claim. He grew up in Pointe à la Hache, a small town on the main channel of the Mississippi River. As the crow flies, Pointe à la Hache is not that far from Grand Isle, only about fifty miles. But driving takes three or four hours. Even by Louisiana standards, Billy Hingle had to be pretty dedicated to surf.

Billy discovered surfing in 1965 on a trip to Florida. By the late 1960s he found work as a machinist in New Orleans, where he made good money and lived closer to the waves of Grand Isle. On weekends and holidays, Billy raced down to the distant beach with his longboard.

The Louisiana local liked to surf a break called Dips, but there were many others on Grand Isle: Skip Jim, Staubs Camp, Camp Mal Aux Dent, the Point, and the Pass. The Point and the Pass could hold the biggest swell. A jetty jutted out of the East End of the island (where the state park would eventually be built), forming a mini–point break especially during big hurricane ground swells. Fourchon, southwest of Grand Isle at the end of Bayou Lafourche, also had a few breaks. Back in the sixties, before the state built a port at Fourchon, surfers had to paddle across the bayou to get to the breaks there, not the most pleasant prospect with venomous water moccasins slithering nearby.

By the late 1960s, Louisiana's surfing community had grown, but its most dedicated members still numbered fewer than a hundred or so. Surf movies in New Orleans drew the faithful from across southern Louisiana to hoot and howl at the screen. If there was anything approaching surf the next day, cinematic stoke drove everyone to the water to emulate the hot moves of surfers from California, Hawaii, or Australia. The movies fired the imagination of Louisiana locals, so that Grand Isle surf would look good, even if it rarely was.

Billy met a beautiful local girl, Jan, the daughter of a man who worked for the oil companies flying helicopters out to the rigs and back. It was perfect. He could visit Jan and surf in his favorite place in Louisiana. Occasionally, he'd travel to Florida for better waves, but Louisiana always called him home. As his he grew older, work and family obligations made trips to Grand Isle shorter and less frequent. He moved back to Pointe à la Hache and got a job on the river as a ferryboat captain. Billy navigated the Mississippi for over three decades. On the side, he had a small oyster farm and a share in a shrimp-boat business. Billy was always working, always on the water. When he finally retired, the old boat captain "took it easy" by hunting gators in southern Louisiana bayous.

Before all of that, there was one last surf trip to Grand Isle. He'd never forget the day. He'd been out for a long while, hours maybe. His wife was on the beach, waving him in. It was way past time to go, which to a surfer, always means time for one last wave. That last wave was a doozy, maybe the best Billy ever caught. It peeled head high off the jetty. He carved his way gracefully to shore before getting in the car with his family for the long ride home. Maybe he was in trouble a little bit with Jan, but she understood. Billy needed that last ride. He'd surf it thousands of times in his memory for the rest of his life.

When I planned the trip to Grand Isle, two things other than surfing excited me: the possibility of staying at the Cajun Holiday Motel and the rodeos that the island is famous for in the summer months. I imagined checking in, swapping my board shorts and flip-flops for jeans and boots, and then heading out to watch Cajun cowboys wrangling cattle while zydeco music pulsed in the background. Unfortunately, I found out that "rodeos" on Grand Isle are actually just large fishing tournaments, much less cool than cowboys roping doggies on an island in the middle of the Gulf. On the plus side, I did confirm the reservations at the Cajun Holiday. I told Zinnia that I had some good news and some bad news about Grand Isle. First, I bragged that I managed to reserve a room at the Cajun Holiday Motel. Without missing a beat, she said, "What's the good news, Daddy?"

After we checked in to the Cajun Holiday, Zinnia asked, "What's the worst motel we are staying in on this trip?" Both of us were thinking that we'd be hard pressed to find worse digs than the Cajun Holiday. The proprietor, Ms. Millie, was genuinely sweet and helpful, but service can only make up for so much in accommodations. The cinderblock barracks of the Cajun Holiday can charitably be described as Spartan. Ms. Millie upgraded us to a room at the back of the motel. These rooms were quieter and darker than the ones on the roadside and evidently much sought-after by the off-duty Coast Guard folks, who made up most of the motel's clientele in the off-season. Unlike our Galveston hotel, there was no gas leak. Still, most of the charm of the place could be found in its name and proprietor. "If you want luxury, go to Florida," one online reviewer concluded.

We dined at the Surfside Grill. Ms. Millie recommended a different place, but we managed to get lost on the only road in town. As we pulled into a vacant lot to turn around, a dude in front of the Surfside Grill desperately flagged us down and waved us into one of his many vacant parking spaces. The nautical kitsch decor immediately welcomed us into the Surfside, but the place was absolutely deserted, a bad sign on a Saturday night. Mark, the owner, chef, and parking attendant turned us over to his sole employee, Miss Joy, to take our orders. As you can tell by the titles, "Ms." Millie and "Miss" Joy hailed from southern Louisiana. Mark did not.

Hearing Grand Isle locals addressed as "Ms." or "Miss" coupled with their first names struck me as quaint and distinctly southern. When I taught middle school kids in Mississippi for a few summers, the other teachers and I referred to the kids in a similar manner. I taught "Mr. Kedric Carter" and "Mr. Chris Perkins," for instance. The mixture of the formal and familiar captures something unique about the relationship between strangers and locals in the rural South. After years of living in the West, where casual familiarity flattens out social graces, it was actually refreshing to see an older, more traditional form of personal interaction.

Miss Joy had never been asked why Grand Isle folks called their fishing tournaments "rodeos," but she wasn't particularly defensive about what I viewed as false advertising either. She said the rodeos were a big deal on Grand Isle, with fishing being the main driver of local tourism. Looking around at the empty restaurant, I thought that either the fish weren't biting or we were about to get a serious case of food poisoning.

The fishing must have been bad. After Mark made us a delicious hamburger and tacos, he came out to chat us up. It turned out that he was a surfer from South Padre Island, Texas, who had lived in Hawaii and Costa Rica. He said that the surf in Grand Isle could be pretty good. "You should have been here four days ago," he said. The onshore winds that often roar across the island turned offshore for a few hours of blissfully groomed chest-high surf. Mark told us that Fourchon had the best waves in the area, but that the Homeland Security officers who guard the port there were pretty particular about who surfed the break and the things they carried.

Talk about locals only! Evidently boards are okay with Homeland Security, but backpacks are a nonstarter. Mark told us that the pass at the beginning of the island sometimes saw good surf. A rock pile near his restaurant occasionally channeled swell. Neither of these spots were working the weekend we visited. He suggested that we try the pier in the state park at the east side of the island.

The next day, Zinnia and I woke up early, hoping that dawn would bring respite from the onshore winds. Initially, I thought our prayers had been answered. The wind remained stiff but not overwhelming as we walked out of the Cajun Holiday. Fishermen were getting their boats ready. Some were already out on the bay, rivaling the local sea birds in patience and forbearance. We crossed Louisiana 1 and walked up the ten-to-fifteen-foot levee that defends the island from storm surges.

Most surfers, especially southern ones, will recognize the mixture of anticipation and hope that courses through your body when you approach shoreline dunes. You can hear the waves breaking before you see them. In your mind's eye, they are perfect little caverns, peeling left and right from A-frame peaks. The seagrass atop the dunes gives some indication of wind, but sometimes you don't even want to look. You want to live in that moment of possibility. It's the moment before you unwrap a birthday present, imagining all of the gifts you could be getting before the open box reveals the actual one. The gift may be awesome. It may suck. But it is finite. How can a real number compete with infinite possibilities?

I had already mind-surfed a dozen amazing waves by the time we clambered up the Grand Isle levee. When we crested the hill, an onshore wind of about twenty knots smacked us in the face. It blew the seagrass flat against the sea side of the levee. The waves crumbled over about knee high, maybe thigh high at best. They broke chaotically about twenty yards off shore. I resigned myself to a hike.

Just in case, we decided to check the pier at the state park to see if it was any better. In fact, it was worse. More onshore wind. Just knee-high chop. No one else braved the swimming beach that morning. A swarm of voracious mosquitos tore into our flesh. Fleeing the insect plague, we climbed up to the top of an observation tower. The waves looked even smaller from above. The white caps extended out to the oil rigs on the horizon.

At least, we could learn something, I thought, making Zinnia read the park's informative panels on the history and ecology of Grand Isle. The only part of the panels that piqued Zinnia's interest concerned pirates.

Swashbucklers like Jean Lafitte had used Grand Isle as a home base for smuggling and attacks on Gulf Coast shipping. According to legend, ghost pirates still haunt Grand Isle and the Louisiana Gulf Coast.

The state park information center primarily focused on the natural world of the Gulf. The center corrected a misperception that I had about the oil rigs. I foolishly assumed that the primary function of these rigs was pulling raw crude from beneath the sea floor to convert into the fossil fuels. According to the state park panels, however, oil production appeared to be merely a happy side benefit. The rigs fostered sea life in the waters off Grand Isle, drawing hundreds of species to their support pilings like a manmade reef system. Colorful illustrations depicted schools of fish swimming happily beneath the rigs. Turns out, Exxon found Nemo . . . and gave him a sweet marine sanctuary.

Big Oil raised the second Grand Isle surfer whom I interviewed, Mike Barton. His dad flew helicopters out to the rigs as a contractor for Humble Oil (later Exxon). Servicing the rigs was dangerous work. John Barton had to lead rescue missions in storms without the guidance of modern navigational aids. He flew by sight. In storms, that meant flying blind.

Helicopter company pilots, oil workers, and their families lived in camps on Grand Isle. Camps, the local term for neighborhoods, suggested impermanence. The companies hired private buses to take the kids to schools in Galliano, Louisiana (an hour and a half each way). As a result, the oil company kids grew up segregated from the Grand Isle locals, despite the fact that they shared a strip of earth so narrow at points that one could toss a rock across the landmass. The camps were more than just separate neighborhoods, Mike Barton came to realize. They were separate worlds.

Mike started surfing in 1966, about a year after Billy Hingle, but Billy was five years older and had his own car. Because of their difference in age and status, Mike didn't surf with Billy much. He looked up to the older surfer as a local hero. In fact, Billy sold Mike his first board, a used, nine-foot, six-inch Dewey Weber Performer.

After a few years of surfing the Weber, Mike downsized to shorter boards. Maybe it was the shift to short boards. Maybe it was hours in the water. Maybe it was the zeitgeist of the late 1960s. Mike realized that he didn't need a weatherman to know which way the wind blew. For surf in Grand Isle, the wind needed to blow hard out of the southeast for several days with an approaching low front. Then, if the wind swung around

*Atlantis on the Gulf*

offshore from the northwest, the waves cleaned up and held their size for a time. That magic could last an hour or a day, but when it came, Mike found a way to get into the water. He calculated the number of times he could play hooky as a senior and still graduate. Mike earned his degree without an absence to spare.

There were two surf shops in Houma (sounds like "Hoe-ma"). Houston surf entrepreneur, BJ Williamson, owned one. A Louisianan named David Dutha owned the other. BJ assembled a surf team with the hot young kids from Houma. Dutha's team had a motley crew of Grand Isle folks. Mike surfed for Dutha. There were so few surfers in southern Louisiana, the two teams ginned up a friendly rivalry just to keep things interesting.

Mike started going to college at Louisiana State University. He worked on an oil rig for a short while during a summer to earn money. Mike admitted that he only lasted a few weeks. He especially didn't like swinging from a boat to the rig in bad weather, across four or five feet of stormy seas. This gave the Grand Isle local a new appreciation for his father's job and a sense that his destiny lay elsewhere. After a vacation in California, Mike realized that LSU's academic prestige (meaning its proximity to the ocean) couldn't compare to the University of California, Santa Barbara. With more consistent ground swells pumping out of the Pacific, Mike found himself in heaven. Yet the breaks near Santa Barbara had a familiar backdrop to the ones in Grand Isle—offshore oil rigs.

Like other marine life, Louisiana surfers actually have a love-hate relationship with the oil industry. On the Gulf Coast, rigs have brought high-paying jobs to a region that would otherwise rest largely on the seasonal, service-sector economy of tourism. Over the course of the twentieth century, oil companies drilled 181,000 wells in Louisiana. Surfers and other southern Louisiana residents were happy to find work in the more lucrative fossil fuel industry. Conservationists looking to regulate or roll back offshore drilling activity had a tough sell in the Pelican State. A spokesperson for the environmentally conscious Surfrider Foundation acknowledged the "real need for oil" and the importance of "existing offshore [drilling] activity" in a state like Louisiana.

Surfers rely on the oil industry far more than any of us want to admit. Whether you live in Houston or Mobile, Pasadena or Berkeley, if you surf, you drive. Car culture has long been integral to surf culture. Billy Hingle couldn't have learned to surf in Grand Isle without the GTO convertible that got him to the distant break. Surfers that I interviewed on the East Coast waxed nostalgic about their Deuce Coupes and Econovans. The famed Woodies (wood-paneled wagons) popular with surfers in the early 1960s guzzled gas like there was no tomorrow. The Volkswagen vans that replaced Woodies as surfers' vehicle of choice in the late 1960s got better gas mileage, but they were still not exactly fuel-efficient.

A massive oil spill off the coast of Santa Barbara in 1969 catalyzed the modern environmental movement and complicated the romance between surfers and their cars. Workers for Union Oil (now Unocal) received a waiver from the government in January 1969 to drill without standard safety procedures on the new California well. After the drill tapped the undersea reservoir, oil gushed up through the rig. Workers capped the well, but oil escaped through cracks in the sea floor. Three million gallons of crude spewed into the sea, creating the biggest oil spill to that point in U.S. history. Black waves curled onto the southern California coast around Santa Barbara, killing thousands of sea birds and countless other marine animals.

Pictures of the Santa Barbara spill and the resulting ecological devastation added a sense of urgency to the young environmental movement. Americans celebrated the first Earth Day just over a year after the spill. New state and federal laws regulated not only offshore oil drilling, but everything from clean air and water to coastal real estate development and automobile emissions. Sadly, according to historians Peter Westwick and Peter Neushul, "surfers were notably absent from the environmental response to the Santa Barbara oil spill." In fact, surfers didn't organize the Surfrider Foundation until fifteen years after the 1969 Union Oil disaster.

Still, the Santa Barbara spill affected us all. It influenced my life in ways that I did not fully understand until decades later. My first surfmobile was a 1972 Buick Skylark. My grandfather, the original owner, only bought American cars. He refused to buy goods made by the men that killed his brother in World War II—a boycott he maintained his entire life. Aside from patriotism, he bought the car because of its muscular V-8 engine. The Skylark roared to life at the slightest touch of the gas pedal. My grandfather seemed unconcerned that the car got a paltry twelve miles to the gallon. Little did he know that new environmental laws passed after the Santa Barbara oil spill kicked in for the first time in the 1972 model year, making his Buick Skylark slightly "greener" than its predecessors.

This particular Skylark was also quite literally green—"sea mist" green. Sea mist probably seemed pretty cool in the earth-tone decade of the 1970s. By the 1980s, the car's paintjob had aged to puke-colored perfection. Salt and sun destroyed the interior, shredding the upholstery and cracking the steering wheel. I plastered a rainbow of surf stickers on the windows and every square inch of the exterior. Despite a budding environmental consciousness, I felt an uncomplicated love for the first car that carried me to the ocean.

My surfing buddy Alexander and I cut our teeth on environmental activism in high school. We wrote letters to our congressman to save the whales, dolphins, turtles, and a host of other marine animals. We religiously snipped the plastic rings of six packs, although later reports suggested that this ritual saved very few sea birds. We drove my Buick Skylark, without any sense of irony, to candlelight vigils for coastal conservation at the College of Charleston. I remember distinctly looking around at one such candlelight vigil, my mind laser-focused on a vital political question: were any of these college girls single? I didn't find love in the environmental movement, but I couldn't imagine being a surfer and anything other than a conservationist.

When I eventually moved to the environmentally conscious city of San Francisco, I found myself a mile and a half from my local break. I drive to the beach in a Toyota Prius, a hybrid which runs on a mixture of gasoline and self-righteousness—found in deep wells throughout San Francisco. But still, I drive to surf. I also live forty-five miles from the university where I teach. Carpooling only slightly diminishes my sasquatch-sized carbon footprint. Surfing gave me a deep love of nature, a sincere concern for the environment, and a vehicle to destroy the very oceans that are the lifeblood of the sport.

The ecological consequences of mixing oil and water are nowhere more apparent than in the Gulf. Author Jack Davis dubbed it "an American Sea" in his masterful study of the region's environmental history. "There is a kind of nourishing energy out in the Gulf that doesn't pump from a well," Davis writes in one lyrical passage. "It is the wholeness of living things, the dynamic energy moving from sun to plant to animal." The Gulf of Mexico holds 643 quadrillion gallons of water and hides billions of barrels of crude within its depths. People in the region rely heavily on both, though the mixture yields as many problems as solutions.

For decades, tar balls washed up on otherwise pristine Gulf shores. Natural seepage rising from the ocean floor created some of this tar. But Gulf Coast surfers and environmental watchdog groups speculated that much more came from small leaks on rigs or ships releasing oil and waste into the sea as they emptied their bilge tanks—a process that is illegal in U.S.

waters. Oil and tar contaminated Galveston beaches so much when Boog Cram was growing up that he and other surfers carried baby oil to help wipe the crude off their bodies. In recent years, regulations and industry changes have dramatically reduced the amount of tar that shows up on Gulf Coast beaches.

Some surf shop owners like Boog Cram argue that environmentalism is not just good for the planet; it is good for business in the long run. Boog recognizes that regulating the oil industry reduces revenue along the Gulf Coast and raises gas prices around the country. Replacing single-use plastic bags in surf shops with biodegradable or multi-use bags also hits his bottom line. But lately, Boog and others have started to see that the trade-off for these short-term costs in the long term is a healthier coastal ecosystem, better fishing, better surfing, and ultimately, more tourist dollars.

The real wake-up call for many on the Gulf Coast came in 2010. That year, the Deepwater Horizon rig, run by the BP oil company, exploded forty miles off the coast of Louisiana. The accident resulted in the biggest oil spill in U.S. history. It also killed eleven workers, leaving about a hundred others struggling to escape the burning rig.

Like most rig workers, Mike Williams wasn't a surfer. He was an electronics technician overseeing a station near the center of the Deepwater Horizon. He was talking to his wife on the phone a little after 9:30 P.M. on April 20, 2010, when he heard a warning about gas pressure rising underneath the rig. These warnings happened so often, he later testified, that everyone basically tuned them out. He got off the phone when he started hearing the constant beep of an alarm from a nearby office. A few seconds later, the lights on his computer console popped and the engines nearby began spinning out of control.

Williams tried to leave his office just as an explosion blew the steel safety door off its hinges. Carbon dioxide gas began flooding the area. Barely able to breath and unable to see, Williams crawled along the floor until he reached a second door. Another explosion blew this door inward, throwing the electronics technician against the opposite wall.

When Williams recovered enough to get out of the rig, he saw two lifeboats. "I seriously considered launching a lifeboat by myself," he admitted, "because I knew that something really, really bad had happened." Instead, Williams made his way to the rig's bridge, where he heard the Mayday call go out on the radio and talked to the captain about abandoning ship. The order eventually came, but there was no time for Williams to get in a life raft. He jumped to the surface of the Gulf one hundred feet below.

"I remember closing my eyes," Williams told an interviewer for *60 Minutes*, "and saying a prayer and asking God to tell my wife and my little girl that Daddy did everything he could and if, if I survive this, it's for a reason." He survived, swam through burning fuel beneath the rig, and made it to a rescue vessel. His harrowing tale formed the basis for a 2016 Hollywood drama about the disaster.

By the time Williams shared his story with the media and government investigators, the true scope of the disaster was already coming into focus. Nearly five million barrels of oil spilled from the rig before BP was finally able to staunch the flow of crude into the Gulf. In June of 2010, President Barack Obama addressed the nation on the spill. "You know, for generations, men and women who call this region home have made their living from the water. That living is now in jeopardy." The president made a promise that day. "Already, this oil spill is the worst environmental disaster America has ever faced," he said. "But make no mistake: we will fight this spill with everything we've got for as long it takes. We will make BP pay for the damage their company has caused. And we will do whatever's necessary to help the Gulf Coast and its people recover from this tragedy."

The fight and recovery took years. The federal government levied an $18.7 billion fine on BP—the largest in the nation's history—after finding the company guilty of manslaughter and lying to congress about the accident. The spill affected 1,100 miles of coastline. Tar balls and oil continued to wash up on Gulf shores from Grand Isle, Louisiana, to the Florida panhandle for years. The oil released into the water devastated every link in the food chain of the Gulf ecosystem. NOAA scientists documented mutations in fish and shrimp populations along with dramatic increases in the number of dead dolphins and turtles washing up on the Gulf Coast. The economic impact was equally devastating. Fishing and tourism industries along the Gulf Coast lost tens of millions of dollars and thousands of jobs.

Gulf Coast surfers had a fish-eye view of the BP oil spill. N.O. Surf Shop, the only core shop in Louisiana, survived Hurricanes Katrina and Rita, but the BP spill and a national recession forced the owners to close up for good in September 2010. You could still surf Lake Pontchartrain that year, but Louisiana officials closed Gulf Coast beaches due to health concerns. Some locals were undeterred. "You're not going to keep people who want to surf out of the water," one Fourchon charger told a New Orleans journalist. "The water has always been pretty funky. That's never stopped me. Just bring some gallons of water and rinse off."

Mike Barton remembered that he didn't even need to wash off after the BP spill. By 2010 the California transplant had a vacation home in Grand Isle that brought him back to southern Louisiana for long visits. He surfed every chance he got. Sharing the skepticism of many with ties to the oil industry in southern Louisiana, Mike argued that the Deepwater Horizon spill was sensationalized by the media. Local people made lots of money off of the cleanup and settlement. (Oystermen got thousands of dollars an acre for beds that were hurt when BP released fresh water to stave off the slick from shore. Shrimp boat captains leased their boats to FEMA.) Mike never saw oil on the beach from the spill. In fact, he remembered far worse slicks from accidents on the rigs when he was growing up that never even made the news. To him, the real environmental problem in southern Louisiana was not the oil, but the dead zone for local fishing from the fertilizer and pesticides flowing down the Mississippi River into the Gulf.

The Mississippi basin is "America's kitchen sink," environmental historian Jack Davis explains, "and the river itself, the drainpipe." Tons of fertilizer from farms in the basin drained into the Gulf through the river, creating hypoxic conditions as the fertilizers fueled massive algal blooms that died, decomposed, and then strangled the water of oxygen that fish needed to survive. The dead zone cost the Gulf over $80 million in tourist revenue. Mike Barton saw declining fish stock and angler tourism in southern Louisiana with his own eyes. This slow death made few headlines, but sometimes the worst calamities are the least sensational ones. To Mike, this was the real tragedy. The BP oil spill represented the cost of a dangerous but vital industry. The Gulf would heal itself in time, he believed.

Other Grand Isle surfers didn't share Mike Barton's sanguine view of the BP spill. *Surfer* magazine interviewed Kent Hornbacker (aka Kajun Kent), a Fourchon local who had been surfing in Louisiana for two decades at the time of the Deepwater Horizon disaster. The spill cost him his job and his waves. As Kent explained to *Surfer*, BP barricaded the beaches at Grand Isle and Fourchon for months after the disaster. Skeptical of the company's motives in closing down the beaches, Kent concluded, "It feels like they're policing their own crime scene."

Louisiana surfers who shared Kent's view decided to take action. Along with fishermen and other coastal residents, in May 2010 surfers joined the artist John Quigley to demonstrate against what they saw as BP's crimes, the same week Mike Williams shared his Deepwater Horizon survival story with *60 Minutes*. Williams's account completely eclipsed the protests that Quigley organized with southern Louisiana folks devastated by the spill.

John Quigley describes his work as "aerial art," which allows people and community to send a collective message about the environment. Louisiana fishermen and surfers laid their bodies and boards end-to-end and intertwined on the beach. Together they spelled out the phrases "Never Again" and "Paradise Lost."

Kajun Kent chose another form of protest, finding solace in satire. He penned an ode to BP's oil to the tune of the *Beverly Hillbillies* theme song. The original lyrics recount the dumb luck of hicks who find oil gushing out of their backyard, giving them the means to live a lush life. With tongue in cheek and a wink from beneath his fedora, Kent sang alternate lyrics: "Come and listen to my story about a fun little wave / the one we're all out here tryin' to freakin' save / deep down inside, I hate to be rude / But out of BP's hole came some bubblin' crude."

Seven years after Kent sang these words, Zinnia and I were determined to surf the "fun little wave" that he described. After reading the panels at the state park about the positive effects of the offshore oil rigs on local marine life, we noticed a sign warning us that we would be swimming at our own risk if we entered the Gulf. This appeared to be a reference to the lack of lifeguards, not the water quality. There was also a purple flag flying at the entrance to the pier, indicating dangerous marine life (particularly stingrays) in the water. Some sea life had clearly rebounded since the oil spill.

The dangerous marine life warnings combined with the tiny surf to drive us away from the park without dipping a toe in the water. We stopped by Yum's diner to get some homemade biscuits, cinnamon rolls, coffee, and juice. On a whim, I asked the lady at Yum's if the stingrays were bad this time of year. Not at all, she said. In fact, she had just gone to the beach the day before and there were no rays or jellyfish. I decided to give the surf a try.

We swatted at mosquitos during a photo shoot in front of the Cajun Holiday Motel before heading over the levee. To my surprise, the wind had dropped from gale strength to a stiff breeze, meaning that the Gulf was no longer white-capped all the way to the marine sanctuaries (ahem, oil rigs). Zinnia stayed on shore at first to take pictures, and I jumped right in, forgetting to put the leash on the board. Since the break was only twenty or thirty yards out and thigh high at most, I figured paddling after wipeouts wouldn't kill me.

The author with the Bingo Board outside the Cajun
Holiday Motel in Grand Isle, Louisiana.
*Courtesy of the author.*

Despite the assurances from the folks at the diner, I stepped lightly and slid my feet on the bottom to avoid the stingrays. My Florida grandmother taught me this "stingray shuffle." I taught my daughter. Zinnia asked me if sliding your feet really scares away stingrays, and I assured her that it does—although it's not kook-proof. Rays have stung me more than a few times in the Gulf. None swam under foot this day.

The water on the Gulf Coast of Louisiana is a warm chocolate brown. It's laden with silt from the Mississippi. As I looked down at the earthy solution sloshing across the deck of the Bingo Board, I thought about snowmelt from Minnesota, rainfall from Wisconsin, soil from Iowa farms, dirt from Missouri construction sites, and tailings from Kentucky mines. Half the continent from the eastern side of the Rockies to the western slopes of the Appalachians drains down this river system. It sweeps the wetlands clean of plant and animal matter, mixing the biological and mineral into a dark, rich tincture in constant, slow-motion churn. All of that geology and ecology flowed through my fingers as I ran my hands through the water and waited for a wave to emerge from the Gulf.

I'm not sure that what I caught was an actual wave, but the magical inertia of the Bingo Board kept me moving toward the beach for a good five seconds after I stopped paddling and stood tall. At the end of the ride, I threw both arms into the air with a huge claim as if I'd been spit out of a double-overhead barrel. I even hooted a "Yeehaw" for myself, since no one else was going to cheer for me as I rode the wild Louisiana surf.

Zinnia documented the moment for posterity, and I went in to get her. We paddled around together. I pushed her into a few waves that were so gutless they were actually pretty tough for her to ride. As a beginner, you don't want to go too fast for fear of losing control, but if you go too slowly, it's hard to maintain your balance. After a few rides and a few more wipeouts followed by frantic dogpaddling to avoid stingrays, Zinnia had had enough of Louisiana surfing. We rode a few on our stomach and then called it a day. As we walked back to the Cajun Holiday, the mosquitos started dive-bombing us. The weaker wind signaled feeding time for the local bloodsuckers. I'll say this for Grand Isle: what it lacks in waves, it makes up for in mosquitos.

Back at the hotel, a couple of the fishermen struck up a conversation with me, based mostly on the novelty of the Bingo Board. They complained about how bad the fishing had been that morning because of the "big" waves. Commiserating, I told them the surf had been just as bad. Grand Isle must have sighed with frustration at the ungrateful human visitors. I could almost hear the island scold us in a Cajun cadence, "Y'all gonna miss me when I'm gone."

# 4

# *Surf City, USA*

## *Mobile, Alabama*

After we left Grand Isle, we hauled ass toward Alabama. The languid southern Louisiana bayous ebbed and suburban New Orleans flowed around us. We resisted the allure of the Crescent City and crossed the border into the Mississippi, entering the Magnolia State south of the "most southern place on Earth"—the Mississippi Delta. Delta residents wink at the geographical impossibility of this claim while nodding at its undeniable cultural truth.

Zinnia missed another history lecture and autobiographical monologue by napping through this part of the trip. She's heard vague tales of her father teaching in freedom schools in the Delta. These weren't the famous freedom schools of the 1960s, when the KKK killed civil rights activists for trying to register to vote. No, I taught in a freedom school program during the late 1990s—a faint echo of 1960s idealism.

"Mr. ES-TEEZ, you sound half-redneck and half-surfer," one Delta kid told me, before advising, "Drop the redneck." It was sage advice and a painfully accurate assessment of my "teacher voice" at that time. Those kids smelled blood in the water the first time I waded into their classroom. They circled like a shiver of ravenous bull sharks. Every afternoon, I'd return to the teacher house with a hoarse voice and a feeling of defeat.

My boss, the founder of the program, had little sympathy. He gave the teachers and students the same tough love. Sink or swim, he'd be pushing you under to make you earn it. When the teachers arrived in the Delta, we were horrified to learn that our house lacked air conditioning. We endured three sweltering days and nights in the Delta before the veteran teacher who owned the place returned and asked, "Why isn't the AC on?!" Our boss smiled at the rest of us sadistically. Welcome to Mississippi.

Part of me wanted to take Zinnia on a battlefield tour of my greatest defeats in Mississippi, but there's no surf in the Delta. Neither the Yazoo River nor the mighty Mississippi produce rideable swells, at least not survivable ones. Biloxi and the promisingly named Waveland do get occasional surf on the state's Gulf Coast. No one agreed to an interview in these beach towns, so we raced across Mississippi to get to Alabama. Zinnia snored unconvincingly, sure that if she opened her eyes I would bore her to death with more stories.

Palisades of pines guarded both sides of the highway as we drove eastward. The monotony of these interminable pine tree vistas all but required musical accompaniment to maintain consciousness. Zinnia had largely ceded control of the radio to me as she pretended to nap. For much of Mississippi, I listened to country stations, a regime broken only by Zinnia's radio revolution, leading to a Top 40 reign of terror—featuring Justin Bieber and Bruno Mars.

The compromise between country and Top 40 turned out to be classic rock. From Texas through Florida, classic-rock stations came in loud and clear, making it the soundtrack for much of our trip. Much to Zinnia's chagrin, the distorted guitars and feral wails of dad-driven noise pollution began in Houston.

Houston's classic-rock station is called "the Eagle." If you have fled the world of "terrestrial radio" for satellites, podcasts, and digital music, you may not realize that classic-rock stations are still awesome. Their names pair strong definite articles with inspiring nature themes: the Wolf, the River, the Hawk, the Bone, or (slightly less natural, but no less manly) the Rocket. Sometimes these names are related to their call letters. Other times, they seem to be products of some all-male boardroom at Clear Channel, Infinity Broadcasting, or Soulless Media. Houston's "Eagle" had an actual affiliation with its call letters KGLK, although these letters could have just as easily morphed into "the Kegel." Naming a classic-rock station after a pelvic exercise seems like an opportunity to diversify the listening audience.

Rush, Led Zeppelin, Aerosmith, and Lynyrd Skynyrd provided reliable opportunities for scream-alongs, steering wheel drum fills, and hands-free air guitar solos that satisfied a middle-aged dad and mortified his preteen daughter. I'd been inflicting such songs on Zinnia since she was little. She knows all of the words to classic road songs like "Ramble On" and "Tuesday's Gone." Despite herself, Zinnia occasionally lapsed into harmony with Robert Plant or Ronnie Van Zant before sheepishly glancing around to see if any passing drivers could see her rocking out. Her dad felt no such shame as we rolled toward Alabama.

~~~~~~~~~~~~~~~~~~~~~~~~~~~~~~~~~~~~~~~~~~~

Few would mistake Mobile, Alabama for Surf City, USA. Situated on a bay with no ridable waves, Mobile is connected to the Gulf more through its port than beaches. Like Houston, many Alabama surfers hail not from the small seaside communities along the Gulf, but from the nearby city and its leafy suburbs. That's where Zinnia and I found Mike "Tank" Young and his dog Spot.

When we arrived at Tank's place, the first thing I noticed was an old personalized license plate nailed to his fence. Underneath the motto "Stars Fell on Alabama," Tank had added his own personal mantra: "SURF-IT." The man that met us at the door bore a striking resemblance to Santa Claus, if Santa Claus had a long, white ponytail to match his bushy white beard and a southern drawl to match his jolly laugh. I can only guess that Tank's nickname came partly from his Santa-like physique. His hand dwarfed mine as we shook in greetings.

When I called Tank to confirm our interview, he told me that Zinnia and I should crash at his house. He just had to move his hunting clothes off the guest bed, and we'd be welcome. I later learned that Tank hosted lots of traveling surfers, folks from Hawaii, California, and nearly every point of the compass. I didn't want to impose, and it turned out that Tank's dog Spot, a pit bull mix, was a far too enthusiastic host. During our interview, Spot licked and pawed Zinnia so energetically that I worried the dog's exuberance would underscore the "hospital" in hospitality. Before things went that far, Tank banished Spot to the yard.

Tank decorated his dimly lit man cave with comfortable, cushy furniture—the seat of honor a well-loved, Archie Bunker–style recliner. Hunting and surfing memorabilia hung on the walls. As we spoke, classic surf documentaries played silently in an endless loop on his TV. These distractions made for a tough interview setting, but they were not enough to hold Zinnia's attention. A master of electronic parenting, I handed Zinnia a device on which she whiled away the time with a game called *Subway Surfers*. I kept telling myself that listening to all of us old guys "talk story" about wave-riding back in the day would increase her stoke. Instead, she tuned us out. Her digital avatar skimmed across the flashing screen.

Tank kindly arranged for two other longtime Alabama surfers to join us: Clif Dodd and Gene Gabel. Between the three of them, they covered several decades of surfing in the state. Tank was the biggest character of the group and the most jubilant storyteller. Gene and Clif complemented Tank's enthusiastic nostalgia with more critical analysis. Born in the mid-to-late 1940s into military families, both Gene and Clif fit the classic mold of baby-boomer surfers. They caught wave-riding fever from the movies and music pumped out of southern California in the early 1960s.

~~~~~~~~~~~~~~~~~~~~~~~~~~~~~~~~~~~~~~~~~~~~~~~~~~

Two distinct subgenres of surf music swept across America in the early 1960s. On the one hand, the instrumental blues rock of groups like the Ventures and Surfaris served as the perfect sonic backdrop for movies and television shows of the era. The Ventures charted the first hit of the genre in 1960 with "Walk Don't Run," and the Surfaris followed with "Wipe Out" a few years later. The true godfather of instrumental surf rock was Dick Dale, an East Coast transplant to Southern California, who picked up surfing and guitar in the 1950s. Dale spliced the Middle Eastern melodies favored by his Lebanese dad into the blues rock of 1950s wizards like Link Wray to create an intriguing hybrid sound. Dale's cover of the traditional Greek tune "Misirlou" became his biggest hit in 1962, but I'm partial to his surfy 1963 take on the Jewish folk tune "Hava Nagila." An audio effect known as reverb enshrined Dale's guitar lines within a cavernous hall of echo. Epic guitar solos captured much of the attention given to the genre, but the rhythm sections of instrumental surf-rock bands lent their tunes a vital danceability. The leg-shaking cadences of songs like "Surfing Drums" and "Surf Beat" fueled the genre's success miles from any ocean.

If instrumental surf rock traced its ancestry back to the blues and jazz of the 1950s, the other subgenre of surf music that exploded onto the pop charts in the early 1960s owed a debt of gratitude to the preceding era's doo-wop bands. The syrupy harmonies of Jan and Dean's "Surf City" gave way to the lusher vocal arrangements of the Beach Boys' string of hits. Brian Wilson's manic musical genius underscored these harmonies with three-minute pocket symphonies. Even though Brian Wilson only stuck his toes in the water for album cover photo shoots, his talent in the studio gave surf music staying power beyond its mercurial rise in the 1960s.

These songs harnessed real surf lingo and name-checked famous surf spots, but historian Matt Warshaw argues that they mostly fell on deaf ears for real California surfers. "We hated that crap," big wave pioneer Greg Noll scoffed with a typically blunt assessment. That was just "whiny, cornball music," dismissed another champion surfer of this era. "More than anything," Warshaw concluded in his magisterial *History of Surfing*, "surfers' disregard for the Beach Boys and Jan and Dean came down to authenticity—or lack thereof." In other words, most vocal surf music wasn't made by real surfers, but by (and for) kooks.

Still, this music rode the radio waves across the country, carrying with it the surf craze. In "Surfin' USA," the Beach Boys wondered what would happen if everyone had their own ocean as perfect as the Pacific. For kids listening to surf music in Kansas or Montana during the early 1960s, this required a rich imagination, but for kids in Houston or Mobile, it just required a radio, a full tank of gas, and a short drive to the Gulf Coast. These kids might have started out as hodads (1960s slang for kooks), but some of them became real, lifelong surfers.

Clif Dodd listened to the Surfaris. Gene Gabel liked the Ventures, Jan and Dean, and the Beach Boys. In the early 1960s, transistor radios lay along the Gulf Shores like driftwood. When Alabama surfers came in from the beach, they might catch a bite to eat at the Hangout, pumping dimes into the jukebox to make up their own summer soundtracks. In the late 1960s when he was in the army, Gene and his buddies would crank up the volume of classic surf rock on eight-track tapes during their long journeys from barracks to the beach. By the 1970s, Alabama surfers partied (and crashed) in rooms at the Sunnyland Motel. The motel's owner, Walter Ferguson, didn't surf, but he took a liking to the sunburned tribe, hiring many of them to work at his motel and gas station. Parties at "Fergieland" soon became legendary. Woe unto other, unsuspecting hotel guests who stopped for a quiet night's rest and found anything but, as the surfers rocked and rolled until the early morning hours.

Talk of music inspired Tank to jump up out of his recliner and retreat to his room to dig up an ancient artifact—an old cube of a weather radio. The Radio Shack instrument recalled a time when surfers really had to be meteorologists. Half of the times Gene, Clif, and Tank drove to Dauphin Island or Gulf Shores, they'd race down the white sand to a break that was flatter than the surface of a bathtub. To avoid such seemingly inevitable disappointment, Tank cranked up the weather radio. "We would listen to the report from Grand Isle, Louisiana," he told me, "and if it said winds out of the south-southwest at fifteen to twenty, seas six-to-eight feet, off we'd go." Alabama surfers even called the Coast Guard occasionally to get an inside line on incoming swells. Eventually, surfers could call one of the local shops like Les Stinson's Natural Wave Surf Shop, to get updated surf reports.

All three of the Alabama surfers admitted that the infrequency of good waves meant that swells took priority over everything else in their lives when they were younger. "If there's a front out in the Gulf," Gene chimed in, "you're leaving work early or skipping school or whatever it was." "We did that a lot," Tank agreed in his best stage whisper, furtively looking over at my impressionable daughter to see if she was listening. "She's not going to do that," I assured him. "What do they say?" Gene asked with a laugh. "*We* might be dumbasses, but that doesn't mean *you* should be." Zinnia didn't even look up from her game.

Since he was ten years younger than Gene, Tank's earliest musical memories of surfing lay on the other side of the counterculture divide that the Beach Boys managed to straddle with their psychedelic, orchestral pop album *Pet Sounds*. Tank listened to that and the old surf rock, but Santana, the Allman Brothers, and Pink Floyd soon eclipsed the early 1960s tunes in his surf soundtrack.

~~~~~~~~~~~~~~~~~~~~~~~~~~~~~~~~~~~~~~~~~~~~~~~

By the 1980s, these psychedelic rock bands had rebounded onto the radio in the form of classic-rock nostalgia in that way that popular culture feasts on itself every few decades. As a result, I grew up listening to many of the same songs that Tank, Gene, and Clif loved. When I first learned to surf in South Carolina, the local classic-rock station was 96 Wave (WAVF), which began broadcasting in 1985 with the actual sounds of waves breaking before smoothly segueing into 1960s and '70s arena rock. Occasionally, a new band would snake its way onto the classic-rock airwaves. The summer that I learned how to surf, U2 released *The Joshua Tree*, which became the soundtrack to my first surf sessions.

On the way to the beach, 96 Wave pumped "Where the Streets Have No Name" into my brain. That song creeps into your consciousness like the first rays of dawn as silence gives way to the swelling wash of organ chords. These chords flow into the Edge's iconic delayed guitar pattern. The notes cascade onto the listener from a seemingly infinite height. The song's repetition is both meditative and propulsive. A California desert originally inspired the album, but the brilliant malleability of the music makes it a perfect soundscape for almost anywhere. "Where the Streets Have No Name" seemed just as apt a description of the blacktop that stretched between Charleston and Folly Beach as it did sand-swept California roads lined with Joshua trees.

Music matters to surfers because it forms the soundtrack not just of our journeys to the beach, but also our sessions. The last tune you hear before you hit the water jangles around in your head as you bob and weave in the ocean. During our Mobile interview, Gene Gabel remembered one session when he kicked out after a long ride just in time to see his buddy pitch over the falls in a heinous wipeout. Gene's buddy surfaced, cackling wildly at his own misfortune and humming the rollicking instrumental hit "Classical Gas," which dominated the airwaves that year. There must be surfers who listen to NPR or morning shock jocks on the way to surf, but I can't imagine why. No epic session ever started with *All Things Considered* or a zoo crew's zany hijinks.

My surfing buddy Alexander shared my love of 1980s rock acts like U2 that recalled the grandeur of 1970s arena rock or alternative bands like REM and Drivin' N Cryin' that echoed their southern rock predecessors. But Alexander preferred the psychedelic folk rock of the Grateful Dead and the electrified blues of masters like B. B. King. As often as not, his beat-up Honda Civic carried us to the ocean, so he called the tunes, making me a de facto Deadhead and wannabe bluesman.

When both Alexander and I left Charleston for school, we entered extended periods of landlocked surf droughts. Mine lasted roughly a decade, with brief coastal interludes like a summer waiting tables in San Francisco. Most surfers suffer through such dry spells when school, work, or family responsibilities curtail time in the water. The music that originally inspired me to surf temporarily took the sport's place in my heart. I learned guitar and bass, in part, to make up for the increasingly kookish distance from the ocean my path had taken. This was the 1990s, an era when a pox of singer-songwriter sentimentality infected coffee shops and bars across the country. Caught up in the cultural moment, I wrote a song about my self-imposed exile from the ocean. Sadly, no one could mistake "Neptune's Tears" as a masterpiece of surf music. Happily, it was an instrumental tune. Imagine the awful lyrics! God only knows.

When Gene Gabel started surfing in the early 1960s, other Alabamians would joke at gas stations between Mobile and the Gulf that the thing on top of his car must be a giant water ski. One day, he saw another car with boards on the roof coming back from the beach. Both he and the other driver literally ran off the road with excitement. The other guy, Leon, remained one of Gene's buddies more than five decades later.

Alabama surfers learned from each other in the tiny Gulf Coast Surf Club, Young Wave Hunters, and other groups. Mostly, they learned through trial and error. After Clif bought his first board, he knew that he was supposed to wax it, but he didn't know how. He put some of his mom's furniture polish on the board and headed to the beach. The waves were chest high and choppy, rough going for any beginner. He paddled, and as soon as he tried to stand, he slipped right off the polish-slicked deck. "I just busted my tail falling off the board. Every time I tried to get up, I'd go bam!" Something wasn't right. Clif bought some paraffin wax, melted it in a tin, poured it on the board, and then roughed it up. That did the trick—less slipping and more sliding.

Alabama can't claim any secret big-wave spots or even consistent mid-range breaks, but the state's tiny coastline does contain a few fun breaks that keep the locals stoked despite long periods of frustratingly small surf. Today, Dauphin Island catches the most waves. Old-timers get nostalgic about the heyday of the Alabama Point jetties before dredged sand tamed the break. The rock jetties jut out from Perdido Pass, where a river cuts through the barrier islands. These jetties refracted and focused swells from hurricanes and larger storms in the Gulf. Sure, there was a long paddle and the rip could occasionally pull you miles down the beach, but these were small prices to pay for waves that crested over head high on epic days.

Assuming the role of raconteur, Tank recalled just such a day at the jetties. It was a hurricane swell, but he couldn't remember which one. When Tank and his buddies first paddled out, the waves were four, five, even six feet on the sets, about as good as it got. Over the course of the session, as the storm approached the Alabama coast, the waves continued to grow. Tank looked around and realized that his buddies had all caught waves and headed to the beach. He was alone. He turned his attention back to the Gulf. Seeing a massive set approaching, he paddled like mad towards it. His only chance to avoid getting steamrolled by white water would be cresting the heaving swells before they broke. He made it over the first wave, an eight-footer. Made it over the second, a nine-footer. Made it over the third, a ten-footer.

Tank's friends looked like specks on the beach. "The rip was so bad," he recalled. "How bad was it?" Gene cracked, with perfect timing, egging Tank on. The rip was so bad that it dragged Tank two miles from the jetties down to Terry Cove. His friends walked down the beach, keeping pace with him, but there was little they could do to help from the safety of shore. No one wanted to paddle back out to play the hero. Finally, Tank summoned the courage to catch a wave. When the wave hit the outer sandbar, it jacked up into a monstrous fifteen-foot face. "Scared the ever-living hell out of me," Tank recalled. "I surfed it. I made it in. All my friends hugged me and thanked God."

"Then you hit the showers, right?" Gene joked, acknowledging what we all knew—that this was a glory-days sports story with more than a few feet added to the wave heights. We also all understood that feeling of being out past the limits of our ability in a situation beyond our control—the kind of session that reminds one how small and insignificant humans are in comparison to the vastness of the ocean. Thinking back to those moments in our surfing lives, we forgave Tank his enthusiastic exaggerations.

It helped that Tank didn't take himself too seriously. At one point, the conversation turned to "men in gray suits," a quaint Australian euphemism for the sharks that often ply their trade in the same waters as surfers. The Alabama Point jetties and Dauphin Island have more than their fair of shark sightings. Gene, Clif, and Tank had all seen sharks while surfing. Gene and his friend Leon ran into a few at Johnson Beach. Clif saw one at First Street. Not to be outdone, Tank recalled the day he charged out in the channel at the jetties right after the movie *Jaws* opened in theaters. Paddling hard to avoid the rip, Tank froze mid-stroke when he saw a massive maw open wide next to his board. He was so close that he caught sight of the shark's last meal caught in its teeth. He yanked his hand back in the nick of time, before the plastic bag he mistook for *Jaws* floated by harmlessly. Tank's friends teased him for years about his courage in the face of certain death.

As Gene, Clif, and Tank grew older, they began to travel both for jobs and waves. Gene went into the army and did a stint in military intelligence at the Pentagon, necessitating 300-mile surf trips down to the Outer Banks. Clif went into the navy, hoping he'd stay close to the water. He got to surf in California and Virginia, but also ended up working for two years in Idaho at one of the navy's inland nuclear power facilities. The closest he came to surfing there was sliding down snow-covered hills on his longboard. Tank traveled to Hawaii and met some of the icons of 1970s surfing, sharing sessions with Buttons Kaluhiokalani.

Surfing broadened these Mobile natives' horizons, exposing them to different cultures and ideas. Gene tried vegetarianism for a while. Surfers like him brought a "West Coast vibe" to Mobile. In the days before the internet

Tank Young, Clif Dodd, and Gene Gabel (*l to r*), behind Tank's
house in Mobile, Alabama. Note the personalized license plate
with Tank's motto "SURF-IT" nailed to the fence.
*Courtesy of the author.*

and 24-7 global media coverage, traveling and surfing made Clif Dodd feel
less isolated than many of his Alabama neighbors. Tank grew out his hair
and learned a new appreciation for the natural world.

As much as surfing and traveling changed these guys, they remained
proud southerners. Tank lived and died for Crimson Tide football. When the
big Alabamian talked about his love for the environment, he bemoaned the
fact that it was hard to organize a local Surfrider chapter. He also explained
his philosophy in a way that echoed Ducks Unlimited more than Earthjus-
tice. "Well, being at one with the ocean is one thing," he said. "It's like going
hunting. You get out into the woods to enjoy nature. To clear your head.
There's nothing like paddling out and sitting there and breathing the fresh
air and watching the waves and catching a wave." Clif Dodd's globetrotting
had broadened his horizons without altering his political trajectory toward
rock-ribbed Republicanism. When he wasn't shaping and painting beautiful custom surfboards for his kids and grandkids on the weekends, he was
teaching Sunday School at his church.

The conversation wound down. Zinnia emerged from her electronic
game. Clif drew me a map to a couple of good breaks on the Alabama coast

and just across the state line at Perdido Key in Florida. Zinnia tried to hide the impressive scratch Tank's dog Spot had left on her cheek. We waved goodbye and headed to the hotel to decompress before hitting the beach the next morning.

Zinnia and I followed Clif's hand-drawn map to the Alabama coast. Sure, we could have used my cell phone, but what would have been the fun in that? We did get lost a few times, through no fault of Clif's directions. After a few diversions through the piney woods of southern Alabama, we finally ended up in Orange Beach. High-rise hotels and condos protruded from the dunes like snaggled brown teeth along much of the once-pristine, lightly developed Alabama coast.

Approaching the state line, we saw a bar creatively called the Flora-Bama. The place turned out to be a cultural center for the coast. "If you're looking for the Redneck Riviera, you will find it there," historian Harvey H. Jackson III wrote of the Flora-Bama. The bar sponsored mullet-tossing contests on the nearby beach and was decorated with the bras of female patrons. Most nights, Jackson claimed, you could yell "Bubba" and fifteen people would turn around.

Across from the Flora-Bama and next to the sign that read "Welcome to Florida: We're Open for Business," we found a vacant lot where we parked for free. Zinnia and I decided to surf our way from Alabama to Florida. As Tank promised, the sand was "sugar-white," a stark contrast to the silt we sifted through in Louisiana. A stiff onshore wind nearly obliterated the anemic swell in the water. One short-boarder beat us to the break, bobbing about fifteen yards offshore. The guy didn't seem to know how to stand up, much less ride his board. Still, he easily outgunned his two buddies, who were armed only with boogie boards.

Dragging the Bingo Board against the stiff breeze, we reached the water line. The lack of waves and surprisingly biting wind did not inspire enthusiasm in Zinnia. She wrapped the leash around her ankle and several eye rolls later, paddled past the sea reeds to the first sandbar. Random white caps roiled the surface of the water, occasionally breaking with enough force in the direction of shore to approximate waves. Zinnia took a few of these and even made it to the open face of a knee-high screamer. I caught one or two outside waves and rode them triumphantly several feet past the sandbar. Laughing at the futility of the situation, we took one final belly ride together that carried us across the state line into Florida.

Back at the car, a guy about my age strolled by carrying a rental long-board under his arm. His flip-flops slapped a happy rhythm on the asphalt of Perdido Beach Boulevard. The dude called over to say thanks. He hadn't surfed in ages, but seeing Zinnia and me thrash around in the shore break motivated him to get a board to do the same with his kids.

A few weeks later, Clif Dodd checked in to see where we decided to go surfing and how the waves had been. I told him about the magic of the Flora-Bama lineup. He responded with two grainy, digital images of an eight-foot alligator swaggering across the road just a stone's throw from where we'd paddled out.

On the short drive to Pensacola, Zinnia spied a life-size cardboard cutout of President Donald Trump in the window of a welding shop. We pulled over to investigate. The welding shop was closed. The owner had plastered the doors with an impressive array of signs and stickers. One sign warned that the premises were "Protected by Smith & Wesson." Another proudly proclaimed support for Florida's stand-your-ground law. By contrast, an AME church across the street had a sign that announced "Everyone Welcome" for Sunday services. As inviting as this message was, the church lacked a life-sized Trump giving the thumbs-up to passersby.

"I'm not sure this is a good idea, Daddy," Zinnia wisely observed as we debated whether to check out the welding shop window display. I argued that despite all of his protestations, the shop owner clearly wanted visitors to come and take selfies on his property. Zinnia mugged for the camera. She flashed me a nervous smile and stuck out her thumb and pinky in the shaka sign, aping the president's goofy grin and enthusiastic thumbs up. Survival instinct and parenting skills kicked in. We sprinted back to the truck and headed for Pensacola.

# 5
# Charlie Don't Surf
## Pensacola, Florida

Instead of throwing down big bucks for a nice hotel near the beach in Pensacola, I found a humbler establishment downtown. Sight unseen, the place looked perfect. Just north of an hourly rate flophouse on the quality and price scale, this hotel promised proximity to everything. Directions suggested that it was close to the highway—a little too close, it turned out. A massive concrete viaduct wrapped around much of the structure, obscuring all possible views except for the picturesque parking lot.

Venturing out for a walk our first night in town, Zinnia and I discovered a beautiful, old Pensacola neighborhood. We strolled past a historical marker honoring the state's first Black junior college, named for famed educator Booker T. Washington, and on to a small patch of quiet greenery known as Lee Square. The square, part of a former military post, had been renamed for the commander of the Army of Northern Virginia in the 1880s. A few years later it became the site of Pensacola's thirty-foot-tall monument to Confederate war dead. According to the inscription, the soldier perched atop the statue and others like him were "uncrowned heroes of the southern Confederacy whose joy was to suffer and die for a cause they believed to be just." For decades after its construction, the monument stood proudly as the centerpiece for Confederate Memorial Day celebrations in town. By the time Zinnia and I found it and read the inscription, this monument and others like it throughout the South had long been objects of controversy. This battle over Confederate memorials gained new urgency as a result of the Black Lives Matter movement. The mayor of Pensacola proposed taking down the Lee Square monument two months after our visit, and the city council eventually agreed, voting to remove the memorial and change the name of the park back to Florida Square a few years later.

On the recommendation of local folks, Zinnia and I dined at Jerry's Drive In. Despite the name, Jerry's is mostly a sit-down place these days. Opened in 1939, the restaurant relishes in its throwback appeal. The kitchen fryer gets a workout every day and night. You can get fried mullet, grouper, shrimp, steak, chicken, oysters, livers, gizzards, hush puppies, onion rings, and of course, five varieties of French fries. Zinnia and I stuck with the bacon cheeseburgers, which were as delicious as advertised. In terms of decor, Jerry's goes for a "more is more" philosophy. Pigs, chickens, banners for dozens of college sports teams, and signs from each decade since the restaurant's founding line every inch of wall space. Our booth had a bumper sticker of recent vintage that read:

Capitalism<br>
— pays for —<br>
Socialism

Unfortunately, capitalism didn't pay for our meal (directly). I gladly paid in cash, since Jerry's doesn't take credit cards. Zinnia and I waddled back to the car, fat and happy. We slid into a food coma back at the motel with dreams of surf the next morning.

I woke up to not one but two surf reports. One of the guys I was interviewing in Pensacola texted to say that there was ridable surf, but it was—surprise, surprise—a little mixed up due to the wind. Tom Grow, a longtime local surfer who lived across the road from the beach gave me the live report, optimistically predicting that the wind would die down a bit before coming back up later in the morning. I should surf at the Pensacola Pier with Zinnia first thing, he advised, before we headed to his house for our interview.

One advantage of sleeping next to an on-ramp is that you can roll out of bed directly onto the highway. Zinnia and I made it to the pier in record time. There were already six or seven guys out in the water. The waves were waist-to-stomach high, as big as we'd seen them in the Gulf of Mexico on this trip. The flags at the pier snapped audibly on their poles, flying parallel to the beach on a strong side-shore wind.

Unlike the onshore winds which had plagued us for much of the trip, the side-shore winds didn't destroy the surf, but they did make for some rough surface conditions and bumpy takeoffs, especially when we were headed into the wind going left. Luckily, Zinnia and I are both regular footers when we surf, meaning that our right foot is closer to the back of the board, and we face the wave when we ride to the right. (Strangely, both of us skate as "goofy-footers," with our left foot near the back of the board.)

Like most regular-foot surfers, we feel more comfortable facing the wave and going right, which for us is "front-side," as opposed to going left with our back facing the wave (back-side). The direction of the side-shore wind meant that there would be plenty of rights for us. The trick would be finding ones that were gentle enough for Zinnia to catch.

Regardless of the wave size, paddling out for the first time at a new spot always gets the adrenaline pumping. People told us that Pensacola had some of the best waves on the Gulf Coast. This session proved them right. As we approached the water's edge and looked at the first daunting shore break of our trip, Zinnia admitted that she was a little scared. I confessed that I was a little nervous too. (Of course, I wasn't *really* scared; I just knew you were supposed to say stuff like this before risking the death of your only offspring.) The empathy pep talk worked. Zinnia strapped on the leash of the Bingo Board. We waited for a break in the wave action. After the last wave of a set, we launched into the sea.

Zinnia and I tandem-paddled relatively easily to the first sandbar, where the waves were breaking a bit bigger than they had looked from the beach, maybe four feet on the sets. I ended up treading water for the first twenty minutes, because it was too deep for me to stand and push Zinnia into waves. She rolled into the whitewater on a wave that was about waist high and got a good ride. It boosted her confidence. The next wave was bigger. She rode it on her belly to the inshore. I got tossed like a ragdoll after she took off. When I popped back up, I was proud that she had managed to hang on to the board. After a couple more waves, Zinnia had enough. She got out and searched for seashells, collecting one from each place we visited.

Once Zinnia went onto the beach, I took the Bingo Board back out to put it through its paces. As Tom Grow had predicted, the wind subsided a bit. The waves cleaned up just enough for some longer rides of maybe five or six seconds. Admitting the pitifully short length of these rides, I can almost hear non-surfers asking, "Is that what all the fuss is about?! Five or six seconds?"

If you look at it rationally, there is no way that surfing makes sense. With other sports, you are constantly in motion or playing for an hour or two with a few timeouts or breaks. Performance art is the same. A dancer doesn't wait for twenty minutes, dance for six seconds, run to the other side of the room, wait ten more minutes, and repeat the process. But dancers practice their skill on a stable floor in a room or hall. Surfers don't have it so easy. We must find a beach where waves *can* break in a certain way, wait until the waves *are* breaking that certain way, and finally, *catch* the wave that breaks that certain way. Only then can we dance.

On my first wave at the Pensacola Pier, I took off behind the peak. Staying in a low crouch, I ploughed my way through the mush of white water that broke in front of me to get to the open face. The Bingo Board proved faster than I thought and the stability of all that extra foam served me well. My second wave had even more open face. I connected it to the inside, where an oncoming wave made for a perfect little ramp. The Bingo actually responded as I shifted my weight to my back foot and leaned over the inside rail toward the wave's face. This turned the Bingo up to the breaking lip. Smacking the lip with the bottom of the board, I floated over the oncoming whitewater, and glided down smoothly to the flats in front of the wave.

Nearly every ride that day turned out like that. The Bingo kept surprising me with its suppleness, especially given that I was such a novice longboarder. Eventually, I started to feel guilty about Zinnia sitting alone on the beach. Taking one last ride in, I looked longingly at the horizon. I could see Pensacola's surfing future, but it was time to learn about its past.

Zinnia and I headed west from the pier, past Peg Leg Pete's seafood place to a beautiful pink house with white trim just across the road from the beachside dunes. On the phone, Tom Grow bragged that he had the perfect living room for our interview. He hadn't lied. From the bay windows, you could peek over the dunes at the vastness of the Gulf.

Tom invited his friend Scott Bush to join us. The two men had been surfing buddies for six decades by the time Zinnia and I sat down with them. They finished each other's sentences like an old married couple. This easy rapport and longtime friendship belied dramatic differences between the two guys. Tom was a retired marine biology professor who spent his days shaping clay into beautiful pots, vases, and other works of art. His politics leaned to the left, and he wasn't shy about expressing them. Scott was equally outspoken in his conservative views. After a long and varied trade career, working mostly for the government on or near military bases, Scott's artistic outlet remained surfboard shaping. His productivity had slowed in recent years, but he had probably shaped over a thousand boards in his life.

Both Tom and Scott were the sons of military men. Tom's dad had gotten out of the navy not long after World War II and settled in Pensacola, where he worked as a civilian contractor. Scott's itinerant childhood reflected his father's many years in the Marine Corps. He bounced around from North

Lifelong friends Tom Grow (*l*) and Scott Bush stand in front of Tom's house overlooking the Gulf of Mexico in Pensacola Beach, Florida. *Courtesy of the author.*

Carolina to California to Florida. "The military messed me up," Scott said by way of explanation. "Every two years, I'm ready to go." When he left a town, he'd always leave "part of my history behind."

Military deployments call the cadence of life along much of the southern coast, but particularly Pensacola and the Florida panhandle. More than 55,000 active duty military personnel were stationed in Florida when we traveled there, 16,000 of them at the Pensacola Naval Air Station. In addition to the naval air station, a navy dive center, two Air Force bases, and several Coast Guard stations wrestled for branch supremacy along 100 miles of coastline. The comings and goings of all these service personnel have long made this stretch of the "Emerald Coast" more cosmopolitan than outsiders would guess given its unofficial nickname: Redneck Riviera.

Tom Grow credits navy guys with introducing Pensacola locals to surfing in the late 1950s. Scattered references to wave-riding can be found in Pensacola papers as far back as the 1920s and '30s, but the sport didn't take hold until the late 1950s, when two of Tom's lifeguard friends watched in wonder as a navy pilot from California hit the beach with a board from back home. "Whoa," Tom remembers the lifeguards saying, "we didn't realize you could do that here!" They immediately came up with a scheme to make their own board by gluing Styrofoam blocks together and then glassing the surface with polyester resin. Unfortunately, polyester resin melts Styrofoam. Back to the drawing board. The Pensacola locals coated their Styrofoam board with rubber-based paint and then glassed the whole thing. Whether or not this Frankenstein project was a "surfboard," the lifeguards were proud of their work. "It's alive!" they must have said. So was the Pensacola surf scene.

Tom Grow and Scott Bush both caught their first waves in 1959. Tom took his first ride in Pensacola. Scott worked out the kinks of kookdom at Laguna Beach and San Onofre on either side of the legendary break at Dana Point in Southern California. Within a year or two, Scott's dad had been transferred once again from this surfer's paradise to Pensacola. Scott brought his Velzy longboard, joining the growing line-up of panhandle locals, including Tom, who was hard to miss with a bright yellow, nine-foot, six-inch Hobie.

By 1962 Tom and Scott were itching to get out of Florida. When Tom's brother joined the navy, they followed him out to Southern California. On the sixty-three-hour bus ride from Pensacola to San Diego, they lost track of both the miles and the number of hands of canasta. That summer trip was the first of many Pacific pilgrimages the guys made in the 1960s, suggesting that the distance between the Pensacola surf scene and its better-known California cousins was not nearly as great as one might think.

Surfing La Jolla's famous Windansea, the two Floridians traded off waves with each other and a hundred of their closest friends at the perpetually crowded spot. After a good ride one day, Scott had almost gotten back out to the lineup when a set approached. He was just three or four good paddles from where Tom sat, comfortably bobbing on his board beyond the impact zone. Those fifteen feet turned out to be the difference between easily cresting the set waves and a much less desirable alternative. The two friends made eye contact. Tom watched as Scott's face contorted from the smiling memory of his last ride to fear of the oncoming wall. Scott wasn't going to make it. Time slowed. He held on with white knuckles as his board went vertical like a tombstone before flipping backward in the pitching lip. The two friends still chuckled about it decades later. Tom laughed a little harder than his buddy.

In between these surf trips and stints working on the West Coast, Tom tried (and largely failed) to pursue higher education. Scott tried (and largely failed) to earn money at a random assortment of jobs. The two friends learned that the owner of Hutson Hardware wanted to make surfboards to capitalize on the popular craze. The owner asked Scott and Tom if they could make boards. "Sure!" they immediately said. Neither had made a board before. They'd seen guys shape in California. How hard could it be? They started by simply glassing the foam boards that hardware store already sold. Then, they bought unshaped blanks and began carving their own line in earnest. Scott had a better feel for shaping, so Tom became the glass man. When I joked about the number of boards they must have thrown away before they perfected the craft, the two men corrected me nearly in unison. "We sold every board we ever made!" They shaped and glassed for several shops in Florida and California before eventually creating their own company—Design Line custom boards.

Tom described surfing in Pensacola as "a frustrating process of waiting for the surf to come up, hoping the conditions are good, and constantly checking to see if things have changed." He argued that the tricky combination of wind and inconsistent swell made Pensacola a difficult place to learn to surf. "Some of the best surf I've ever had has been here, but those times are few and far between."

By the late 1960s and early 1970s, Tom and Scott found themselves elder statesmen of a young man's game. They were still in their twenties! Yancy Spencer became the most famous Pensacola surfer in that era due to his unmatched competitive drive and business savvy that helped him found the successful chain Innerlight Surf Shops. A statue of Yancy Spencer at the Pensacola Pier memorializes his importance to the local scene. Cities don't erect statues to folks like Scott Bush and Tom Grow, even though surfers of their generation paved the way for the generations that followed.

To reward Zinnia for bravely battling the surf at the Pensacola Pier and stoically sitting through Tom and Scott's interview, I agreed that she could skip my second interview of the day. This meant she would be hanging out by herself at the downtown Pensacola hotel for a few hours. I'm not really sure how cool (or legal) this was, but I'm hardly the first parent to treat cable television as a babysitter. Zinnia promised me that she would read and draw for "a while" and then watch TV. I'd estimate that she read for approximately .02 seconds after hearing the snick of the lock on the hotel room door. Thanks, Disney Channel and Cartoon Network.

I headed to a downtown surf shop called Waterboyz for the next interview. The name of the shop, with its entirely unnecessary "z" plural, sounds like a rap-metal band from 1995. (I should know, because I played bass and guitar that year for a hip-hop group called Mad Stylz.) Despite the mockable name, this was the coolest surf and skate shop I had ever seen. If a fourteen-year-old Steve had designed heaven on earth, it would have looked like Waterboyz. There was an indoor skate park with several different ramps. The walls were lined with racks of multi-colored surfboards from tiny fish to massive longboards. A ten-foot-high tunnel rack displayed an impressive array of skateboard decks. The seating area of a café in the store doubled as a band performance space with amps and drum kit set up for impromptu jam sessions. Kids of all ages treated the shop as a community center, while parents typed away on laptops and sipped lattes. It looked and felt exactly like California. There were no rednecks at this Riviera.

Waterboyz was the brainchild (and nickname) of a surf crew led by Sean Fell and Kaipo Robello. As a kid growing up in an upper-middle-class Pensacola family, Sean played sports like golf and tennis before surfing lured him away from the country club to the beach. In the water, he met Hawaiian transplant Kaipo Robello, whose island-honed skills earned him immediate credibility in the Pensacola lineup. Sean, Kaipo, and their buddies shared a house out at the beach after graduating from high school in the mid-1980s. Kaipo surfed for Yancy Spencer's Innerlight surf team and occasionally worked at the shop along with other members of their crew.

Innerlight inspired the guys to start their own successful screen printing business, which evolved into the Waterboyz shop.

---

Larry Martin and his buddy Mike Cotton walked up to my table at Waterboyz. Larry stuck his hand out in greeting. He was a tall, gangly guy whose goofy, loping gate belied his seventy-two years. We decided to head outside to the patio for the interview. Rain threatened and music speakers competed with traffic noise, drowning out half of our conversation. A light drizzle did nothing to dampen Larry's spirits. He loved talking about his past, particularly his role in running the China Beach Surf Club during the Vietnam War.

Like most everyone I interviewed in Pensacola, Larry's dad had been in the navy—over twenty years of a career that began with action in the Pacific theater during World War II. As a kid, Larry loved his dad's stories about his adventures in the navy—the dangerous tales of combat and the funny ones about shore leave. He treasured pictures of his dad as a skinny teenager in places like Guadalcanal. Larry's favorite photo showed a shirtless kid wearing bell-bottom pants and holding an M-14. By the time that kid retired from the navy in the 1960s, he was a man who had seen the horrors of war and now wanted to raise his family in peace on the Gulf Coast.

Larry's dad bought him his first surfboard from Hutson Hardware for the king's ransom of $140. Sure, Larry had "surfed" foam boards and rented used logs, but the nine-foot, six-inch longboard accented by a blue fin from Hutson was the first real board he ever owned. Scott Bush shaped it; Tom Grow glassed it—the 115th board to emerge from their collaborative partnership. In fact, Scott had shaped Larry's newest board too, fifty years after crafting the first one.

Surfing quickly eclipsed other aspects of Larry's life. After graduating from high school, he made a half-hearted attempt at junior college. His classmates were ex-military guys with a world of experience. Larry felt that he couldn't keep up. More to the point, the books, homework, and classes couldn't compete with the surf. Larry's course load dropped below eleven units. Uncle Sam sent him a draft notice. Soon, he was headed to Vietnam. His parents would obsessively watch nightly news reports during his deployment. It became their vigil to bring him home safely.

Larry Martin was just one of the many southern surfers I met who served in Vietnam. Southerners found themselves overrepresented in nearly every military branch during the war. Higher poverty rates in the

South meant fewer college draft deferments or private sector alternatives to military service. Family histories of military service and strong strains of patriotism meant that southern boys volunteered in higher numbers too. Even though many southern surfers would eventually join the counterculture, I didn't talk to a single one who dodged the draft.

When Larry Martin got to Vietnam, he wasted little time trying to find ways to surf. During a first stop in the Philippines, Larry borrowed a board from one of the naval officers who never actually took it out. Then, he traveled twenty-five miles through the jungle with the board. (It might have been on foot, uphill, both ways, in the snow. The details remained fuzzy.) Finally, Larry arrived at the San Miguel Communications Base on the coast and found surf. Most days, not surprisingly, he'd be the only guy out. As he looked west across the South China Sea, he knew that the shore of Vietnam lay just over the horizon.

Both my dad and my uncle served during the Vietnam War era, but neither saw combat. Uncle Jimmy joined the Coast Guard and spent much of his time posted at the tiny station in Charleston, South Carolina. Knowing Jimmy, he stoutly defended every local bar and cocktail waitress against communist incursion during his time in the service. My dad served as a doctor in the Air Force. As an obstetrician, he mostly delivered babies at the Tyndall Air Force Base near Panama City. Not a lot of combat pay in that line of work.

I shouldn't mock the military service of my dad and uncle. When called to serve, they did, regardless of whether or not they deployed to Vietnam. When I graduated from high school, the Gulf War was heating up. I must have offhandedly said something about it over dinner one night. My mom told me that if I even thought about joining up, she'd kill me before I could sign the papers. Surfing and college were more important to me then anyway. I had the choice that my parents' generation didn't necessarily have.

Wanderlust brought me to the surfing promised land of California. I found land's end not in the magical, sunshine of the Southern California coast, but the mystical, fog-shrouded wilds of Northern California. Years later, I lucked into an interview for a job teaching history just north of San Francisco. I casually mentioned during the interview that I was a surfer. Surfing had cost me a few jobs. Maybe this time it would help me land one.

The chair of the history department at Sonoma State was a surfer from Florida. My prospective boss and I spent five minutes discussing history

Randy Dodgen finishes up his last ride in after a session
at Ocean Beach in San Francisco, California.
*Courtesy of Randy Dodgen.*

and the rest of the time talking about boards and breaks. Six months later, I paddled out at San Francisco's Ocean Beach with my new boss, Randy Dodgen.

Randy's childhood had been split between the East Coast of Florida and Northern California. He caught the surfing bug just south of Patrick Air Force Base, where his dad was stationed on the eastern coast of the Sunshine State. At sixteen, he got his first surfboard. Two years later, Randy was in the navy, headed to Vietnam.

Displaying both the intellectual prowess and propensity to overthink things that would eventually earn him a PhD from Yale University, Randy couched his decision to join the military during the Vietnam War in literary terms. When he wasn't drag-racing cars or surfing, he was reading. *A Farewell to Arms* and *Les Misérables* were favorites. Hemingway and Hugo taught the Florida teenager an ideal of heroic manhood that fired his imagination, but also perhaps played to his insecurities. Disappointed that his son surfed instead of playing football, Randy's dad encouraged enlistment. "He said he thought it would make a man out of me," Randy recalled.

The day before Randy shipped out, he took one final run at the Florida surf. He was still riding his very first board, the ten-foot log, dings patched with duct tape or stuffed with surf wax to keep the sea water from seeping into the foam. The session was going great until he took off on a wave and the nose of his board dug into the water—a common mistake known as "pearling." Pearling on takeoff means that you are too far forward on the board or on too steep a section of the wave. Most of the time that surfers pearl in small waves, they tumble into the water next to their board, which is then carried harmlessly away toward the shore. In the era before leashes, the worst thing that would happen would be a tiring swim to fetch the board bouncing around the shore break. On this occasion, the buoyancy of Randy's board bounced it right back into him, nailing him in the thigh and leaving a deep bruise. Two days later he was on a troop ship in the Philippines, kneading the sore muscle—a bittersweet reminder of surfing and home.

Serving in the navy meant that Randy wasn't humping gear through the jungle on search and destroy missions like guys in the army, but he ended up spending a fair amount of time in the war zone anyway. He manned a landing craft, carrying canisters of napalm, cases of beer, and companies of soldiers. One time, his boat carried a few hundred infantrymen to a landing zone near Cam Ranh Bay. "I looked at those guys," he told me. "They were muddy and exhausted. Nobody spoke, and they all looked miserable. They were in these heavy uniforms in the frying heat." At that moment, Randy understood he was only seeing the fringes of the war. That was as close as he wanted to get.

~~~~~~~~~~~~~~~~~~~~~~~~~~~~~~~~~~~~~~~~~~~~~~~~~~~~~~~~

The relationship between surfing and the Vietnam War is a complex one. Historian Scott Laderman argues in his excellent book *Empire in Waves* that surfing has long been an extension of American military power. Military personnel brought the sport not only to the American South, but to the coasts of Japan, Vietnam, and countless other beaches near U.S. bases around the world. This connection was strong enough that film director Francis Ford Coppola deployed it in one of the most iconic scenes of *Apocalypse Now* (1979). "You can either surf or you can fight," orders Lt. Col. Bill Kilgore (Robert Duvall) as U.S. soldiers are about to rain fiery death on a Vietnamese coastal hamlet near a good surf break. A surfer in Kilgore's unit balks at hitting the waves during the battle, complaining that the Vietcong (VC or "Victor Charlie") control the area. "It's pretty hairy in there. I mean it's Charlie's point," the soldier protests. Kilgore fires back, "Charlie don't surf!" As Coppola intended, the surreal juxtaposition of combat and surfing called into question the whole enterprise of the war. Yet many troops, including southerners, actually did surf in Vietnam. For American servicemen fighting in Southeast Asia, surfing represented a peaceful respite from the conflict. "Surfing was a great morale booster amid the death and destruction in Vietnam," Laderman explains.

All the surfer vets I spoke with dreamed of riding waves in Vietnam, but only one made that dream a reality. Larry Martin arrived in Vietnam at the end of 1967. His official duties involved inventory control at Camp Tien Sha in Da Nang. His least favorite item to inventory—aviation fuel. The pessimistic Pensacola native just knew that VC mortar rounds would score a lucky hit on the fuel depot and blow him to kingdom come.

When Larry arrived in Vietnam, he admitted that he was "scared shitless," but after about a month, he began to venture off base. He'd work eleven days and have the twelfth off. One day, he hitched a ride to nearby China Beach where the lifeguards had a quiver of about six or seven longboards, only half of which were in decent shape. The guards refused to let Larry ride their boards at first, but the Floridian refused to take no for an answer. If he worked the night shift, he'd come down to the beach first thing in the morning. If he worked days, he'd race down to the beach just before sunset. Eventually, the guards took a liking to him. The officer in charge even gave him a pass in exchange for handling board rentals at the beach. The China Beach Surf Club was born.

Larry and one of the lifeguards had a card system for club members who could check out boards after they passed a surfing and swimming test. There were about 170 members in 1968. The club had patches made with a goofy cartoon character that Larry designed. The character was running down the beach, wearing a shit-eating grin and carrying a longboard under his arm. The guys even built a clubhouse. Made with "extra" military building materials, the surf shack measured about sixteen feet square and fourteen feet high with a corrugated metal roof. A loft with two bunks stood above an open space with five or six chairs and some lockers for members. "You had your own locker," Larry told me, "and what you did, you kept your trunks in there, kept your wax in there, kept your flip-flops in there. Soon as you got down [to the surf shack], you got out of your fatigues, put that on, and just forgot about the world."

The world and war weren't so easily forgotten. Larry remembered that one day, he learned about an army nurse at a nearby hospital who had a board to sell before she rotated back to the States. He hitched a ride to the hospital with $125 for the board. As he got to the hospital, he saw a steady stream of helicopters landing with wounded soldiers in baskets hanging off the choppers. Medics rushed out of the hospital to do triage on the wounded. Larry sheepishly asked someone where he could find the nurse, and they impatiently directed him inside one of the hospital tents. "I was going through and they're operating on these guys. I mean they're in there and they've got masks on and they're working on these guys," Larry said. He paid the nurse, and walked back through the operating room, carrying a nine-foot, six-inch surfboard.

Somehow, Larry convinced the navy to ship that board back to the States for him. He had extended his tour an extra three months, so he returned home in 1969. Two decades later, as Hollywood sought to heal the generational wounds ripped open by the war, a studio hired Larry to consult on the hit TV show *China Beach*, which was set at the hospital where he bought the nurse's board and at the beach where he cofounded the surf club. For a sheet-metal worker from Pensacola, being a Hollywood consultant was a pretty cool side gig.

~~~~~~~~~~~~~~~~~~~~~~~~~~~~~~~~~~~~~~~~~~~~~~~~~~~~~~~~~~~~~~~~~~~~

When I first started surfing with my boss and friend, Randy Dodgen, I had no idea he was a Vietnam vet. He never talked about it. We had been surfing together for four or five years at Ocean Beach before he mentioned it casually. I was rambling on about a class I was teaching on oral history and war. Randy said something like, "I was in the navy in Vietnam." "*In Vietnam?*" I asked him. "Yeah." Then, he turned to catch a wave. That ended the conversation. I don't think we talked about Vietnam again for another year or two. When I interviewed Randy almost a decade after that first stilted conversation, he opened up more about his time in the service.

Turned out, Randy's dad had been right about the military making him grow up, but wrong about the end result. "When you go into the military, you get confronted with a lot of your own mythology," he said. "There's nothing romantic about it. There's nothing particularly manly about swabbing the decks and doing the grunt work." Working on landing craft in Vietnam hardened Randy . . . not into a man, but a cynic. Near the end of his deployment, he decided that when he got home, if he got home, he wasn't going to play the game anymore. He'd turn on, tune in, and drop out for a while to become a hippie beach bum. Biding his time in the innumerable hours of waiting that define wartime service, Randy started to doodle. "I remember once drawing a self-portrait." He lost the picture long ago, but archived it forever in his mind's eye. "I said, 'This is what I'm gonna look like six months after I'm out of here,' and there I was standing there on the beach in my baggies with my surfboard and my hair down to my shoulders." By the spring of 1969, he stood on a Florida shoreline, fulfilling the prophecy.

Talking to Randy Dodgen, Larry Martin, and other southern surfers about Vietnam wasn't easy. We had started the conversations about a sport they loved and then shifted to a much more painful topic. Oral historians invariably ride these emotional roller-coasters with the folks they interview. It's part of the process. You hear someone's life story, witnessing their highs and lows on sped-up film. I didn't feel like I'd been in a war talking to these guys about Vietnam, but I felt the powerful poignancy of those memories from a distance of half a century.

After these interviews, I was pretty beat. Zinnia and I headed back to Waterboyz for a low-key dinner at their café. I took Zinnia on a tour of the place, telling her that all it lacked was an old-school video-game arcade. The indoor skate ramps particularly impressed her. She had gotten her first skateboard six months earlier and had just started to shred the parking lots near our house. We also bought Waterboyz souvenirs. Zinnia picked out a wool hat, and I snagged a long-sleeved rash guard, mostly to protect innocent bystanders on southern beaches from being blinded by my not-so-savage San Francisco tan.

In the evenings on this trip, Zinnia and I fell into an easy rhythm. She'd watch a little TV while I wrote up notes on the day. Then, I'd read her a book. On this trip, I read Zinnia the first volume of *The Lord of the Rings*. Zinnia was not the only one clinging to childhood. A total fantasy nerd, I also wanted to read a journey book while we were on our own adventure. In Pensacola, we got to the passage where Sam and Frodo set off from their home in the Shire on the quest to destroy the ring. Zinnia and I were not Sam and Frodo. Our quest was far less epic. We faced no capital-E enemy other than Time. Still, the Bingo Board could have been our ring—no offense to Kirk, who bore little resemblance to Gollum. That board had, in some sense, become "our precious." It was going to be hard to throw it into the fires of Mordor at the journey's end.

It would have been cool to see *The Lord of the Rings* on the big screen during our trip. Instead, Zinnia chose *Wonder Woman* . . . in Pensacola's finest 3D Imax experience! A girl-power movie seemed an appropriate climax to the day. The leading actress was a badass Israeli former combat instructor named Gal Gadot. (Her first name means "wave" in Hebrew.)

Watching the movie with a strong female lead, I realized how bro'ed out this trip had been. Though women have ridden waves with great skill since the origins of the sport in Hawaii, modern surfing has often been male dominated. It was not surprising that most of the guys we met were, well, guys. Still, ever since Gidget helped kicked off the surf craze in the late 1950s and early '60s, women have played an integral role in the sport. The next morning, Zinnia and I interviewed our first "surfer girl." Significantly, Zinnia didn't complain about coming along on this interview. It helped that the conversation took place in a diner serving cake-sized muffins and hot chocolate topped with small mountains of whipped cream.

Lisa Muir was just digging into biscuits and gravy when we joined her at the roadside diner in Gulf Breeze, Florida. She beckoned us over to her table, her warm smile framed by sandy blonde hair. If Hollywood wanted to cast a "surfer girl" in her fifties, they'd cast Lisa in a second. She looked like she could have just toweled off from a dawn patrol session, though she hadn't. In fact, she had to work the evening shift of a new retail gig the night before. Recently divorced, she struck out on her own with a new job and new house. The small talk about this before the interview revealed conflicting emotions—pain from charting a life course alone and joy at a newfound freedom. For Lisa, that freedom meant more time in the water.

A self-described military brat, Lisa had a childhood as adventurous and itinerant as Scott Bush's. Lisa's dad flew missions for the Air Force as a "hurricane hunter," a pilot who intentionally pointed the nose of his plane into the most dangerous storms on the planet. The Air Force sent him and his family to Bermuda and Puerto Rico. Those might sound like idyllic home bases, but imagine taking off from paradise and winging towards the hell of the Bermuda Triangle. When he wasn't flying, Lisa's dad liked to dive. He took Lisa and her siblings along to swim, snorkel, and eventually ride the waves.

Lisa first started surfing Puerto Rican beaches in 1969. She grew partial to the breaks near Rincón. Her parents' divorce and her dad's retirement from the military led her to the Gulf Coast of Florida by the mid-1970s, but she never got Puerto Rico out of her system. For the rest of her life, she'd return as often as possible to surf and visit with childhood friends. As a result of military ties and surfing connections, Lisa rarely made her Puerto Rico pilgrimages alone.

After talking with Lisa for just a few minutes about surfing, I could tell that she was both serious and good. Ironically, shredding asphalt, not waves, first won her a sponsorship. The Brewer skate team took her on tour in California and outfitted her with skateboards and surfboards in the mid-1970s. At the same time, she surfed professional contests all over the Gulf Coast and up and down the Eastern Seaboard. Photos of her graced the pages of *Surfer* magazine in this era. She'd eventually be inducted into the East Coast surfing Hall of Fame in 2002—a welcome, albeit belated, recognition of her pioneering role in the sport.

In the 1960s and '70s, women surfers like Lisa struggled to get recognition for their skills in the water. Most of Lisa's magazine shots didn't show her riding waves. "The only magazine that featured me actually surfing was a local magazine in Cocoa Beach," she explained. Other magazine editors decided, "'Here's a pretty girl walking down a Puerto Rican beach in a really nice bikini,' so that's what they wanted to print at that time." To Lisa, these editorial decisions rested on assumptions about marketing to male consumers.

Lisa talked about the lack of respect for women wave riders in a matter-of-fact way without any real bitterness. This was the era of "women's lib" in second-wave feminism. Lisa truly believed that if a guy could do something, so could a girl. Many of her guy friends didn't feel this way. "I remember being ditched," she told me, "because the waves were either too big or the guys didn't want this girl coming along. I can remember a surf trip in particular where it was no girls. It was all guys heading down to Mexico, and it broke my heart when I was told, 'It's an all-guy trip.'"

Zinnia was nursing the sweet dregs of her hot chocolate when Lisa tired of my questions and directed a few of her own to my daughter. "I heard you were surfing yesterday," she said.

"I was," Zinnia mumbled, embarrassed by the sudden attention. "I only caught one wave."

"Was it a good one?"

"It was okay," Zinnia managed.

Maybe other parents are patient, but extroverted control freaks like me can't sit idly by while their only child refuses to brag with appropriate exaggeration about a surf session. This was a teachable moment. If Zinnia learned nothing else from this trip, she needed to realize that embellishing a surf story was as important as—if not more important than—actually surfing well. "It was a little bigger than she usually surfs," I explained, trying to figure out how big I could say it was when talking to someone who undoubtedly checked the report every day. "The wave she rolled into was probably stomach high."

"Bigger than that!" Zinnia corrected. Attagirl! It was like fifteen-foot Pipe, wasn't it? Gnarly barrels. Sick aerials. (Don't mention the Bingo Board in mixed company.) Zinnia wisely let that sink in before moving on to talk about the "even bigger" waves she rides in California. I let Zinnia roll with this for a good two minutes before hijacking the conversation and mansplaining Northern California surfing to a pro like Lisa, who doubtlessly needed no lecture from me. What was I saying about lack of respect for women surfers back in the day?

As we drove away from the diner after the wonderful meal and conversation, I asked Zinnia what she thought of the interview. "It was my favorite one," she said, with a shocking amount of enthusiasm—by which I mean, there were no eye rolls, sighs, or air quotes. It looked like Zinnia found a role model on the trip after all. Sadly, it wasn't her father.

# 6

# *The Space Coast*
## *Cocoa Beach, Florida*

Driving through Florida alone, I missed my copilot. Zinnia skipped this leg of the trip to spend some time with our family in Florida and go to theme parks. A robotic voice coldly issuing directions from my phone was a poor substitute for my daughter's company. With spotty cell reception, I often didn't even have a robotic copilot. Perhaps this was for the best. Artificial intelligence and I had a relationship about as dysfunctional as the mutual suspicion between Dave and the HAL 9000 computer in *2001: A Space Odyssey*. If I relied on my phone to complete my surfing mission (particularly without the aid of my tech savvy daughter), there was a good chance I'd never escape Central Florida. I imagined my phone stranding me in the Florida hinterlands, responding to my increasingly desperate pleas for directions, "I'm sorry, Steve, I'm afraid I can't do that." Instead of going *mano a máquina*, I used a paper map.

Many of the major roads in Central Florida direct you toward Orlando. The pull toward the city and its theme parks is almost irresistible. I was hell-bent on avoiding the Magic Kingdom, fearing that the traffic would be less than magical. I used a gravity-assist maneuver to slingshot around Disney's orbit and sped toward the beaches of Florida's Space Coast.

If the astronautical action took place at Cape Canaveral's Kennedy Space Center, the nautical capital of the Space Coast was Cocoa Beach. Unlike the Gulf Coast, which had surfers in beach towns, Cocoa Beach was a surf town with beachgoers. A larger-than-life statue froze world champion and Space Coast native Kelly Slater in his glory days. There he was, right off the A1A, forever carving a massive cutback in bronze. Innumerable surf shops and shapers call Cocoa Beach home. There's Ron Jon, of course, but flagship stores for Quiet Flight, Natural Art, and the other renowned surf outfits made the place feel like Mecca, the East Coast equivalent of Huntington Beach or Haleiwa.

Tucked away in the rental annex of Ron Jon Surf Shop, I found the Florida Surf Museum. When I asked the clerk behind the desk where I could find museum executive director John Hughes, the sunburned teenager pointed me to what appeared to be a former broom closet in the back of the store. From this humble headquarters, John and a team of tireless volunteers documented the history of surfing in the Sunshine State.

~~~~~~~~~~~~~~~~~~~~~~~~~~~~~~~

The Atlantic coastline of Florida boasts one of the longest and richest histories of surfing in the American South, but Florida did not start out as a beachgoer's paradise. Surf historian Paul Aho argues that Floridians didn't really embrace beach culture as we know it until the twentieth century. White folks in the Victorian Era avoided the sun, fearing that dark tans marked them as working class or, worse, uncivilized. The Sunshine State's long coastline was more of a backwater than tourist mecca in those days. Poor roads, poorer soil, and a generally inhospitable climate for human habitation limited the number of visitors. As one soldier stationed in Florida during the Spanish-American War joked, "If I owned both land in Miami and hell, I'd rent out Miami and live in hell."

Florida changed dramatically in the twentieth century, particularly with the increasing popularity of seasonal beach resorts and water sports. The first photographic evidence of Floridians "wave sliding" dates back to 1919, when the *Philadelphia Ledger* published a grainy image of the break at Palm Beach. The caption described, "Florida swimmers carrying their surf boards seaward for a thrilling ride on the crest of an inrushing breaker." The author of the article had clearly never lifted one of the Hawaiian-style solid wooden planks, because he went on to note that the Floridians "easily" carried the boards to the beach. Decked out in one-piece, wool bathing suits, these surf pioneers struggled to maneuver surfcraft. There was nothing easy about this sport of kings, but it still looked fun.

Most Floridians in the beginning of the twentieth century rode these boards, if they rode boards at all, on their bellies. The first stand-up surfers in Florida plied their trade in the waters off Miami Beach. The Whitman Brothers—Dudley, William, and Stanley—scrambled to their feet in the 1930s. They competed in the state's first surf contest in Daytona Beach in 1938. After a hiatus during World War II, surfing regained popularity in the 1950s, and competitions returned with a vengeance in the 1960s.

A colorful cast of characters led the sport's resurgence in the 1950s and '60s. None were more colorful than Jack "Murph the Surf" Murphy. Born in southern California in the late 1930s, Murph's family moved to Pittsburgh for a brief stint in the 1950s. In Pennsylvania, the precocious teenager played tennis with college students during the day and violin in the local symphony at night. A move to Miami uprooted Murph once again. He caught southern surfing fever, using his prowess in the waves to woo wealthy tourists and, it later turned out, distract them from his criminal exploits.

Murph the Surf became one of the hottest competitive surfers in Florida in the early 1960s. He won the Florida State Surfing Competition held in Daytona Beach in 1962 and the East Coast Surfing Championship the following year. These victories and a cameo in a Bruce Brown surf film gave Murph the name recognition to open his own shop in Indialantic. Secretly, the Florida surf icon had also moved on to a new line of work as a jewel thief.

The same adrenaline rush that inspired Murph's surfing also influenced his criminal exploits. If this sounds like the premise for a bad action movie, that's because it's actually the basis for *three* bad action movies. Hollywood first projected Jack Murphy's story onto the silver screen in *Murph the Surf* (1975). Two *Point Break* films complete the surf heist trilogy. Undoubtedly, this mini-genre reached its artistic apogee with the 1991 film that starred Keanu Reeves as an FBI agent hunting a zenned-out, surfing bank robber played by Patrick Swayze. Unlike Swayze's wave riding Robin Hood, Murph the Surf's crimes profited only the perp.

A cocktail of booze and cocaine mixed with questionable real estate investments in New York, California, and Hawaii turned Murph to the Dark Side. Revenue from a small surf shop and contest winnings couldn't support the lifestyle to which Murph had become accustomed. He cut his teeth in a number of South Florida burglaries, where he spirited valuables away from the crime scene in a boat and then swam ashore with the loot if cops gave chase. On one job alone, he netted $15,000, but Murph had his eyes on a bigger score.

In 1964 the Florida surf champion learned about a jaw-dropping jewelry collection at the Museum of Natural History in New York. The collection, which had once belonged to the industrialist J. P. Morgan, included the 16-carat Eagle Diamond, the 100-carat DeLong Star Ruby, and the 563-carat Star of India sapphire. Murph and his accomplices cased the museum for a few days. Then, they simply crawled through an unlocked bathroom window after hours and filled a bag with precious gems worth nearly half a million dollars. Two days later, the FBI captured the men in Florida. Authorities recovered most of the gems, including the Star of India, from a bus station locker in Miami, but they never found the Eagle Diamond. The FBI speculated that Murph and his associates had the diamond cut and fenced before their arrest.

For one of the biggest jewel heists in American history, Murph the Surf served only a few years behind bars on Riker's Island in New York. Promising that he had turned over a new leaf, Murph returned to Florida. Yet surfing took a back seat to criminal enterprises once again. In the late 1960s, officials convicted the Florida wave rider of burglary and murder. This time, he faced a life sentence. Murph found religion. After two more decades of incarceration, he won parole, vowing to spend the rest of his life ministering to prisoners and ex-cons.

My San Francisco surfing buddy, Randy Dodgen, told me about Murph the Surf when recounting his time growing up on Florida's Space Coast. Even before he could surf, Randy loitered at Murph's Indialantic shop in the early 1960s. He ogled boards that he couldn't afford, much less ride. Randy peeked into the back room of the shop to try to catch a glimpse of the legendary local in action, but he never did. Still, half a century later, the surfer-turned-professor remembered the smell of fiberglass and resin that wafted throughout the shop. The smell was "one of those Proustian things," he recalled—the only dude I interviewed to reference the French novelist.

Even if most of us haven't read Marcel Proust, every surfer has a sensory memory connected to their early days surfing. For me, the tropical scent of Mr. Zog's coconut Sex Wax carries me back to sweltering summer days outside of McKevlin's surf shop in the 1980s. For Randy, decades of surfing and dozens of shops couldn't eclipse the memory that resin recalled of lazy days loitering around Murph's shop in Indialantic.

By the time he could actually surf, Randy had grown into a tall, gangly teen. He stood six feet one but weighed only a buck thirty when sopping wet. The skinny kid dragged his first board, a used ten-foot log, through the sand so much that he wore a hole in the glass on the rail. As unwieldly as that first board was, it gave Randy a lifelong passion for the water.

The military had brought Randy's dad and family to Cocoa Beach; the space industry convinced them to stay. A bombardier over Europe in World War II, Randy's father eventually retired from the Air Force to work as an electronics technician on NASA's lunar modules. The senior Dodgen joined the workforce of what would become Florida's Space Coast.

Cocoa Beach's booming surf industry owed as much to a 184-pound, two-foot-diameter silver ball as it did to the waves and climate of the Sunshine State. The successful launch of the Sputnik 1 satellite by the Soviet Union in 1957 served as the starting gun for the space race between the United States and the U.S.S.R. Cape Canaveral became the American headquarters for the effort to win this race when President John F. Kennedy promised to send an American to the moon by the end of the 1960s. In Kennedy's 1961 address to Congress, the young president called upon "every scientist, every engineer, every serviceman, every technician, contractor, and civil servant" to give "his personal pledge that this nation will move forward, with the full speed of freedom, in the exciting adventure of space."

Thousands of educated, ambitious Americans—including Randy Dodgen's father—heeded Kennedy's call. They moved to Florida to achieve the president's goal of putting a man on the moon. The population of sleepy coastal hamlets like Cocoa Beach ballooned by more than 1,000 percent in the 1950s, and more than doubled during the frenzied space race of the 1960s. Cocoa Beach even became the setting for a hit TV series about an astronaut and his magical mistress. The silly, almost psychedelic, suburban sitcom *I Dream of Jeannie* epitomized the ethos that anything was possible on the Space Coast of the late 1960s.

Like the oil booms in Texas, the military build-up in Pensacola, or the ascent of aviation in Southern California, the influx of people and money to Florida in the 1960s accelerated the growth of the local surf industry. On a less tangible level, the driven, ambitious people drawn to the pressure-cooker jobs at Cape Canaveral might have also inspired the competitive success of Space Coast surfers, who were the sons and daughters of these high-octane technicians, engineers, and astronauts. They were each, in their own way, trying to harness what President Kennedy had called the "speed of freedom."

For Florida teenagers like Randy Dodgen, this quest for speed fueled not only surfing, but more landlocked pursuits. Randy's surfmobile was a blue-and-white '57 Ford Fairlane. Sure, everybody talked about legendary '57 Chevys, but Ford made a pretty damn good roadster that year too. Randy lived to drag race it on Florida A1A or smaller local roads patrolled by fewer cops. Tearing down the darkened streets of Indialantic, Melbourne, and Cocoa Beach on balmy evenings, the teenage hooligans of coastal Florida imagined that they were Junior Johnson and other southern gearbox heroes, burning rubber just up the coast in Daytona. So went the nights. During the days, you'd find Randy and his friends in the water.

After surfing in California for years, the Florida native had little nostalgia for the waves of his youth. There was usually "no shape, none, breaking over very poor sandbars in most places," he complained. "The places where we surfed were these little breaks where the bottom was shaped mostly by coquina rock that held the sand." Unfortunately for Space Coast surfers like Randy, Cape Canaveral blocked most North Atlantic groundswells, leaving weaker wind swells or the occasional hurricane swell to pump inconsistent surf toward the local breaks. In 1964, Randy surfed the "shark pit" south of Indialantic. There were few sharks, but the name scared away kooks and tourists. Randy surfed the shark pit and the Cape Canaveral jetty with guys like Gary Propper, one of the first pro surfers to make it big from Florida.

~~~~~~~~~~~~~~~~

Long before social media discovered the humblebrag, Florida surf journalists mastered the form. They started with a longboard-sized chip on their shoulder balanced with just the right amount of self-deprecation. "How many times have surfers from the West Coast or elsewhere given you the impression you weren't a real surfer the moment Florida was mentioned?" began one such Daytona Beach feature in 2004. "Is it because our waves are smaller? Because we don't swim with great whites?" Nope. Humblebrag time. "Even if you aren't ready for double-overhead waves or great whites, there isn't a reason in the world to doubt your ability based on the fact that you're from Florida, . . . [because] there are 15 world crowns residing in lowly Florida." By the time I headed to the Sunshine State, its residents could (humbly) boast twenty world titles. Frieda Zamba, Lisa Andersen, and C. J. Hobgood gained international acclaim for impressive world championship runs, but no single surfer put Florida on the map like Cocoa Beach native Kelly Slater.

These champions stood on the shoulders of an earlier generation of Floridians—not giants exactly, but pioneers. Just before I arrived in Florida, longtime surfer and coach Dick Catri passed away. Murph the Surf introduced Catri to wave-riding in the late 1950s. By the end of the decade, Catri left the Sunshine State for Hawaii, honing his skills there from 1960 to 1964. When Catri returned to Florida, he channeled his hyper-competitive nature into a career, coaching successive generations of young surfers for teams sponsored by Surfboards Hawaii, Hobie, and others. Catri mentored Space Coast native Gary Propper, who became the highest-paid American pro surfer in the mid-1960s. In addition to Propper, Catri coached nearly every other competitor of note from the Space Coast for the next several decades. Catri's surf teams struck fear into the hearts of competitors up and down the Eastern Seaboard. As one Virginia Beach vet told me, it was almost impossible to compete with those teams. In Florida, they could surf nearly all year round, and working for Catri, they damn well did!

The weekend I arrived in Cocoa Beach happened to be the memorial for Dick Catri. When a longtime surfer passes away, people in the community gather at the beach and paddle out beyond the break to form a circle with their boards. The saltwater salute to a life well lived can be profoundly moving, but I didn't know Catri. I wasn't part of the Space Coast surf community. It would have felt voyeuristic to join the paddle out. Who was I to horn in on the memorial? I went surfing instead.

~~~~~~~~~~~~~~

I needed a session to wash off the stink of the road. The familiar warmth of the ocean relaxed me. The Gulf Stream current that flows up from South America and through the Caribbean warms the waters off the southern portions of the U.S. Atlantic Seaboard. This oceanic river once helped sailors navigate to the New World. Today, it lures visitors to the temperate waters of southern shores. Northern Californians dream of water temperatures in the 70s and 80s. Floridians take such miracles for granted.

The waves were thigh-to-waist at the county park near my Cocoa Beach motel. The Bingo Board worked its usual magic, getting me into waves that I would never have caught otherwise. For one of the first times on this trip, however, I longed for a shorter, more maneuverable board. There were actual sections of lip to hit and speed to drive me into them. The Bingo Board looked at the lip and cried uncle, so I decided to try walking up to the nose. Some longboarders can do this with a graceful cross-step that's as smooth as a Viennese waltz. I hopped forward like a crustacean. Since I hadn't waxed the front of the Bingo Board, I slipped off the first couple of times I crab-walked forward. Cursing my own stupidity, I promised to give the board a better coat of sticky bumps before my next session.

Quality being out of the question, I opted for quantity of rides. I jumped up, planted my feet on the waxed portion of the board, and angled down the line, staying near the curl until each wave petered out. I caught about twenty waves in a one-hour session. These were not long rides, but they lasted an eternity compared to the waves on much of the Gulf Coast.

I dipped my head in the white water as if trying to get tubed and dragged my hand in a few walls.

Surfers place our hands in the water to slow down, keeping us near the wave's power source when inertia carries us too far out in front of the curl. I didn't really need to slow myself down on these rides, but dipping a hand offered less tangible rewards. Surfers have an innate longing to touch the ocean's surface. Combing our hands through the water gives us the feel of the wave. Somehow, that connection helps us understand the complicated interplay of physical forces going on beneath the surface. Dragging a hand offers a sense of stability, another point of contact, almost like a mountain climber keeping two hands and a toehold on a sheer cliff face. Finally, and most importantly for me, this is a simple way to score style points. On small days, I'm happy to soul-arch down the line, doing nothing more than caress the curl feathering at my waist.

After the session, I casually strolled back across A1A in flip-flops with the board under my arm and a towel over my shoulder. In that moment, I understood the draw of living in Cocoa Beach. If I had grown up there, I never would have gotten anything accomplished on land. That thought itself somehow snapped me back to reality. Shit! I was late for an interview. I hustled back to the hotel, threw on some dry clothes, and hopped in the truck to go meet Sharon Wolfe at the Cocoa Beach public library.

The library is easy to find. Just hang a right at the Kelly Slater statue. There you are. I found Sharon Wolfe's office in the back of the building near the children's books. She keeps a low profile as a librarian, but the former U.S. surfing champion is a local legend in the water.

Sharon's parents brought her to Cocoa Beach when she was just a toddler in the mid-1960s. Her dad worked at the Kennedy Space Center, of course. She got into surfing at a young age because both of her older brothers surfed, and her family loved the beach. Sharon spent five or six hours a day in the water for another reason. Her dad drank. When he drank, he became abusive—not physically, but verbally—screaming bloody murder at his wife and the kids. It was better to get away, much better to be in the water.

Like most other Cocoa Beach teens in the 1970s, Sharon often surfed at a break simply called Third Street. After sessions and on weekend nights, the surfers hung out in the nearby parking lot of the Apollo Building. The abandoned offices of the Apollo Building represented the declining economic fortunes of the Space Coast after the success of the Apollo program. As the federal government cut back on funding for NASA and the U.S. economy hit the skids, Cocoa Beach's unemployment jumped to nearly 15 percent in the mid-1970s. The tough times continued until the Space Shuttle program took off and cruise ships began bringing hordes of tourists. If Sharon Wolfe sought solace in the surf, she wasn't alone.

Because I knew that she had an illustrious competitive career, I asked Sharon about the difference between "free surfing" just for fun and surfing in contests. She laughed. For Sharon, there was no distinction. Surfing was always fun and always a competition. Every time she hit the water, she and her friends ran mock heats, egging each other on to do more radical maneuvers. By the end of the 1970s, local shop Quiet Flight sponsored Sharon as part of a talented roster that would soon include a young Kelly Slater. She surfed contests from France to Hawaii, working hard at the Quiet Flight shop and a number of other jobs to pay her own way to contests. In the 1970s, professional surfing had stalled in the doldrums of declining mainstream appeal—trapped between the beach-party era of the 1960s and the Day-Glo explosion of the 1980s. Sharon was lucky to make $200 a contest, even if she won. Free boards and clothes were about all she could count on from Quiet Flight, but with limited resources the guys at the shop supported her budding career.

Sharon rarely surfed longboards for competition. She came of age in the shortboard era, a period where not only the boards shrank, but so did the fins. In addition to all of the foam and surface area, longboards got their stability from a large, single fin that acted almost like the keel of a sailboat. The shorter surfcraft of the 1970s had two smaller fins, equally spaced from the center at the back of the board. Without the keel-like center fin and with much less foam, these twin fins turned on a dime. They were "loose," in the parlance of the day. Flow had been the crucial measure of excellence in the longboard era. Speed and power completed the holy trinity of competitive greatness in this era, metrics by which surfing is still judged today.

One day, the shapers at Quiet Flight asked Sharon to bring in her trusty twin fin. "They took it away from me, like literally took my board and said, 'You're riding *this*.'" *This* was a thruster, a three-fin design that became the future of competitive surfing. "I hated it," Sharon recalled ruefully of that first thruster. That board "was so stiff, and I didn't like how tight it was when I was doing turns." At Sharon's suggestion, the Quiet Flight guys went back to the drawing board and cut down the center fin a fraction of an inch. That did the trick. Now Sharon had the drive of a thruster with the looseness of a twin. She would go on to win four U.S. championships with various versions of that board. "That was probably the best thing," she said. "They actually listened to me, a girl."

Despite the reality of competitive surfing being very much a man's world, Sharon told me that she rarely faced overt sexism in the water. The only time she recalled was in Hawaii, training for a contest. According to Sharon, a southern sense of chivalry extended to the water, where guys looked out for local women who were regulars. The other side of chivalry, of course, was the belief that girls needed protection from danger. Melody DeCarlo, a contemporary of Sharon's, told me that she got the most grief from her parents. "They said that women didn't surf," she remembered with a wry smile. "My mother was like, 'No, you can't. You're going to get hurt, you can't do that.'" Melody pointed out women that she idolized like Californian Jericho Poppler and Hawaiian Rell Sunn. If they could do it, so could she. Once Melody's family moved north from the Miami area to the Space Coast, she found more consistent waves. What she didn't find was either rampant sexism or a surf sisterhood. "A lot of women always talked about how they got hassled," she said. "The guys would give them a hard time and everything. I never found that at all." There just wasn't a critical mass of women in the water, in Melody's view, until the mid-1990s. Before then, Melody said, "If you asked a guy if they knew me, it would be easy for them, because I would be the only woman out a lot of the time."

Women did find camaraderie and competition in surf contests during the 1980s, but they also faced a unique set of obstacles. Contests at the amateur and pro levels were separated by gender. Contest organizers often ran women's heats during less favorable conditions. As in other sports, women's prize money and sponsorships paled in comparison to male surfers' potential earnings. Despite these challenges, Florida women did very well in national and international contests. In fact, they dominated the professional surfing circuit in the 1980s and early 1990s. Flagler Beach native Frieda Zamba became the first world champion from the Sunshine State in 1984, going on to win three titles in a row and a fourth in 1988. Then, Ormond Beach native Lisa Andersen won four world titles in a row from 1994 to 1997.

In the early 1980s, Sharon Wolfe appeared to be on the cusp of a similarly stellar competitive career. A magazine photo of her surfing (as opposed to a headshot or an image of her modeling on the beach) was an early mile-stone for women from the South and East Coast. Sharon remembered the day she saw the shot, riding on a plane out to California for a competition. She grabbed the arm of the guy next to her and pointed excitedly to the glossy image in the magazine. "That's me! That's me!" "Um, that's nice," replied the non-surfer in that noncommittal way you engage with a crazy person in a confined space. How could he have known? For the aspiring pro, coverage in a magazine meant Sharon was on her way.

Then the young Floridian's life took an unexpected detour. Her mom was diagnosed with cancer. The dutiful daughter cut back her travel and helped take care of the mother who had protected her from a difficult family life. After her mom died in 1985, Sharon returned to competition. Unfortunately, a window of opportunity had closed. Sharon never stopped surfing, but her competitive career gave way to a family of her own and sessions where she was happy to get three waves before returning to the beach and the responsibilities of motherhood. As the next generation of Cocoa Beach locals, including Todd Holland and the Slater brothers, picked up the torch for Space Coast surfing, Sharon counseled them, perhaps wondering what could have been.

By the 2010s, a critical mass of women surfed in Florida and across the South. Sharon, Melody, and a few others wanted to connect to this new generation, but they didn't want to do it solely through contests. Instead, they launched a surfing exhibit and reunion called Women of the Waves. The inaugural event succeeded beyond their wildest dreams. They began coordinating Women of the Waves weekends that included talks, food, movies, and surfing socials. At the first event, Sharon laid down a big cloth. All the women in attendance put their footprints on it and signed their names. The weekends kept growing until nearly 140 women, ages two to sixty-two, walked in the footsteps of those who had come before, adding their own names to the Women of the Waves.

~~~~~~~~~

The waves on my first day at Cocoa Beach would have been perfect for Zinnia. She would have even enjoyed the two sessions that I had the next day when the swell dropped and I badly timed the tides. As Randy often reminded me, the worst day surfing is still better than the best day at work. Zinnia might not go that far, but she does love the small stuff. Cocoa Beach offered plenty of that.

Surfing the small, summer waves alone, I really felt Zinnia's absence. She texted me from my dad's phone to ask about the waves, simultaneously warming and breaking my heart. She had fun visiting her grandpa in Sarasota, swimming in a pool, playing minigolf, and watching way too much TV.

As any parent knows, pawning off kids is a bittersweet experience, as long as you're not literally pawning them off. That's totally sweet, but also illegal. Imposing childcare responsibilities on grandparents and friends is perfectly legal and downright necessary to maintain parental sanity. I don't care what kind of angel a kid is, even the best of them can channel Satan better than the freaky girl in *The Exorcist*. Zinnia is no different. She tends to yell more at her mom and whine more with me. If screaming tantrums are the blunt force trauma of childish mutinies, whining is the death of a thousand cuts.

This surf trip had certainly seen its share of whining and bad behavior. In exchange for an excessive amount of screen time both during my interviews and in the evenings, I asked Zinnia to read a fantasy book that my first stepdad gave me when I was a kid. Piers Anthony's *A Spell for Chameleon* kicked off an epic series of Xanth novels that were long on puns, cornball romances, and of course, magical creatures. Better still, the land of Xanth bore an uncanny resemblance to Florida, where Anthony wrote the books. How cool was that? We were exploring the magical land that Zinnia was reading about!

Evidently, it was not cool at all. Zinnia has never been a huge reader like her nerdy father. It turned out that on this trip, she wasn't actually reading the book at all. When asked about *A Spell for Chameleon*, my daughter couldn't even recall the main character. I was furious at first, a feeling that quickly morphed into profound disappointment. Zinnia had deceived me, not for the first or last time, I was sure. She'd played the dutiful daughter so well, thumbing through the pages of a book for long spells without retaining any of the magical story. The subterfuge and dedication to laziness actually impressed me. The more dispiriting aspect of my daughter's rebellion was the way it called a lie to my naive assumptions about parenting. I believed that I could mold Zinnia into the bookish nerd that I had been, despite all evidence to the contrary. This incident with the Xanth novel proved that Zinnia was going to be her own person, no matter how much I cajoled, threatened, or loved her. That wasn't going to keep me from trying and, in the process, making her life miserable. Did I mention that the Xanth series includes *forty-one* novels? Piers Anthony was nothing if not punishingly prolific.

~~~~~~~~~~~~~~~~~~~~~~~~~~~~~~~~~~~~~~~~~~~~~

With Zinnia off gallivanting with her grandpa, I had the freedom to investigate the summer nightlife of Cocoa Beach. At first, I thought it would be a good idea to get dinner and beers at the 7-Eleven near my motel. Day-old hotdogs rotating on spits beneath heat lamps somehow didn't turn my stomach. A tall boy of Budweiser would wash away the sour aftertaste of loser. At the doors to the 7-Eleven, I froze. Even through the smudged glass, foggy with air-conditioner condensation, I could see this was not the kind of clean, well-lighted place that Ernest Hemingway saw as the last best hope for the lonely. Harsh halogens illuminated an establishment that was anything but clean. Having crisscrossed the country many times, I was no stranger to the delicacies of 7-Elevens. Slurpees, Nekots, Combos, Doritos, and Rolos leave little doubt that America has perfected culinary chemistry. I weighed these options in a moment of indecision with my hand on one door. A dude came out of the other door with a six-pack. He looked annoyed, grumbled under his breath, and then shuffled toward a rusted-out clunker parked in the same place it must have rumbled to rest innumerable nights before. I turned and walked away.

Instead of the 7-Eleven, I flip-flopped over to a local dive called the Sandbar. I chose it primarily on its unimaginative name. The Sandbar reminded me of places where I grew up in South Carolina, particularly Folly Beach's (in)famous Sand Dollar Social Club. Riddled with aging hippies and plagued by blues-rock jam bands, southern beach bars are the release valves for small, seaside towns. They may not be clean or well-lit, but they offer more than the suicidal sustenance that vomits out of convenience-store microwaves. In the Sandbar, I found the perfect place to sit anonymously and sip a few beers while gazing blankly at televised sports and listening to not-so-classic rock.

The management had decorated the Sandbar with far too much of the surf-themed decor one would expect of a Cocoa Beach dive. A skull-and-crossbones sign welcomed "short boarders only" to the place. I didn't mention the Bingo Board to anyone over the course of the evening, but based on the age and fitness of the crowd, I wasn't the only longboarder. The bar's mantra—plastered all over the menus and walls—promised in a Red Cross lifeguard design that I would get "rescued from ordinary food." Unfortunately, my fish tacos drowned in a humdrum, greasy sauce. Another sign, shaped like a surfboard, advertised (or warned unsuspecting patrons about) "Reggae Fridays."

Luckily, I hit the Sandbar on a Saturday. By my second beer, the southern rock band started sounding pretty good. The bar's soundman appeared to be a spry sixty-five. He sported a gray beard longer than Merlin's. His stick-thin legs jutted out from stringy jean shorts. Fashion aside, this guy was a pro. No architect designed the Sandbar for acoustic perfection, nor did the place have a state-of-the-art speaker system. Yet this guy had adjusted the band's levels with impressive clarity, each instrument surprisingly distinct in what should have been a muddy swamp of sound. The dude clearly knew the band's tunes by heart. Even on the thousandth listen, he sang along with gusto and relished every noodly note. Years dropped off his aging body as he danced—damn near vibrated—to a rhythm of lost youth embedded deep within the band's unending jam. He wasn't alone. A gaggle of vacationing retirees cut a rug in front of the stage, the older women staring adoringly up at the band's lead guitar player and singer.

The long-haired, twenty-something band leader played and sang with equal panache. The rhythm section laid down a rock-solid foundation upon which he carved baroque, curlicue solos. They mixed covers of Hendrix and the Allman Brothers with originals that echoed the songs of their idols. The band only stumbled once, when attempting a Soundgarden tune in honor of that grunge band's recently deceased singer, Chris Cornell. Few vocalists can approach Cornell's feral wail, and the jam band singer didn't prove up to the task. Still, I tipped a beer cup salute to his attempt as the song ground to a halt in a dissonant chorus of guitar feedback.

At the end of the evening, I staggered back to the motel with that feedback still echoing in my ears and a beer buzz fuzzing out everything in between. There would be no dawn patrol the next morning. No matter, I had an interview with another local legend.

When Sharon Wolfe told me that I should talk to a Cocoa Beach surf instructor named Todd Holland, my first thought was, "Hell, yes, I should!" Four years older than me, Todd's pro career took off just as I was learning how to surf. I remembered seeing his photos in all the mags and watching him surf in televised contests. This guy was from the East Coast like me. He wore stupid-loud neon board shorts and wetsuits like me. The difference between us boiled down to ability.

I sat down with the old pro at the School of Surf, which Todd ran with his wife in downtown Cocoa Beach. I soon realized that School of Surf was the second-worst place to hold an interview after Buffalo Wild Wings. People were constantly coming in asking Todd to sign up their kids for lessons, asking Todd when they had to work, asking Todd to take care of their old dog while they ran errands. (Todd subcontracted this last job to me while he signed up yet another kid, and I dutifully petted the stinky beast until he collapsed into a heap of fur and bones near the door.) As a result of all the distractions, we must have started and stopped the interview half a dozen times before really getting down to business.

The old pro sat down somewhat wearily. The hassles of being a public face of the surf school meant that he was always on, always coaching, whether in the water or not. The guy that sat across the table from me was still easily recognizable from his tour days, but of course, he had aged in the intervening decades. When we spoke, Holland had been surfing for forty years. He had filled out a bit, becoming a stockier version of the wiry phenome that I watched blaze through pro contests. The biggest change was in his eyes. They glistened, rheumy windows into the soul of a much older man. Maybe this was merely a physical change, reflecting 1,001 dawn patrols staring into rays of the rising sun. Undoubtedly, those eyes had seen things that amateur surfers will never see.

Before he was an old pro, Todd Holland grew up in an honest-to-God log cabin near Emerald Isle, North Carolina. His dad, a journeyman electrician, built the cabin in the early 1970s, while the family lived in an Airstream trailer. The Airstream kept them mobile, so the senior Holland could take his family along with him wherever he picked up work. Wiring a seafood processing factory kept them in Emerald Isle long enough for Todd to pick up surfing at the age of eight. Within less than six months, Todd had won his first contest. During our interview, he reached back and proudly pointed out the trophy.

By the age of ten, Todd's dad picked up a long-term gig in Florida, and the family moved to Cocoa Beach. Todd quickly fell in with a crew of hot young surfers on the Space Coast who were coached by Dick Catri. In the early 1980s, that team included Sean O'Hare, Todd Propper, Sean Slater, and Sean's runty little brother, Kelly. Catri coached the kids once a week, but they hit the water every day, pushing each other to shred harder with every session.

People often assume that Todd and his crew regularly surfed Sebastian Inlet, an hour south of Cocoa Beach. The Inlet held the best break in the area, due to a rock and concrete jetty that amplified swells to double their normal height and created one of the fastest waves in Florida from the 1970s through the 1990s. Although the Cocoa Beach groms surfed contests at Sebastian Inlet and launched strike missions there as often as they could, the Catri Team that would one day became world-class professionals mostly just surfed the mediocre waves near the Islander Hut snack bar in Cocoa Beach. If you could manufacture speed for radical maneuvers at Third Street, Todd explained, you could draw out those same carves into longer lines and better maneuvers on bigger waves around the world. Todd's version of this "bad waves make great surfers" mantra emboldens every southern surfer to think that they've got a shot at the world tour.

Todd and the other members of the Catri Team practiced daily, with the dream of winning a spot on the U.S. National Team. Todd's exercise regimen out of the water eventually included multiple sets of 100 push-ups and sit-ups each day as well as breathing exercises that enabled him to survive fearsome hold-downs for minutes at a time. On Todd's first trip to California, he placed third in the national championship race for the junior division. That result catapulted him into another level of surfing, coaching, and eventually sponsorships. At the time, two Aussies, Peter Townend and Ian Cairns, coached the U.S. National Team. Together, they revised the scoring system for modern surf competitions. Cairns also resuscitated the world tour of professional surfing. With mentors like Townend and Cairns, Todd Holland got world-class coaching along with access to the heavy winter waves of Hawaii and the rippable summer swells of Southern California.

Barely thirteen on his first trip to the famed North Shore of Oahu in Hawaii, Todd remembers wanting to prove that Floridians could ride the biggest, best waves in the world. Never mind that Catri had already proven that in the early 1960s and Floridian Jeff Crawford had won the Pipeline Masters in 1974. Every Floridian has traveled to Hawaii with the same chip on his shoulder that Todd carried. "That's one thing I wanted to break the image of," he told me, the Sunshine State surfers who were supposedly out of their league on the North Shore. His coaches shared that goal. "They paddled me out at ten-foot Sunset when I was four foot ten and eighty-five pounds." Holland took a heavy beating, but he also faced his fears, so that when he returned, he'd be ready.

Coming up behind Todd, just three or four years his junior, Kelly Slater had started out as something of a pint-sized mascot of the Catri surf team. In his memoirs, years later, Kelly speculated that he got on the team by riding the coattails of his older brother Sean. Perhaps to compensate for his tenuous position on the team, Slater had c-a-t-r-i emblazoned in huge letters across his board. He had always dreamed of a sponsorship sticker, and by god, he got the biggest one possible—even if the "sponsorship" mainly consisted of free advice from Catri.

The Slater brothers initially struggled to make the National Team, though both were excellent surfers. Kelly and Sean tried out for the U.S. team in 1984, balking at their first sessions in huge California surf during the run-up to the trials. The coaches sent Sean and Kelly packing. Todd Holland and another Cocoa Beach local made the cut. Over the next few years, Kelly Slater's skill and confidence grew apace with his physical stature. By 1986, when Kelly faced off against Todd in an East Coast Pro-Am event held in Cocoa Beach, the young gun beat the teenage veteran in head-high waves. At that point, the competition remained a friendly crosstown rivalry. The next contest splintered the Cocoa Beach crew.

The U.S. National Team trials in 1986 saw Kelly Slater not only qualify but win the event. In Kelly's telling of the story, his brother and Todd Holland vied for the last slot on the team. Kelly thought this rivalry was political as well as personal, because he and his brother competed in the Eastern Surfing Association (ESA) while Todd surfed in the National Scholastic Surfing Association (NSSA), which had been founded by U.S. Team coaches Townend and Cairns. According to Kelly, Cairns told other surfers in the contest to let Todd win his heat so that he would beat out Sean Slater for the final slot on the team. Whether the other guys sandbagged the contest or not, in the end, Todd made the team and Sean didn't.

Within five years, both Todd and Kelly would be representing Cocoa Beach on the world tour of the Association of Surfing Professionals founded by Ian Cairns. If Cairns placed his thumb on the scales of the trials event, he furthered the career of one of his Florida stars and fueled the competitive fire for another Floridian who would go on to become the best contest surfer of all time.

The year that he graduated from Cocoa Beach high school, Todd Holland began to compete as a professional on the world tour. Because he joined after four contests had already run, he had to do well if he wanted to qualify for the tour the next year. His parents told him that he had three years to make it; otherwise he was going to college. In one contest held at Margaret River in Western Australia, Holland beat fellow American Tom Curren in a man-on-man heat. Curren, a three-time world champion, was arguably the best surfer of his generation. On that same trip, Holland joined Virginia Beach native Wes Laine in one of the first successful surf sessions at a notorious West Oz break called the Box, a place once deemed unrideable. Holland rode his trademark red-and-yellow boards, along with a newfound confidence, to a victory at the 1990 Op Pro (now the U.S. Open of Surfing) during which he defeated both Tom Curren and the reigning world champion, Australian Martin Potter.

As exciting as it was to be traveling to exotic places and competing with the best in the world, rookies like Todd surfed the tour on a shoestring budget. If Todd lost in the first round of a contest, he won the consolation prize of $300, nowhere near enough to cover airfare, much less food and lodging. To save money, the Florida rookie roomed with other young mavericks like Hawaiian Sunny Garcia. That first year, Garcia and Holland checked into a hotel during a French contest flat broke. One of them had to advance through heats just to pay for the room. But the tour wasn't always such a grind. Todd started winning, going deep into contests in the early 1990s and making enough money to buy a tricked-out new truck. In one memorable stretch, he won two high-profile contests back-to-back, netting $35,000 in a matter of weeks. The giant check he received for one of those contests leaned against the wall of the surf school. In 1991 Todd finished eighth in the world. The future looked bright for the young Floridian. By then, however, Kelly Slater had joined the tour.

Back in the early 1980s, Dick Catri predicted that Kelly Slater would go far in surfing. When Slater joined the world tour in 1990, commentators weren't just asking *if* the Cocoa Beach native would be world champion, but how *many* times he'd win the world title. Slater won his first title in 1992, at the tender age of twenty the youngest man ever to wear the crown. Then, he won five world titles in a row. During Slater's series of title runs in the mid-1990s, he seemed unbeatable. Meanwhile, Todd Holland's place in the rankings yo-yoed between fourteenth and twenty-sixth overall. At a pro contest in France, Holland and Slater faced off in jerseys one last time. Todd didn't tell me about this contest. He may not even remember the particulars of the heat. But Kelly does. He included the judge's score sheet from that heat in his 2003 book *Pipe Dreams*.

Kelly liked to jump out to an early lead in heats, putting psychological pressure on competitors who were already quaking in their board shorts at the prospect of facing the champ. In this heat, Todd paddled hard to gain priority, so that he could pick the first set wave, scoring a solid 8.00 out of 10 on the ride. Kelly's first wave scored a middling 6.33. No matter, pro contests at that time counted each surfer's best four waves. Kelly had plenty of time to make up ground. The champ's next ride, an 8.83, ranked as the best wave in the heat, and he followed that up with a solid 7.00. It wasn't enough to take the lead, however, because Todd scored an 8.50 on his second ride, backing that up with two more rides in the seven-point range. The champ was up against the ropes. He added rides of 7.00 and 8.33 to his heat score. To beat his crosstown rival, Kelly needed only a 6.95. Time ticked down. One final wave came through for Slater. Tense with anticipation, the crowd on the beach wondered if Slater could pull a rabbit out of a hat and catch the magical winning ride at the end of the heat. Not this time. Slater's final wave scored merely a 4.60. Holland had won. On the judge's sheet, which Kelly kept in a file with all of his other results, the champ scrawled a note: "Let Todd get early position on me." Win or lose, Kelly learned a lesson from every heat, remaining a student of the game even as he appeared to be the master.

Todd left the world tour after the 1996 season, returning to Cocoa Beach to face several years in the wilderness. An ugly divorce from his second wife left him nearly penniless. For a time, he barely surfed at all. He worked construction, got an entry-level position at Sea Ray boats, and booked trips for his mom's travel agency. Meanwhile, Kelly Slater signed multimillion-dollar endorsement deals, dated celebrities like Pamela Anderson, and returned from early retirement to win even more world championship titles in the 2000s. Slater heard about Todd's plight. One day, a brand-new, Channel Islands board showed up at Todd's place. It was from Kelly. "He sent me a gift, just out of the blue," Holland recalled. "Kelly helped me get back into surfing. It got me motivated again." Within a few years, Todd found love, started the surf school, and regained his footing. He may have been harried when I talked to him, but he was also happy.

I had two more stops to make before I left Cocoa Beach: the Kennedy Space Center and Ron Jon Surf Shop. I grew up in the wake of the Apollo program's miraculous moon landings and watched the Space Shuttle's awkward, but no less awesome, attempts to make space travel feel like airplane flight. I journeyed to Cape Canaveral on a nerdy hajj.

Just before closing time, the dwindling crowd at the Kennedy Space Center displayed a quiet reverie of the sort usually reserved for tours of cathedrals. Hushed conversations about booster rocket specs and g-forces suggested that I was among my people. Before visitors were allowed into NASA's inner sanctum, we had to endure far too many movies. Hell, we'd seen the movies and watched the launches on TV. We wanted to *see* the space stuff with our own eyes! Sitting in one of the old mission-control rooms, we listened to a recording of august newscaster Walter Cronkite counting down to liftoff, giving any of us who were old enough to remember that familiar tingle of anticipation in our spines.

At liftoff, the doors opened into a cavernous hall, bigger than several football fields and chocked full of the holiest relics produced by American science over the last half century. A gargantuan Saturn V rocket dwarfed all of the other displays. How can one comprehend a vehicle as large as the Statue of Liberty and as powerful as a fleet of passenger jets? Human beings made that. Human beings piloted it to the moon! Ceiling wires suspended the Atlantis Space Shuttle, banking left, as if in midflight. The Atlantis Space Shuttle. The *real* Atlantis Space Shuttle, with pockmarks in the heat shields and everything! A lunar lander, command capsule, moon rocks, space suits, astronaut helmets, zero-gravity bedrolls. I had died and gone to nerd heaven. In the gift shop, I bought Zinnia an old-school NASA Space Shuttle T-shirt. I didn't buy the freeze-dried, astronaut ice cream, but just seeing the package brought back Proustian memories. My tongue recalled the mouthfeel of the weirdly desiccated, sugary, Neapolitan brick. It tasted like the future.

Space is yesterday's future. Sadness and loss always sketch the boundaries of nostalgia. After the Cold War ended, the United States reduced funding for the space program. We privatized it (SpaceX and Boeing) or outsourced it (Soyuz rockets, really?). The weekend after I visited Cape Canaveral, SpaceX fired off a new Falcon rocket from one of the massive launch pads at the Kennedy Space Center. How had I not known about this? Wasn't a rocket launch into space more important than petty political tweets? Twitter wouldn't send humans to Mars or probes to explore distant stars and nebulae. Most important, it wouldn't inspire kids to dream of traipsing around the galaxy. Can I get a witness, Carl Sagan? What about an "Amen," Neil deGrasse Tyson?

On my last morning in Cocoa Beach, I woke up early and hopped across the highway with high hopes. Tiny, ankle-high peelers dashed those hopes immediately. Since I needed a ding repair kit to fix a small crack in the tail of the Bingo Board, I skipped the surf and drove over to Ron Jon Surf Shop.

When I got to Cocoa Beach, I expected all of the real surfers that I was interviewing—the lifers and pros—to share my disdain for Ron Jon, with its in-your-face billboard advertising and its 52,000-square-foot consumer castle. Cocoa Beach locals quickly corrected me. They respected Ron Jon and all that it did for the surfing community. The company donated free space in the back of their rental shop to the Florida Surf Museum. They sponsored local pros on the way up and those on the way down. When Todd Holland lost his major sponsorship after Ocean Pacific declared bankruptcy in 1993, Ron Jon picked up the slack and stabilized his career. They still sponsored his wife as she transitioned from competitor to coach, just as they sponsored a number of groms with dreams of becoming the next Kelly Slater. It turned out that Ron Jon was a model corporate citizen. Maybe the Ron Jon folks weren't exactly Robin Hoods, but they profited off tourists and ploughed some of that money into the local surf economy.

Still, entering Ron Jon's flagship store initially seemed to confirm my worst fears about the place. The whole first floor was nothing more than a glorified sticker, magnet, towel, and T-shirt warehouse. And Ron Jon branded the hell out of everything. I wouldn't have been surprised to see a Ron Jon toilet brush that cleaned "with the power of surf." Then again, who can fault them for running a business like . . . well . . . a business?

Wondering if I could get actual surf equipment at Ron Jon, I braved the T-shirt and sticker gauntlet of the first floor and raced up to the "core" shop upstairs. I still needed a small tube of epoxy resin to repair the Bingo Board. A clerk asked if he could help me find something. "Nah," I sniffed, "I'm just getting something to repair a few dings." I carried my small sack of core purchases proudly downstairs.

As I made it to the door, the display of boogie boards caught my eye. Zinnia had been begging for a boogie board all trip, something to let her ride waves when I had the Bingo Board and vice versa. I balked. Sure, I surf with really talented boogie boarders in California, but something about buying a kook sponge went against every soul surfer bone in my body. Staring at the Ron Jon boogie boards, I realized how stupid that was. True watermen and women enjoy the ocean. They don't draw stupid distinctions between water sports, surf shops, or types of surfers. Soul surfers are an integral part of industry marketing. Contest surfers have soul (and talent) to burn. I decided to embrace the commercial juggernaut at the center of surfing. I picked up the most garish boogie board that I could find. A factory in China tatted that board with a sweet flame design and of course, a Ron Jon logo. With my new stick picked out, I marched to the register next to the T-shirts and magnets. Cha-ching.

~~~~~~~~~~~~~~~~~~~~~~~~~~~~~~~~~~~~~~~~~

I've only seen Kelly Slater surf in person once. In 2011 the world tour came to San Francisco for a one-off contest at Ocean Beach. Most of the spots on tour are either world-class waves or places where the surf industry moguls think they can hawk their wares to the most potential customers. With an inconsistent and punishing beach break, San Francisco fell decidedly into the latter category, as the home of booming tech and biotech companies. Like other Bay Area surf fans, I bleated my way sheep-like to buy a sweat-shirt and watch the pros. At thirty-eight, Slater had passed his prime but still ripped with the whippersnappers rising up to challenge him.

The waves that November day were awful, five to eight feet and torn up by a side-shore wind under partly cloudy skies. Still, the pros pulled off unbelievable maneuvers. I watched folks launching impossible aerials. One contestant, Californian Pat Gudauskas, smacked the lip, grabbed his board, flipped upside down in the air, and rolled completely over to continue the ride. Unfortunately, Gudauskas's ankle crunched beneath him after the trick, ending his run. Gabriel Medina, a rookie and future world champion from Brazil, won the contest, but Slater surfed well enough to win several heats. At the end of Kelly's final heat, he caught a classic Ocean Beach close-out just after the horn. I watched the champ disappear in a crush of white water that I knew from personal experience was unmakeable. I turned away, unwilling to watch my hero humbled by an inevitable beating. Then a roar erupted. I looked back just in time to see Slater emerge miraculously out of the whitewater. That wave didn't count and probably didn't even rank in the top 1,000 rides of his life. For almost anyone else, it would have been the ride of the year. The Cocoa Beach native nonchalantly rode to shore and collected his eleventh world title, becoming both the youngest and oldest man ever to claim the crown.

As I left Cocoa Beach and thought about Kelly Slater and the other surf-ers who hail from Florida's Space Coast, I wondered if it was accurate to call these folks southerners. Some people say that Florida isn't *really* southern, that the further south you drive, the further north you go. Or some such nonsense. Was Sharon Wolfe really a southern surfer? Todd Holland? Kelly Slater? Yes. Sharon lived for a decade in San Diego, but she longed to return to Cocoa Beach, ultimately, forsaking the famous waves of California for the far more finicky surf of her hometown. Todd Holland's love for country music, the fiddle, and jacked-up trucks distinguished him from most folks on the world tour, and when it was time to retire, there was only one place he could imagine living.

What about Kelly Slater? He was a citizen of the world—at home in Fiji or France, Huntington Beach or Cocoa Beach. Early in his memoirs, Kelly meditated on the nature of growing up as a "good ole boy," someone who loved to hunt and fish so much that he often slept with his fishing pole when he was a kid. "I wonder if growing up around fishing poles, guns, and alligators made me a redneck," he mused. Then, he concluded—correctly, I think—that being a redneck is a "state of mind," not necessarily a function of geography, hobbies, or habits. By that definition, Kelly Slater was no redneck. Then again, the very fact that he had to ask the question suggested that he remained a southerner at heart. If a southerner can surf like Kelly Slater, there's hope for us all.

# 7

# *Have Boards, Will Travel*
## Daytona Beach, Florida

I drove due north. My compass needle would not point south again. There were strange breaks to surf and more strangers to meet, but in some sense, I was headed home. A sadness tinged this moment, as it does just over the halfway point of every journey. I hadn't passed the point of no return—nothing so dramatic—but more miles had faded in the rearview mirror than stretched out in front of me. Midlife crisis, anyone?

Without Zinnia, I drove alone. Solitary road trips afford time for contemplation. I've logged thousands of miles by myself, careening back and forth from the Carolinas to California and nearly every state in between. On these trips, the monotony becomes meditative. The physical pain of driving dulls your senses. The passing countryside blurs into a smear of color and light—the subdued earth tones of cultivated fields and untended forests accented by the garish neon of roadside attractions. These visions can yield enlightenment, but just as often they bleed into a profound sense of loneliness.

The short, uneventful trip from the Space Coast to my next stop, in Ormond Beach, fit this latter pattern. I merged onto I-95. The gravely gray asphalt recalled family vacations, traffic jams, and surf trips up and down the East Coast. But those trips were rarely solitary affairs. There were always copilots or coconspirators, siblings to rival for backseat supremacy. Not this time. I stuck my already sunburned left arm outside the open window. The din of diesel engines and howl of the wind drowned out my depressing internal monologue.

When I arrived at Ormond Beach, I checked into a bland, cheap chain hotel just off the interstate. The beige walls and institutional furniture perfectly suited my mood, allowing me to wallow in the misery of a traveling salesman. I couldn't muster the energy to do much except watch TV, lying on a bedspread of synthetic fabric—coated in a thin layer of plastic for maximum longevity and minimum comfort. I leaned back against the faux-wood headboard and stared mindlessly at an NBA Finals game. The two poorly matched teams confirmed the game's predetermined outcome just a few minutes after tipoff, as the score grew more and more lopsided. Still, the players ambled up and down the court for hours, distracting me from any deep thoughts. At the final buzzer, there were perfunctory high fives and smiles for the camera, but everyone looked more exhausted from the performance than the gameplay. The remote control winked out the flatscreen. I sank into unconsciousness beneath over-starched sheets and comfortless comforter.

~~~~~~~~~~

The first Daytona-area surfer that I interviewed requested that we rendezvous at Starbucks around noon. I wanted to meet earlier, but Renee Eissler pushed our interview back a few hours. She needed time to feed all of her birds and cats, most of which she had rescued. "So you're the neighborhood's crazy cat lady?" I said on the phone with a bit too much familiarity. Renee rolled with this. "Yes, I guess I am," she replied wryly. Renee Eissler was comfortable in her own skin.

A bit of a jock in high school, Renee excelled at sports. When she tired of tennis, she fell in with a surf crew near her home on the ocean side of Daytona Beach Shores. This was 1965. Renee grew so obsessed with her new sport that she lugged her heavy, three-stringer longboard to the beach almost every day. Before long, she held her own in competitions with Florida's best. Dick Catri recruited Renee to join his legendary Hobie Team. Surfing for Catri, she went to the U.S. Nationals in Virginia Beach and then to the World Championship in San Diego.

Renee placed ninth in the 1966 World Championship contest, but as often happened with women surfers, journalists barely noticed her athletic skill. When her photos graced the pages of *Sports Illustrated* and *Life*, the lens focused on Renee (and her bikini) on the beach. "Vibrant Renee Eissler may not have won in the water," read a classic *Sports Illustrated* caption, "but was a winsome winner ashore." The North Florida native kept the articles and photos in a scrapbook. She liked the media attention and the surf competitions, but she *loved* the travel. Trips for contests inspired a lifelong wanderlust.

Surfers are a notoriously nomadic tribe. The waves always break better, cleaner, or less crowded down the coast, at the next point break, hidden cove, distant pier, or freshly brewed sandbar. The first generation of American surfers in California fled their increasingly crowded home breaks for uncrowded waves of Baja. In the late 1960s and '70s American surfers began making pilgrimages across the South Pacific, skipping across endless archipelagos of Indonesia, Tahiti, and Bali. "Surfing was increasingly about the search, the journey, the discovery," argued historian Scott Laderman in *Empire in Waves*. For Laderman, surf tourists of the 1960s and '70s represented the soft power of American foreign policy during the Cold War. Although global surf trips veritably "dripped with the trappings of empire," the surfers themselves left relatively light footprints in the countries they visited, when compared to other American tourists or military operations. Surfers often sought not only uncrowded waves, but genuine cultural exchanges.

Renee Eissler counted herself among these seekers. Her globetrotting made all but the most intrepid surf explorers look like homebodies. As a college junior in 1967, Renee spent a semester at sea, circumnavigating the globe. She traipsed through the Iberian Peninsula, falling in love with Spain and Portugal. Unable to pass through a war-torn Suez Canal, her ship headed down around West Africa toward the Cape of Good Hope. Renee used her college French to barter in Senegal and crashed with a South African surfer she knew from the World Championships. The African season of her endless summer included wild safaris and epic surfaris in rarely ridden breaks. Crossing the Indian Ocean, Renee and her friends caught up with the Maharishi Mahesh Yogi one day after the Beatles visited him. They sailed up through Asia, stopping in Kuala Lumpur, Hong Kong, and Tokyo before turning east toward Hawaii. Renee surfed her way around Oahu and had the same question that every traveling surfer asks in Hawaii. Why leave?! When she met her mom in Los Angeles at the end of the semester at sea, Renee broke the news that she wasn't returning to the Sunshine State. Instead, she flew right back to Honolulu to finish up college and keep surfing in the Aloha State.

After college, Renee hit the road again—this time, with the Peace Corps. She learned Portuguese for a posting in Brazil. She strolled down the streets of Copacabana and surfed the beaches of Ipanema before being posted in northern Brazil near Recife. She surfed there too. Her whirlwind posting came to a screeching halt when she came down with a serious illness and had to fly back to the United States for treatment and recuperation. Disappointed that she hadn't been able to finish her Peace Corps posting, Renee sought another way to travel, serve, and surf. She ended up teaching elementary school art for a year on Saint Croix in the U.S. Virgin Islands, where finding consistent surf spots proved much more challenging than teaching. Sailing, diving, and snorkeling kept her in the water between swells. With the end of the school year, Renee headed back to Florida. She was already planning her next adventure as she unpacked her bags.

~~~~~~~~~~~~~~~~~~~~~~~~~~~~~~

If anyone could give Renee Eissler a run for her money in terms of globetrotting, it'd be William Finnegan. The son of a Hollywood producer, Finnegan bounced back and forth between Hawaii and Southern California during his childhood. The phenomenal surf memoir *Barbarian Days* chronicles Finnegan's epic journeys in search of waves from Hawaii to Australia to Fiji. Finding *Barbarian Days* was like stumbling on a secret surf spot. My buddy Randy dropped the hardback in my mailbox not long after it was published. It was the middle of a semester, and I had papers to grade, articles to write, and tenure files to review.

After just a few pages of *Barbarian Days*, all that work went out the window. The book contained the best surf writing—hell, the flat-out best writing—I'd ever read. When Finnegan wrote about the years he spent in San Francisco, chasing the winter swells of Ocean Beach with local legends, I recognized not just the people and the beach, but individual droplets of water spraying off peeling waves that felt so real, they might as well have blown off the page. Finnegan won the Pulitzer Prize for *Barbarian Days*. A member of the slacker tribe proved that surfers could collect more than sunburns. But the book was no longer the secret spot that meant so much to me on the first reading.

Thumbing through a surfing magazine one day, Finnegan recalled coming across a list of the top ten surf spots in the world. He had surfed *nine* of the ten breaks! If *Surfer* ever publishes a list of the ten worst surf breaks, I hazard a guess that I will have charged nine of the ten. It's not for lack of trying. I've traveled to Hawaii. Each time, visions of being spit out of a cavernous barrel at Pipeline fill my head on the plane ride over. Dozens of magazine articles, films, and contests made me long for a trip to Hawaii, but if I'm being honest, the greatest inspiration was the 1987 movie *North Shore*.

*Have Boards, Will Travel*

Produced by Bill Finnegan, father of the *Barbarian Days* author, *North Shore* cast an army of surf legends in roles both big and small. Pipeline master Gerry Lopez zens his way through the film, just as you'd expect of a guy who coolly styled out of the gnarliest barrels on the planet. The rest of the cast includes a who's who of the sport's luminaries, including Derek and Michael Ho, Corky Carroll, Mark Foo, Mark Occhilupo, and Shaun Tomson. Most of my 1980s heroes leapt from the pages of surf magazines onto the big screen in *North Shore*. The best and worst casting decision was tapping Hawaiian waterman and extreme-sports beefcake Laird Hamilton to play the film's villain. Hamilton's hilariously wooden performance as a pro-surfing bad boy turns a poorly scripted, clichéd coming-of-age story into a cult classic.

*North Shore* begins in landlocked Arizona, where a young shredder named Rick Kane wins a wave-pool contest to become the state surfing champion. Rick ploughs his prize money into a trip to Hawaii. Cocky from his wave-pool victory, Rick heads straight to Oahu's North Shore, where he is humbled by the waves and humiliated by Hawaiian locals. As the reigning surf champ, Lance Burkhart (Laird Hamilton's character) struts around the island like a bantam rooster with slightly more gravitas than the cartoon character Foghorn Leghorn. Burkhart joins a group of Native Hawaiians in putting the newcomer Rick in his place, until the haole (white kook) meets a happy-go-lucky sidekick nicknamed Turtle. Taking Rick under his flipper, Turtle introduces the newcomer to his boss, a reclusive shaper named Chandler. Chandler trains Rick in a montage that walks the kook through wave-riding history, from ancient Hawaiian logs to modern shortboards. Rick gains not only skills and knowledge, but "soul" and (of course) a beautiful Hawaiian girlfriend.

Film critics derided *North Shore* as a soggy knockoff of the wildly popular *Karate Kid* franchise, in which an old sensei similarly teaches a young apprentice not just about sports, but about life. As a B-movie classic, however, *North Shore* succeeds despite itself, becoming something greater (or at least a hell of a lot funnier) than the limited budget and vision of its producers. For a kooky kid from South Carolina (which might as well be Arizona to the surf world), *North Shore* struck with the force of lightning.

My mom took my brother and me to Hawaii for the first time in the summer of 1990. We rented dinged-up shortboards at a Honolulu surf shop. The guys at the shop pointed us to Ala Moana Bowls, which was "small" that day, but still breaking in speedy hollow lefts at a size the Hawaiians called three to four feet. My brother and I paddled out through the channel to the break. As we got to the lineup, we saw Shaun Tomson, the famous South African pro. Torn between begging for an autograph and acting aloof, we opted for the latter strategy. Of course we were used to surfing with pros. They came to South Carolina all the time. No big thing.

The next day, we went back to Ala Moana Park and decided to surf right in front of the rocky breakwater at a place that called Flies, or maybe In Betweens. Surfers have named every square inch of coastline in Hawaii, so it was hard for a haole to figure out where one break ended and another began. Luckily for us, the swell had dropped a bit from the day before, registering only two to three feet Hawaiian. Still, surfing over reef for the first time is scary regardless of the size of the waves. I'd bounced off the sand bottom of the Atlantic Ocean a million times and come up shaking half the seafloor from my board shorts without a scratch. Reef wipeouts were different, the sharp rocks chomped like rows of jagged teeth just beneath the surface. The crystal-clear water hid nothing beneath its surface. I spied sea life nonchalantly going about its business and oblivious that it could become the garnish in a human skewer, when I face-planted onto the reef.

I was eighteen and immortal, so I didn't give the reef a second thought. On one of those rare days when the crowds had found something better to do, my brother and I had the wave almost to ourselves. Since my brother's a goofy-footer, and I'm regular, we split the peak. He'd go left, and I'd happily head right, carving away on shoulder-high slices of liquid paradise.

On a second trip to Hawaii, after I had surfed for a while in California, I carried an unwarranted cockiness. I swaggered down to one of the beach stands that rent crappy longboards. The clerks seemed unimpressed with my not-so-casual mention of my exploits charging heavy surf in San Francisco. "Whatever, haole," they might as well have said as they happily took my money, suggesting that I surf in front of the Royal Hawaiian, where all the beginners surf. "What about out there?" I asked, pointing to a break right in front of their shack. "Nah, the tide's too low for that spot." They might have mentioned patches of exposed reef and sea urchins, but I was already headed out to prove them wrong.

I paddled out easily over increasingly shallow reef, finding "key holes" through which to sneak out to the break. I sat up just outside the takeoff zone, amazed that I had the place all to myself just off the world-famous Oahu beach where tourists lay packed like sardines. I smiled, self-satisfied. A small, waist-high roller popped up. I took off at a lazy pace fueled more by warm sunshine than ocean motion. Near the end of the ride, the wave

*Have Boards, Will Travel*

seemed to steepen up. Seeing a section of dry reef, I jumped off the board, already thinking about the next ride.

My foot touched down on the reef. Just as I put my weight on it, I felt a stinging sensation. Needles of pain punctured the sensitive pad. Jumping off of the reef only deepened the wound. By the time I got to the beach to inspect the damage, I had to wipe away a surprising amount of blood. More than a dozen sea urchin spines the size and color of small pencil lead points lay embedded within my foot. I hobbled back toward the surf shack. The clerks just shook their heads and asked with mock innocence, "How was it, brah?" I showed them my foot. Their facial expressions said "We told you so, dumbass!" They explained how to care for the wounds.

On my last trip to Hawaii, I finally got to see the winter swells that pound the North Shore, but I didn't surf them. When my family got back to the South Shore, I paddled out at a break not far from Ala Moana. A sizable crowd of tourists and hotel workers on break had already staked out the best takeoff spots. I snagged a few rogue waves that broke away from the pack, flopping awkwardly at the end of rides to avoid the army of angry urchins just below the surface. Several spine-free sessions boosted my confidence. Sunny days blurred together and mellow rides in small surf became the norm.

During one session, some guys in an outrigger canoe came out. No one told me how outriggers fit into the priority system of catching waves, but like a motorcyclist on a freeway with 18-wheelers, I yielded. After a ride, I angled back to my usual spot away from the crowd. The guys in the outrigger were paddling like mad to catch a wave outside. I was about to hoot them into it, when they started to turn in my direction. Too late, I realized that were headed straight at me. I ditched my board and got as flat on the reef as I could, basically hugging a family of sea urchins. I asked the urchins about the cost to replace a rental board smashed to pieces by an outrigger canoe. Only when I scratched back up to the surface did I realize how much damage that canoe could have done to me. Shaking with excess adrenaline, I inspected the board. Not a scratch. It had passed unscathed between the canoe's hull and pontoon. A couple of the other surfers came over to check on me. I thanked them and said everything was fine. I took one more wave. As I flew home, the winter waves of Northern California didn't seem so bad.

~~~~~~~~~~~~~~~~~~~~~~~~~~~~~~~~~~~~~~~

When Linda Baron started surfing in Daytona Beach in the mid-1960s, she almost had no choice but become friends with Renee Eissler. The two recognized each other as kindred spirits right away. Linda's dad had been a lifeguard on New York's Jones Beach in the 1930s, where he first started riding waves on massive, fifteen-foot-long lifesaving boards. When he moved to Daytona Beach in 1964, one of his first stops was the local surf shop. He snagged a few boards for the family. The Barons spent their free time at the beach, where Linda hooked up with Renee.

I met Linda at the plant nursery that she and her husband, Dave, own in Melbourne Beach, Florida. Dave had just had hip surgery, so we planned to meet back at their house a few blocks from the beach for an afternoon interview. The house, as one might imagine, was beautifully landscaped, wrapped in lush greenery and accented with bird-of-paradise flowers and other tropical blooms. It felt like I had been transported from Florida to Hawaii—no coincidence, it turned out.

After a few years competing in local contests and working in a surf shop to save money, Linda Baron convinced her parents to let her attend college in Hawaii, following in her friend Renee's globetrotting footsteps. Linda fell in love with Oahu's South Shore breaks from Diamond Head to Ala Moana, while taking classes in physical education at the Manoa campus. She worked at the Waialae Country Club and met the brother of Hawaiian surf legend Duke Kahanamoku. After a few semesters, Linda returned to Florida to finish up school, realizing perhaps that she'd never complete a "degree" in surfing.

Ironically, surfing helped Linda get her first post-college job at the newly opened Disney World in 1971. Disney imagineers built an impressive wave machine at the Orlando theme park. The machine pumped swells across a manmade lagoon onto a beach near the Polynesian Village. The company recruited Florida surfers in the early 1970s to exhibit their skills just off Surfrider Beach. Linda Baron happily signed on. She worked various jobs around the lagoon, but when she heard the wave machine turn on with its distinctive *whoosh*, she grabbed her board to catch the wave. "They could make all different sizes," she remembered, "but the best waves were lefts, and they would break shoulder high and walled up all the way to the beach." For a goofy-footer like Linda, it was the perfect set up. One day, they dialed the wave machine up to full power and a tsunami washed away half of the Polynesian Village beach. Unfortunately, the finicky machine broke down constantly, costing Disney more than it was worth to run it. Missing real waves, Linda moved back to the coast, where she reconnected with Renee Eisler to hit the road once again.

In the early 1970s, it seemed like nearly every American surfer left home in search of wild adventures. Linda and Renee joined the exodus. Working in a travel agency, Renee came across some crazy ideas for overseas excursions. A trip on a dilapidated freighter through the Caribbean held particular appeal for two surfer girls on a shoestring budget. In the summer of 1972, Renee and Linda flew down to Saint Croix to start their adventure. "All the way down," Linda remembered, "we'd stop at islands during the day and look for surf and sleep on the boat at night." They hit Saint Thomas, Saint Kitts, Antigua, Dominica, and Saint Lucia, crashing with Peace Corps volunteers and an international tribe of long-haired backpackers. Bunks were stifling and cramped belowdecks on the *Federal Maple*, so they slept topside under a spray of West Indian stars. According to Renee's diary, they ate breadfruit, drank lime squash, danced to steel-drum bands, hiked to waterfalls, swam at secluded beaches, and politely turned down two marriage proposals from Caribbean suitors. They saw "well-formed breakers" on the eastern side of Antigua, but didn't have time to surf them. In Barbados, they scrounged up a couple of boards and surfed a break at Christ Church, where they finally "got some really good waves" together. They hitchhiked from one end of Grenada to the other, past Grand Etang Lake in a dormant volcano crater at the top of the island. "What sheer beauty," Renee wrote. "Misty all the time, very rainy and lush—sweet smelling! Definitely tops Hawaii or any of the islands for beauty and lushness." One more trip on the "ugly" *Federal Maple* took them to their final destination in Trinidad. Their wanderlust sated for the moment, they flew home to Florida.

Not long after Renee and Linda got back, Linda found a new travel buddy. Dave Grover met Linda in church and took her surfing on their first date. "It was one of those crazy, huge, chunky, awful days," Linda recalled. Just the fact that she paddled out impressed Dave, but then Linda started catching waves. "She was far advanced to most girls in surfing that I'd ever met," he recalled forty years later. "She had won contests in Daytona Beach." Dave had surfed his way around Europe and the Bahamas. He charged Pipeline in the 1970s. Linda knew that if they got married, she wouldn't have to worry about simply settling down. Dave and Linda smuggled Bibles through the Iron Curtain into Eastern Europe on their honeymoon. They taught all of their kids to surf and ski. One daughter moved to Hawaii and surfed professionally. After two hip surgeries, Linda admitted that she was starting to slow down. That meant surfing the North Shore of Oahu *only* once or twice a year.

Dave Grover styles into a soul arch on a wave in the Caribbean in the late 1960s.
*Courtesy of Linda and Dave Grover.*

I woke up early in the morning on my second day in the Daytona Beach area. Through bleary eyes, I peered groggily at the surf report on my computer. Bad news. One-foot waves lapped gently at the shore. Another flat day in North Florida. On a whim, I scrolled through the cameras at nearby breaks, checking New Smyrna Beach. The surf report called it two to three feet and "fair"—undoubtedly an optimistic assessment. I waited through the interminable advertisement that featured hipster models frolicking in beautiful waves somewhere else in the world. I was in such a sour mood that I almost closed the computer in resignation, opting for more sleep. Finally, the camera's live feed blinked into view. There were waves! At first, I couldn't judge the size, but they broke far cleaner than I expected. Just before the website went to another ad, a surfer took off on a waist-high, glassy peeler. I slammed the computer shut and grabbed the Bingo Board. No time for breakfast. No time to figure out directions. Time to surf.

Forty-five minutes later, after several wrong turns, the truck was bumping along the sand just over the mandated ten-to-fifteen-mile-per-hour speed limit toward the rock groin at the end of New Smyrna Beach. Dozens of surfers were already out, catching small, beautiful rollers going left and right. It was the first real crowd that I'd surfed in since California. No wonder. New Smyrna Beach was apparently the only surfable break along the North Florida coast.

I paddled toward the end of the lineup nearest the groin away from the two or three main peaks. It turned out that I needn't have worried about the crowd or aggressive localism; the lineup was all smiles and chitchat. Serious shortboarders made impressive moves on unimpressive surf and longboarders carved graceful lines. I just sat and watched for a while before picking at the leftovers of the regulars. I turned on an inside wave deemed too small and mushy for the locals. After just a few strokes, the Bingo Board sailed into it, gliding along a gently rippled thigh-high bump that shimmered in the Florida sunshine. As it petered out, that wave added my smile to the rest of the ones in the lineup.

Ten or fifteen minutes later, an especially chatty longboarder apologized for getting in my way. He hadn't. Clearly, the guy wanted some moral support and camaraderie. We struck up a conversation between sets. He was about ten years older than me, somewhere in his late fifties with way too much sunscreen slathered unevenly across his face. He admitted that he was just getting back into surfing after a break of several decades. As a result, he consciously decided to ride waves only to the left, because as a goofy-footer he felt more comfortable on them. If I wanted, he said, I could take off going right on any set waves that came through. This was music to my ears. I parked next to this guy and started taking every right peak that rolled our way, astonished when my friendly neighbor took off going left even into guaranteed closeouts.

The guy was super nice. He stayed out of everyone's way, apologized when others even glanced in his direction. He wasn't a great surfer, but a good citizen, better than me for sure. The Bingo Board caught waves far outside of most folks who had smaller boards. It took all of my will power not to be the greedy asshole who paddled for absolutely everything. Instead, I tried to match the saintly mindset of the goofy-footed Good Samaritan. I thanked folks who had given way to my priority. After each ride, I sat patiently on the side of the lineup, gradually working my way back toward the peak as other folks took their turns. At first, I had looked down on my

Linda Grover nails the takeoff on the North Shore of Oahu, Hawaii, in the 2010s.
*Courtesy of Linda and Dave Grover.*

new chatty friend as a kook, but I soon came to realize that his positivity and selflessness turned a small, mediocre day into one of the most fun sessions that I had on the entire trip.

From the beach, surfing seems to embody an individualistic quest for freedom. Surfers might sit in packs, but once the waves arrive, it's everyone for themselves. Once a surfer takes off on a wave, it's a solo enterprise. This is certainly true in most contests. Despite the fact that there are "teams" of sponsored surfers who push one another and train together, only one surfer hoists the trophy at the end of the final heat. Even in the most crowded free-surfing sessions, the surfer closest to the wave's peak gets the right to ride the wave alone as other riders must pull back or kick out to give way.

But as with most human endeavors, surfing is a very social sport with camaraderie at its core. I knew this before the trip, but the interviews underscored the truism. The tightness of the Waterboyz crew or the decades-long, odd-couple friendship between Scott Bush and Tom Grow suggest that blood is only thicker than water if the water isn't salty. "Todos son hermanos del mar," explains one character in Kem Nunn's surf novel *Tapping the Source*. Nunn twists this sentiment into a noirish nightmare. Surfing lineups are just as likely to be riven by sibling rivalry as bound together in brotherly love. Still, friendships made in the water prove surprisingly durable, sturdier than those built on solid ground.

Walker Fischer had been surfing northern Florida for six decades when I sat down to interview him at the Ormond Beach Library. For five of those decades, Walker had surfed mostly with one other person—his buddy Kent Coleman. Walker and Kent met at Daytona Beach's Seabreeze High School in the early 1960s. Gregg Allman, of the Allman Brothers Band, was in their class. Renee Eissler went to school with them too.

Walker was not an athletic kid. He had tried his hand at traditional team sports and excelled at none of them. But Walker had always felt a connection to the water. "My parents told me that the first time I saw the ocean—and I couldn't have been much more than two or three—I just went right in," he said. "They had to come and drag me out!" When the surf craze hit in the early 1960s, Walker found his sport. He and his buddy Kent started surfing on the very same day in the spring of 1962. They split the cost of a mass-produced, pop-out surfboard. The manufacturer hadn't even bothered to sand down a sharp edge around the rails, which sliced up the boys' hands every time they paddled out. With natural athleticism, Kent stood up almost immediately. Walker took a little longer. Both fell in love with riding waves.

Aside from their love of surfing, Walker and Kent were polar opposites. In riding waves, Walker found a sense of self-confidence for the first time in his life. Kent always had confidence to burn. Walker was a proud political conservative. He attended Furman University, a Southern Baptist college, where he studied history and participated in the ROTC program. Then Walker shipped out to Vietnam. Kent was a "wild and crazy guy" who partied his way through several degrees at the University of Florida, easily mastering the stock market and, later, law school. When Walker came back from Vietnam, he went to work in radio and public relations in Saint Augustine, where he could surf in his free time. Kent moved back to the coast as well, relocating to Jacksonville. Walker said his buddy never really

Walker Fischer (*l*) and Kent Coleman not long after they started
surfing together in Florida during the early 1960s.
*Courtesy of Walker Fischer.*

Kent Coleman (*l*) and Walker Fischer surfing together in
Florida in the 2010s. Photo by Kathleen McCammon.
*Courtesy of Walker Fischer.*

worked a day in his life. He always had some kind of hustle going in golf games, poker tournaments, and the like. Kent labored diligently at only one thing—a life of leisure.

Surfing was the glue that kept this odd couple together. The two buddies met in the water whenever they could. They never surfed contests, never connected to other folks in their respective local breaks, never really got into shortboards, even when longboards became woefully uncool in the 1970s and '80s. During one particularly bad nor'easter, they rescued two girls who got swept out to sea by a wicked rip current.

The highlight of Walker and Kent's surfing life came on Halloween in 1991. Unbeknownst to them, a "perfect storm"—made famous by a book and movie of the same name—brewed in the Atlantic. That storm threw waves as high as thirty feet into the Eastern Seaboard from Nova Scotia to Florida. The storm surge washed away sections of A1A and killed two people in Daytona Beach. Without modern forecasting, Walker and Kent were blissfully ignorant of all of this as they headed to the beach to soak up the warmth of the Indian summer. "Have you ever been out in surf so big that you could hear it crack when it broke?" Walker asked me. It was too hairy even to paddle in that day as the wave faces approached double-overhead.

"Kent took off on a wave," Walker recalled, tensing up at the memory. "I swear to God, I thought he'd never come out. It was one of those waves where you can just—*whooooosh*—down he went, didn't see him, didn't see him, didn't see him, didn't see his board pop up, and there he is! Just heading for the beach, just riding it out." Mesmerized by his buddy's ride, Walker ignored the incoming set waves. By the time he turned around, he was staring into the teeth of a monster. "I grabbed the board, and I started crying, 'Oh my God, I'm going to die!'" Somehow, he punched through the wave just before the lip came crashing down. He felt the adrenaline of that session for days.

Walker and Kent had hundreds of surf sessions together. By the 2000s, the sessions became shorter and less frequent, but both men still cherished their time together in the water. Walker had moved back to Ormond Beach to take care of his ailing parents. As Walker's dad's health began to fail, Kent came down for a surf session to cheer up his buddy. Kent returned to Daytona Beach to speak at the funeral a few days later. He gave a heartfelt tribute to the man who had been like a surrogate father. A week later, Kent himself was dead. The sudden heart attack shocked everyone who knew him, but the loss devastated Walker. "It affected me quite a bit at the time," he admitted, "but now it's . . . when I'm on the beach or in the water I just think back on all those great times that we had for fifty-two-something years. It was quite a run."

Randy Dodgen and I had been surfing together for only about four or five years when he nearly drowned in front of me. It was an early spring day. An onshore breeze muddled up middling, chest-high surf. Unseasonably mild weather convinced my wife, Carol, to bring Zinnia out in a baby sling. Randy's daughter, Grace, also joined us. Carol rocked Zinnia to sleep and watched Grace splash around on a bodyboard. Randy and I had an entirely unremarkable session. We probably caught a dozen rides, though I barely remember a single one.

After less than an hour, we took one last wave together to rejoin Carol and the kids on the beach. The ride petered out in the mid-break where we began paddling for an inside wave. Ocean Beach isn't as notorious as a place like the Wedge in Southern California for its fearsome shore pound, but it can still pack a surprising punch when set waves sneak through to the inshore and jack up in shallow water. One minute Randy and I were talking. Then I was sliding off my board at the shoreline, expecting to see my friend. Instead his board floated up next to me. Randy was nowhere to be seen. His leash had snapped. I looked back out toward the lineup. There he was, floating facedown about twenty-five yards away.

Suddenly, I heard the quasi-tribal drums, piano rolls, and epic guitars of the theme song to *Baywatch*. I transformed from Steve into a buffed-out lifeguard in the mold of David Hasselhoff. As the Hoff, my wetsuit morphed into swim trunks, two or three sizes too small. My board became a red life-saving buoy that spun magically on my hand like a Harlem Globetrotter's basketball. I knew what I had to do. I had to flex my pecs for a few minutes, letting the sunlight play off the baby oil glistening on my chiseled torso. Then I had to go save my buddy.

Moving in slow motion—even though time was of the essence—I high-stepped into the surf. My powerful quads pumped through the shore break. My biceps rippled with bronzed perfection. I slung the buoy over impossibly broad shoulders and dove into the water with the grace of a dolphin—if that dolphin looked like a roided-out, Mr. Universe–era Arnold Schwarzenegger. As I approached the lifeless body of my friend, the chorus of the *Baywatch* theme song reached a crescendo in my ears.

The song stopped. Time sped back up. The Hoff disappeared, and I was just Steve again. I struggled to get Randy to shore while keeping his neck immobilized. Eventually, I gave up on stabilizing his neck and just dragged him to shallower water. Another surfer raced over to help. We carried Randy to the beach and rolled him onto his side. Salt water flooded out of his mouth. He came to and immediately began to wretch.

Someone on the beach called 911. The paramedics arrived. I jumped in the ambulance still wearing my wetsuit and booties, leaving the boards with the other surfer who had helped carry Randy up to the beach. When we got to the hospital, I called Randy's wife. By the time she arrived, Randy's condition was stable. The doctors kept him at the hospital overnight for observation. Their best guess—he had gone down hard in the shore break and banged the side of his head on the bottom. The blow must have knocked him unconscious.

I don't remember when I next spoke to Randy or what was said. We probably just made small talk about the surf or college basketball. I undoubtedly cracked some dumb jokes. He probably laughed politely, perhaps holding his tongue from the characteristic comebacks and putdowns that usually mark our banter. We rarely talked about the accident. Sometimes, he'd tell people the story when I was around, I think as a form of gratitude. Other times—like now—I'd tell the story, so I could play the hero.

For the next few years, Randy's wife made him wear a helmet in the water. He hated it, but he understood. As the accident faded into memory, the helmet came out less and less. Eventually, he stopped wearing it altogether. Things basically returned to normal—dumb jokes and wicked comebacks. One day, when I was riding one of Randy's longboards, I snapped the thing clean in half. I expected him to be pissed or at least give me grief for breaking the board in small surf. Instead, Randy said I didn't owe him anything for the board. We'd call it even.

My aunt brought Zinnia to Ormond Beach after their side trip to the Orlando theme parks. Zinnia talked excitedly about her days at Disney World and at Universal Studios. She drank butterbeer at Harry Potterland and rode rollercoasters until her great aunt cried uncle. Listening to Zinnia's stories about the amusement parks, I realized that this was the part of the surf trip she'd remember for the rest of her life—not the waves, the interviews, or the hours connecting to her dad. On the one hand, this saddened me. On the other hand, it meant that she was still a kid.

The next day, we headed for Saint Augustine. We only had time for a brief stop. If we could do just one thing in Saint Augustine, we had to go to the old Spanish fort. I'd been a nerdy kid weaned on *The Lord of the Rings* and *Dungeons & Dragons*, and the fort in Saint Augustine was as close to an American "castle" as I was ever likely to see. The place held a certain magic for me, and I hoped that it would cast a similar, historical spell on Zinnia.

Driving up to the fort with surfboards strapped to the top of the truck, Zinnia and I got some funny looks from the other tourists. Armed only with a park brochure, we joined the Bermuda shorts army in storming the battlements. Oppressive heat and humidity reduced Zinnia's patience for her father's dorky history obsessions.

"Did you know?" started many, many lectures and subsequent eye-rolls on our trip. If those three words strike fear and dread in the hearts of teens everywhere, imagine them weaponized in the mouth of a history professor and know-it-all father. "Did you know that the coquina rock underneath the breaks we've been surfing is actually what made the Castillo de San Marcos such an impregnable fortress? The rock was porous enough to withstand the impact of cannonballs without shattering. British colonists from South Carolina and Georgia besieged Saint Augustine twice in the early 1700s, but were unable to capture this fort!" Zinnia wandered out of the room before I finished the first "Did you know?" I hustled to catch up with her.

Taking a different tack, I decided to draw my daughter's attention to the fascinating artifacts in display cases throughout the fort's interior. "Look at these cool old coins" or "Check out these awesome uniforms," I begged. Finding neither coins nor uniforms all that cool, Zinnia simply said, "Come on, Dad!" She raced through the fort, stopping only for obligatory photos at the front gate and on the parapets, overlooking the old town. This was before her obsession with social media, but she had already mastered the poses that define her generation.

A few years later, I asked Zinnia if she remembered going to Saint Augustine. "You mean the Castillo de San Marcos?" she responded. "Did you know it was constructed from porous coquina rock that proved surprisingly resilient in the face of British cannon fusillades?" Okay, that wasn't exactly her response. At least she remembered the parapet selfies.

We retreated along the course of the British invaders and headed up to Georgia. I lived in Georgia for two years and never once took a surf trip to the coast. There may be epic swells that sweep into the barrier islands just south of Savannah, but I've never seen or heard tales of them. Still, hope springs eternal. We stopped at Jekyll Island, a nicely manicured resort with beautiful lawns, beachside villas, crystal clear pools, and absolutely no waves. Zinnia and I watched a seven-year-old gamely try to boogie board in toe-high surf. I didn't talk to him, but I'm pretty sure that he would have said, "Dude, you shoulda been here yesterday. It was double-over-toe, pushing ankle high!"

# 8

# *Whitewater*

## *Charleston, South Carolina*

As we drove into Charleston, I felt like a stranger in a familiar land. I knew the rhythm of the seasons intimately—the fall hurricanes that produce sick swells and occasionally sicker property damage; the rare winter sleet that brings the town to its knees, releasing joyous children from school; the pollen-painted spring days perfect for outdoor art and music festivals; the summer sun that burns beach sand to white-hot embers by approximately 11:46 A.M. These seasonal rhythms remain, but since I'd left town, many things had changed. Developers cultivated new condos from once impoverished neighborhoods. Quicktalk from Ohio, New York, and New Jersey accelerated the slow cadences of Lowcountry conversations. Stores and restaurants came and went. Children grew. Elders passed. A native son became a prodigal one.

Southern cities like Charleston rarely rebuff prodigal sons. But behind the warm welcomes and *How y'all been?* there's just a hint of suspicion. The suspicion seems to ask, "Charleston wasn't enough for you? *We* weren't enough for you?" One person never asks questions like this of me—my brother, Phil. Whenever I come back to Charleston, we do three things: (1) play music, (2) drink booze, and (3) surf Folly. Only the order changes.

Phil woke up at 5:45 A.M. on Father's Day—our first day in a weeklong stay at Folly Beach. The latch of the front door clicked as he left to go surf. I reluctantly rose a few minutes later, reminding myself that this is what I call "vacation." The waves at the Folly Beach Pier swirled in a disorganized mess from winds that had howled all night. Still, the faces were two to three feet with occasionally bigger sets. Phil must have been telling himself this as he stretched on the beach. Lord knows that was the only reason to consider getting wet at first light. Against my better judgment, I threw on some board shorts and a rash guard to go join my brother. The trusty Bingo Board had proven it was equal to such slop. Phil and I figured that we could get away with a long Father's Day session if we hit it early.

Returning to surf my home break after years away was not quite like riding a bike—I still fell off—but more akin to wearing an old concert T-shirt, comfortable despite its threadbare appearance. The inconsistent southern beach breaks on this trip were reminiscent of Folly, but none matched the place where I first learned to surf. I quickly recaptured that Folly feeling. Taking off, I could imagine my fifteen-year-old self scratching into the ancestor of the same wave thirty years earlier.

The waves all broke left, a result of the howling side-shore wind. As a goofy-footer, my brother was stoked. Even in the slop he out-surfed me. It wasn't just the lefts. Phil rode a nine-foot board crafted by Will Allison, a legendary North Carolina shaper whose boards are works of art emblazoned with iconic abalone seahorse designs. No competition for the Allison, the Bingo Board barely held its own.

My breakthrough that day was cross-stepping the board, which I first accomplished in the flats in front of the wave. The move is both functional and stylish, allowing the rider to move forward on the board for added speed or backward for more control. It resembles the grapevine step in dancing, where one advances sideways by crossing one foot over the other. A tourist on the pier snapped pictures with his camera. Although he was probably just taking shots of the ocean and beach, I imagined that he was getting great magazine cover shots of me, cross-stepping the chop.

Only three other guys joined us. Phil dubbed one of them "Mustache Man Bun," or MMB for short. MMB was a thirty-something longboarding hipster—the kind of guy who drank both PBR and artisanal IPAs "for the taste." I immediately assumed he was a kook, based on his devotion to fashionable facial hair and a gender-bending bun. MMB proved that you shouldn't judge a hipster by his coiffure. In subsequent sessions, MMB always paddled out, regardless of the conditions, and thus was pretty damn good in that effortless way of someone fully committed to surfing.

Zinnia came down to the beach, waving me in to give her a turn on the Bingo Board. She struggled to get into the waves. Eventually, we just started riding waves together and she would stand up after we made the drop with me stabilizing the back of the board. We took a couple of waves in this awkward mockery of tandem surfing, laughing the whole time.

Zinnia Estes steps toward the nose of her board in front
of the whitewater at Folly Beach, South Carolina.
*Courtesy of the author.*

On one wipeout, we pearled so badly that our brains got a saltwater rinse through our sinuses, but we popped back up into the sunshine all smiles.

Phil let me ride the Allison. Sure, the Bingo could catch anything, but the Allison gave up nothing in paddling speed, while offering far more maneuverability on the wave face. The session ended too soon, as the lifeguards ascended their chairs, signaling the conclusion of the morning session at the pier. There would be more waves in the afternoon, followed by painkillers (the cocktail) and fish tacos at the Surf Bar. A perfect Father's Day in the South Carolina Lowcountry, it felt like home.

Foster and Lilla Folsom literally wrote the book on *Surfing in South Carolina*. When I asked people around Charleston for interview suggestions, the Folsoms ranked at the top of most lists. The Charleston area natives met and dated in college. A few decades later, they reconnected and got married. The Folsoms split their time between the Carolina coast, where Foster remains a lineup regular, and Nova Scotia, Canada, where the couple flees before the armies of tourists descend upon their beloved town.

Foster grew up at Folly Beach, where his mom ran a tourist home. The sand was Foster's daycare center and the ocean his afterschool program in the 1950s and '60s. He remembered sharing boards with his friends until he finally got his own one February. He immediately went out in the freezing winter waves, despite the fact that he had no wetsuit. The days warmed quickly. Then came summertime. The living, as they sing in *Porgy and Bess*, was easy.

Other barrier islands near Charleston developed upscale resorts and reputations, but Folly Beach remained proudly rough around the edges. Foster distinguished his crew from the "Bubbas." Fistfights occasionally broke out between surfers and Bubbas—nothing serious, just a bit of culture clash. Still, the Bubbas and surfers went to school together, fished together, drank together, smoked together. Their families knew one another. The line between Bubbas and surfers at Folly Beach was a pretty thin one.

When I asked Foster about race relations, he remembered white friends who'd drive through Black neighborhoods in Charleston, lobbing eggs or green tomatoes at folks just walking down the street. "There was nothing they could do about it," he recalled somberly. Foster heard "the N-word tossed around routinely, discussed at the dinner table." This wasn't only a problem in Charleston, of course. Tom Grow acknowledged of some friends in Pensacola, "When I went to high school, and what they would do on the weekend is go what they call 'nigger knocking,' go looking for some Black guy to beat up." Tom and Foster didn't participate, but as Foster explained, the everyday nature of such virulent racism forced some "serious soul searching."

As for Black surfers at Folly Beach in the 1960s, there were none. Black people "did not come to the beach to surf, to swim," Foster explained. "They did not come to the beach, thank you very much, except to work." Black Charlestonians had Mosquito Beach, a marshy riverfront property known more for its voracious insects than rideable surf. By the mid-1960s, as the civil rights movement heated up, local activists protested beach segregation with wade-ins at Folly. "There was shit going down that you don't have any concept of," Foster told me. "Imagine being on the beach and turning around and four Black kids come out, and you look up and every redneck on the beach is coming screaming down around them. These guys were brave. I mean, they were brave. They had a lot of balls to do what they did."

Foster graduated from high school not long after these protests. He left Charleston to surf and occasionally attend college classes in Cocoa Beach, Florida. The South Carolina surfer faced culture shock on the Space Coast in the mid-1960s. "The people that were there were intellectual and were liberal," he said. "The average parent was a PhD. All of a sudden, I got to see something that wasn't quite so conservative, you know. My parents had been raised in the Deep South, were extremely typical. I came back, and I'm still the liberal in my family of very conservative, right-wing, bigoted bastards."

Not everyone on the Space Coast shared such liberal sentiments. My buddy Randy Dodgen's dad had traveled all over the world in the military and worked on the lunar lander for NASA, but he retained the conservative social views of his upbringing in Alabama. The senior Dodgen believed in the separation of the races, though he employed an African American housekeeper. Randy described his family as "casual racists." The Dodgens were clearly not alone. Many Space Coast beaches were racially segregated by custom if not by law up through the 1960s. A decade earlier, assailants had bombed the home of the founders of the Brevard County NAACP chapter on Christmas night in 1951. No one was ever convicted of the attack, though subsequent investigations suggested that the Ku Klux Klan members were to blame with rumored support from local law enforcement. Unsurprisingly, there were no Black surfers or even swimmers at the Brevard County beaches where Randy learned to surf in the 1960s.

Contrary to myths about African Americans' lack of aquatic ability or interest, there is a long history of Black participation in water sports. Historian Kevin Dawson argues, "From the age of discovery up through the nineteenth century, the swimming and underwater diving abilities of people of African descent often surpassed those of Europeans and their descendants." Dawson also found archival evidence that Africans began riding waves on rafts and mats, positing that "surf riding" developed independently on the shores of the African continent, though it never reached the level of cultural prominence that it did in Hawaii.

The Native Hawaiian origins of surfing are not lost in the lore of wave-riding, but as one Texas shop owner ruefully admitted, the American public came to view surfing as a "white boy sport." This racial metamorphosis did not happen by chance. In the nineteenth century, Christian missionaries denigrated Native Hawaiian wave-riding as "immoral" and the "root of lasciviousness," but the sport survived. Pictures of Native Hawaiians riding waves inspired a South Carolinian named Alexander Hume Ford to relocate to Honolulu in 1907. As he explained in *Collier's* magazine, "There is a thrill like none other in the world as you stand upon a [wave's]crest." Ford began surfing the beaches of Waikiki the year he arrived, introducing the sport to fellow American writer Jack London. In 1908, Ford founded the racially exclusive Outrigger Canoe Club, where membership became synonymous with the island's white elite. The South Carolina transplant eventually started the *Mid-Pacific Magazine* explicitly to promote surfing, tourism, and white migration, so that Hawaii could be "redeemed from the Oriental, fortified, and Americanized." As he was raised in the Jim Crow South, Ford's years surfing in Hawaii never shook his belief in racial separation. "I have learned that where race prejudice has been overcome, race preference remains, and it will never be otherwise, and it should not be."

The segregation that Ford exported to Hawaii defined Black and white beach culture in his native region. Racial segregation of beaches and pools contributed to the decline of African American swimming in the twentieth-century American South. During the Jim Crow era, southern communities reserved the best beaches for whites only. Wrightsville Beach, North Carolina, passed a law in 1930 prohibiting African Americans from walking on the beach, although an exception was made for Black women taking care of white children. In response to such prohibitions, African Americans created alternative recreational areas like Highland Beach on the Chesapeake Bay in Maryland, the Freeman Beach resort near Wilmington, North Carolina, and Bethune Beach south of Daytona Beach, Florida. Such segregation wasn't restricted to the American South. Black beachgoers in Southern California were largely restricted to a Santa Monica beach dubbed the Ink Well.

Southern surfers of a certain age remember racial segregation as a fact of life in their communities. In the Daytona Beach area, Renee Eissler acknowledged that hundreds of African Americans came to work in the hotels, but they weren't allowed to be on the ocean side after sundown. In the Florida Panhandle, Tom Grow remembered, "When we started surfing, you didn't come to this beach if you were Black."

~~~~~~~~~~~~~~~~~~~~~~~~~~~~~~~~~~~~~~~~~~~~~~~~~~~~~~~~~~~~~~~~~~~~~~~~~~~

When I was still in Florida, one of the folks I spoke with told me he knew a longtime surfer in Charleston I should contact. Charleston's still a pretty small city, so I shouldn't have been surprised when I called the guy, and he immediately said, "I know who you are, Stephen. We're cousins!" It turned out that Hal Coste was my mom's first cousin, still spry and surfing at age seventy-one. Hal was out on his boat when I first got in touch with him, but we set up another time to chat at his house on Sullivan's Island. As a bonus, Hal said he'd invite his longtime buddy Tom Proctor over too.

There's a bit of a friendly rivalry in the Charleston area between people who surf on Folly Beach, south of the city, and those who surf the Isle of Palms and Sullivan's Island, northeast of town. The two groups formed their own clubs in the 1960s: West Coast East and the Carolina Surf Club. They locked horns in local contests. There was overlap, given the small size of the South Carolina surfing community and numerous family connections. Another one of my mom's cousins actually surfed with the Folly Beach crew back in the day. My cousin Hal admitted that Folly Beach usually had better waves. In fact, when people called him up for the Isle of Palms surf report, he'd quickly demur: "Oh God, we're probably knee high at best, but I hear its waist to chest over at Folly. I'd go there if I were you."

The Coste side of Hal's family has lived on the islands since the 1830s. One ancestor, Louis Napoleon Coste, sailed as a privateer for the Confederacy during the Civil War. Another was a "surf man" (aka lifeguard) who earned a Coast Guard commendation for a perilous ocean rescue in the 1890s. Hal's house sat on the back side of Sullivan's Island, tucked up under a beautiful canopy of trees. Out in the yard, two sawhorses propped up the half-finished hull of a wooden boat that Hal was building by hand. Like most island homes, Hal jacked his up on stilts to protect the living quarters from hurricane storm surges. A workshop sanctuary hid beneath the house. His tools lay on a long work table. A quiver of old boards nestled snugly in the low rafters overhead.

Hal Coste and Tom Proctor exhibited the easy rapport that came from six decades of friendship. They started surfing in 1962, founding the Carolina Surf Club underneath Tom's parents' house a year or so later. Their fondest memories from that time were of club members cramming into a single car to travel up or down the coast for surf contests. The contests didn't really matter. Neither man harbored delusions of a professional surfing career. They just loved getting away from their parents and having fun. Reminiscing about that time rolled back the years until they joked like teenagers. "I lost my virginity in the back of Tommy's car," Hal offered in a stage whisper. "I knew you were going to bring that up," Tom groaned. Hal continued, "She looked up at me with her brown eyes, and she said, *'Baaah baah.'*" He delivered the punchline with the well-practiced sound of a bleating sheep.

When I asked Hal and Tom to talk about race and surfing, they started with some context on the civil rights movement in Charleston. Mass demonstrations hit the South Carolina Lowcountry in the early 1960s. Tom's dad couldn't avoid the protests, as the manager of a soda fountain and lunch counter at Hunley's Drugstore in the city. Lunch counters became the front lines of the movement after college students began sit-ins in Greensboro, North Carolina, and Nashville, Tennessee, in 1960. The protests spread like wildfire across the South. African Americans could buy goods at the drugstores, but they were not allowed to sit and eat at the whites-only lunch counters. The restaurant in Hunley's Drugstore was no different. When Black Charlestonians began sit-ins, Tom's dad hung a sign in the window that read, "NAACP: Niggers Ain't Acting like Colored People." "That put him right in the middle of the controversy," Tom recalled. "Every Saturday—which was the busiest day on King Street in downtown Charleston—the Blacks would sit in at the soda fountain. My dad turned out the lights and everybody sits there and stared at each other all day. He wouldn't serve anybody. They'd just sit there." The demonstrations went on for months, until white merchants finally agreed to serve Black customers.

The Civil Rights Act of 1964 made such discrimination in public facilities illegal. Yet segregation continued in private clubs and housing developments. Tom and Hal got jobs lifeguarding on the Isle of Palms in 1965. Although a handful of Black families called Sullivan's Island home, they rarely went to the beach, and the Isle of Palms was entirely off-limits unless African Americans were working for white families on the island. "Isle of Palms was a private beach at the time, because all the perimeter was owned by J. C. Long," Hal explained. "In order for a Black family to get onto the beach, they would have to cross private land—that buffer zone—all around the island." If African Americans came to the beach, lifeguards like Tom and Hal "were instructed to go up and find a payphone and call the police—and they would come down and very diplomatically try to explain to them that they can't be here."

Tom and Hal didn't relish their jobs policing racial boundaries of the segregated beach, but the two watermen proudly took responsibility for rescuing swimmers. Many of the surfers I spoke with risked their own lives to save beachgoers swept out by rip currents. Tom told me that he had to pry one frightened swimmer off of the Isle of Palms pier piling. The struggling swimmer clung to the pier with a death grip as barnacles on the post cut him and Tom. Eventually, Tom managed to get the guy to let go and dragged him to safety. Hal made a similar rescue with his sailboat. Goading his friend into the oft-told tale, Tom intoned, "It was a dark and stormy night. The sea was very angry, my friends. . . ." Joking aside, Hal had steered his boat through nasty currents near Sullivan's Island jetties to rescue the swimmers. The Coast Guard gave him a lifesaving medal, the same one that his great uncle had earned a century earlier.

~~~~~~~~~~~~~~~~~~~~~~~~

For me, surfing and beaches always provided an escape from the problematic racial history and politics of Charleston. If this was true of my time at Folly, it was even more true of my move to San Francisco. Adopting the style of a California surfer, I imagined that I had transcended my redneck roots. But surfing and the move to San Francisco were not panaceas. Northern California might have been politically liberal, but "San Francisco values" didn't inoculate the Bay Area from racism. If anything, surfing and San Francisco created segregated bubbles that were only liberating if you weren't Black. By the 2010s, African Americans made up only about 6 percent of San Francisco residents. Most of these Black residents lived in the city's eastern neighborhoods, far from the beach.

In some ways, San Francisco was simply becoming more like other American beach towns. In the 2010s, less than 1 percent of the residents of Folly Beach were African American, compared to almost 28 percent of Charleston County. African Americans made up less than 2 percent of the populations of Cocoa Beach, Gulf Shores, and Grand Isle. Lest you think this was only a southern phenomenon, the same skewed demographics held true for Santa Cruz, Malibu, and Huntington Beach, California.

The lineups at San Francisco's Ocean Beach were no more diverse than the ones where I grew up. More women surfed at Folly Beach than OB. More Asian Americans paddled out at OB, but the dominant demographic group at both breaks looked a lot like me: white dudes. As I thought about the many ways that surfing equaled escapism, I wondered if racial homogeneity was part of this equation.

The City Surf Project in San Francisco seeks to remedy this problem. Given surfers' notorious lack of motivation for anything other than waves, I wouldn't have been surprised if the nonprofit had trouble maintaining supplies of staples, post-it notes, and pens. But the idea behind the City Surf Project was brilliant. Building on the growing popularity of for-profit surf camps, the nonprofit created a camp and school field-trip program for San Francisco kids who might never otherwise hit the waves. The staff and volunteers "connected underrepresented youth to the ocean and themselves through surfing."

After finding a million excuses not to volunteer, I finally took the plunge during a break from teaching. I usually worked with kids from Mission High School, on the east side of the city. Even though San Francisco is a peninsula that measures only seven miles by seven miles, some of the kids on the east side of town have never been in the ocean, much less surfed. The City Surf Project usually takes kids to a break south of San Francisco in the small town of Pacifica.

Linda Mar beach is tucked into a small, picturesque Northern California cove with cliffs to the north and south, protecting it from much of the swell that marches unhindered to assault Ocean Beach. Houses dot the southern hillside, tumbling down to an old boat dock. A hiking trail winds up the undeveloped northern bluff, with million-dollar views of the Pacific Ocean rewarding joggers who make it to the top. Linda Mar also boasts "the world's best Taco Bell," which was tastefully constructed of natural wood and steel right on the sand at the end of the public parking lot. Say what you will about the fare at Taco Bell (or the wisdom of placing one on the beach), even their "authentic" Mexican pizzas taste good after a session in the waves just off the restaurant's deck.

The students from Mission High spilled out of the white van into the parking lot next to the Taco Bell. They laughed and jumped around with nervous energy, seemingly oblivious of the cold wind that had inspired me to pull my wool beanie down over my ears. The project staff told the volunteers that the kids ranged widely in terms of skill level and swimming experience. Some belonged to the school's surf club. They could paddle out alone. Others were total novices who couldn't swim. One kid nicknamed Jack had just immigrated from Mongolia and had never seen the ocean before coming to the United States.

After pulling on wetsuits, we circled up on the beach. The surf club members led us through a series of stretches. Then they hit the waves while the project staff explained the basics of paddling, popping up, and water safety to everyone else. The waves weren't huge, probably waist high, but that was still daunting for the newbies. The staff asked me to work with the Mongolian kid, Jack, who had caught the hang of surfing amazingly fast in his previous outing. When I pushed Jack into whitewater, he jumped to his feet with surprising grace. He rode several waves effortlessly. A few rough wipeouts shook his confidence. Jack started to get frustrated with himself and with me. After a while, Jack asked to go in and get some water. Coincidentally, he switched instructors.

I next worked with Everett, a beefy kid who said he played offensive line in football. He sported the beginnings of a mustache that he'd clearly never shaved. "Are you from the South?" Everett said after I went through a long-winded introduction. "You sound a little like my uncle from Virginia." The kid had a good ear. He scored brownie points for knowing that Richmond had been the capital of the Confederacy during the Civil War. Everett had surfed a few more times than Jack, but he lacked Jack's innate sense of balance. City Surf Project provides beginners with huge soft-top boards. The largest of them, which Everett rode, measured maybe eight by three and a half feet. You needed a pretty large wingspan just to paddle them.

What Everett lacked in natural ability he made up for with persistence. The kid wiped out again and again, took beating after beating on the paddle out. Nothing phased him. He talked nonstop except when he was under-water, although I'm not even sure he stopped then. After about an hour of treading water and wading next to Everett, I was wiped out. I said, "Hey, are you okay? You want to take a break?"

"No way, I could do this all day!" he replied.

"Let me put this another way, Everett. *I* need a break. So we're going in to the beach to rest."

"How long?" he asked, disappointed.

"Five minutes." The stoked beginner allowed the break.

Everett told me that in his last session he'd only caught one wave by him-self. He wanted to try again. I told him to go ahead and paddle out. I'd wait for him in the shore break. The kid got obliterated by a set wave, roiling the huge soft-top in a soup of whitewater. He popped up still talking; the fish below breathing a sigh of relief. I rescued the board and pushed him out to the takeoff spot. When the next set wave came, I yelled, "Paddle, dude!" He missed the wave completely, of course, but he was now perfectly positioned to catch the second wave in the set. I thought he might get crushed, but the wave creased right behind him and carried him involuntarily shoreward. He could have pearled. He could have lost his balance. He could have eaten it. But instead, he held on, shot out in front of the whitewater. "Pop up, Everett!" I yelled. He did. He rode the thing all the way to the beach. There were more rides, but I don't really remember them. All I know is that we were the last two people in the water.

Stone Singleton's dad couldn't swim, even though he grew up on James Island, just south of the Charleston peninsula. One day, when Stone's grandmother caught his dad splashing around in one of the picturesque little creeks near their house, she grabbed him by the arm, popped him, and dragged him home while chastising him for going in the water. The young boy never forgot the incident and never learned to swim, but he resolved to raise his son without that same fear of water. Stone learned to swim as a toddler. When he turned eleven, his dad bought the family a kayak. Before their maiden voyage, the father put on a life preserver and tied two empty milk jugs to it for extra protection just in case the tiny vessel flipped. The father and son shared many aquatic adventures in the waterways around Charleston.

Stone Singleton was one of only a few Black surfers I interviewed on my journey through the South. His dad could still remember a time when African Americans were not allowed to go to Folly Beach. By contrast, Stone's mom had grown up in Jamaica, where swimming was woven into the fabric of life. A stewardess for Air Jamaica and later a nurse, Stone's mom won his dad's heart with her worldliness and ambition. Stone's dad had played football at the University of South Carolina and then returned home to the Lowcountry to coach and sell insurance. They poured all of their love into their only child.

Stone fished his first surfboard out of a dumpster. The last owner had broken off the nose and one of the fins, wisely giving up the board as a total loss. Stone decided to rebuild the thing, even though he'd never surfed a day in his life. Several hours and coats of fiberglass later, Stone had the jankiest Frankenstein of a surfboard, with a new nose that leaned hard to the left and an asymmetrical fin setup. The dedication to restoring the dumpster board proved that Stone was serious about learning to surf. Eventually, with his dad's help, Stone went down to Money Man Pawn and got a used six-foot, ten-inch Seasoned surfboard.

Some of the guys in the West Ashley High School surf club took Stone out on his first hurricane swell. Even though he swam competitively all through school and would eventually work for five years as a lifeguard, that first hurricane swell humbled Stone. An avalanche of whitewater buried the novice surfer. "I got pulled down to where I saw nothing but black. It took me thirty-five minutes to get out," he told me. "But it's funny how, when you struggle with something like that, you just want it more."

I asked everyone I interviewed about the relationship between race and surfing. As a civil rights historian by training, I view race relations as central to southern history, but I also know that it's hard to talk about race with a complete stranger. I waited until halfway through interviews before

Stone Singleton tucks into a nice little barrel off the South Carolina coast.
*Courtesy of Stone Singleton.*

I broached the subject. These best-laid plans went awry. In the small talk before one interview, when I explained that I had written books about civil rights, an interviewee joked, "Well, I'm a racist!" I laughed awkwardly, and moved on to the questions. Perhaps the joke had been a way to test me. If so, I am not sure whether I passed that test. When I asked about race in another interview, a family member of one of my interviewees chimed in: "Swimming is not part of a Black person's culture. You know, really, they've done studies where the back of their legs just don't have the same ability to swim—just the makeup of the muscles are different." None of the surfers themselves echoed this. Instead, they offered historical and cultural reasons for the lack of racial diversity in southern lineups. Most argued that times

*Whitewater*

were changing and that the contemporary culture of wave-riding was more color-blind.

As one of just a handful of Black surfers in Charleston, Stone Singleton was in a unique position to judge whether or not surfing lineups actually were color-blind. Of course, I had to ask Stone about race, but doing so felt shitty. Stone seemed intent on setting me at ease. Even though he grew up in Charleston, he's got what can only be described as a California vibe—laid-back almost to a fault. Stone says "cool" as much as I do—which is to say, too much. For me, adopting a California surfer shtick was an inoculation against being perceived as a hick. Better others think I was a California poser than a South Carolina redneck. I read Stone's California vibe as something else. On the one hand, he is trying to buck stereotypes, embodying a surfer identity that flies in the face of assumptions about southern Black manhood. On the other hand, Stone's refrain of "It's cool" may be a way of setting southern white folks at ease, a constant affirmation that things are okay. It's cool, but it must get exhausting.

I asked Stone how non-surfers viewed surfers in Charleston, and he paused before answering. "People saw a Black guy surfing, and it was just like, 'Whoa, what is going on? This is strange, this is weird—is he going to die? We didn't think you guys could swim!'" Stone almost always paddled out with a friendly crew, but he still got funny looks. Strangers sometimes splashed water in his face as they paddled by. Willing to fight for his place in the lineup, Stone never really needed to do so. His surfing ability and support from other locals eventually quashed such racist hassles. Still, he relished opportunities to travel to more diverse places like Costa Rica.

In thinking more broadly about the relationship between race and surfing, Stone seemed to be of two minds. At one point, he expressed idealism about the ocean being, if not a utopia, a place where the sun and surf created a color blindness that one wouldn't find on land. Some of this idealism, I think, came from his parents' optimism. They wanted the world to be their son's oyster. "It doesn't matter what you look like," his parents taught him. "You do what you want." Relating this lesson to his surfing life, Stone argued, "You can't put a color on the beach. You can't put a color on the ocean. You can't put a color on a surfboard." Yet at the conclusion of the interview, after he'd talked about some of the challenges he'd faced breaking into the lineup, Stone offered a more wistful conclusion: "I'm just hoping that one day there will be more people in the lineup that look like me, eventually," he concluded. "But it's going to come with time."

# 9

# *The Shape of the Past*
## *Cape Fear Coast,*
## *North Carolina*

One month after I left Charleston, my brother put the Bingo Board up for sale. He pocketed a $25 dollar profit. As much as I dogged on the Texas log, it pained me to see it go. I can't say that I loved riding it or that I'd never find another like it. Crappy longboards are worth their weight in fiberglass. Yet when I looked at pictures of the Bingo in all its school-bus-yellow glory, I experienced a twinge of regret. Maybe I should have asked Phil throw it under his house to save it for me. Eventually, I could sweep away the spider webs, wipe off raccoon poop, and bequeath it to Zinnia as her birthright. Instead, I hoped that the Bingo had become a present for some Lowcountry kid, stoked on his or her first board. Maybe that grom was already stroking into thigh-high shore break at Folly Beach.

A momentous year passed between the two southern surf trips that I took with Zinnia. After we got back to California, Zinnia started studying for her Bat Mitzvah. From her room came voice-cracking ancient melodies only a bubbe could love. I'm not Jewish. But based on a single viewing of *Fiddler on the Roof*, I understood that *tradition* mandated this painful form of ritual humiliation in my wife's family and faith. For Zinnia, studying Torah proved almost as hard as learning to surf on the Bingo Board.

Early in the school year, Zinnia's English teacher required the students to write an autobiographical essay. Zinnia called hers "Half Southern," arguing that my ancestry complimented the Jewish identity she inherited from her mom. The dutiful professor's daughter even had a thesis statement. "Southern stereotypes about people that ate BBQ all day and went to rodeos," she explained, "couldn't penetrate my bubble of proud for my southern family and half-identity."

The essay chronicled the first surf trip from Zinnia's perspective, adding observations that I had missed and moments I had forgotten. In Galveston, "the fish jumped all over" and "one even jumped over the nose of the board." She wrote about the "slow pitter-patter of rain" that peppered our drive through southern Louisiana, a drizzle that eventually became a violent downpour. Zinnia likened it to "a monster scratching at our window." In Charleston, before we headed to Folly Beach, she noted that history surrounded us, admiring the beautiful, handcrafted sweetgrass baskets and the "clippity-clop of the horse's shoes against the hard, cold cobblestone streets." Surfing was different in the South. "Maybe everything is different in the South," she wrote, but not in the ways most of her California friends thought.

If the autobiographical essay gave Zinnia an opportunity to reflect on the southern half of her background, the Bat Mitzvah offered a chance to ponder her Jewish heritage. She had to read passages from the Torah and write a speech, interpreting the passages for the congregation. Golden sunlight shined down from a high bank of windows in the sanctuary onto the bimah (podium) where Zinnia chanted from the Torah. She stood there in a new pair of Vans skate shoes and a white dress, her shoulders covered by a tallit (prayer shawl). She felt nervous but betrayed none of that anxiety as she chanted in Hebrew and then offered her interpretation. In her speech, Zinnia talked about the importance of music in the Torah and in her life. She also discussed surfing and the way it connected her to her family. Something may have gotten in my eye at that point in the service. During my blessing, I quoted the great Jewish philosopher Spock, urging my daughter to "Live long and prosper." Something must have gotten in Zinnia's eyes as they rolled to the side in an unmistakable expression of love for her father. The coming of age ceremony had done its work. Zinnia had become a young adult. At the end of the Bat Mitzvah service, my wife and I experienced what can only be described as a "bubble of proud."

The week after the Bat Mitzvah, Zinnia and I left San Francisco for the second leg of our southern surf trip, flying to Raleigh, where we met up with my high school surfing buddy Alexander Krings and his daughter, Sasha, for an adventure along the North Carolina coast. Raleigh is decidedly not a surf town. It's a lush, leafy place with trees lining almost every roadway. To shake off the stiffness of the cross-country flight, we walked from Alexander's house to a park where Sasha and Zinnia climbed a massive wing-nut tree. Dusk settled on the city. The girls clambered down from the tree and started to catch lightning bugs.

Zinnia's childlike enthusiasm for the lightning-bug hunt came as a welcome change from the raging teenager mode of the Bat Mitzvah weekend. Carol and I had bribed her to study Hebrew with the promise of her first cell phone. That was a deal with the digital devil. Zinnia immediately got sucked into social media. We made a rule that she couldn't post more than two selfies a month. She quickly bent that rule, uploading photos with her friends that weren't "technically" selfies. I felt powerless to stop this. Letting go of that control as a parent—at least a little bit—seemed part of acknowledging that Zinnia was starting to make her own choices.

The phone stayed in Zinnia's pocket while we were in Raleigh. Alexander gave us a tour of his family's cozy home, but his pride and joy was outside the house. As a botanist at North Carolina State University, he had turned his yard into a laboratory. A stunning variety of plants and trees sprouted up in nearly every corner, each taking root in a unique soil or fertilizer mix, calculated to cultivate a specific genus or species. In stark contrast to the manicured lawns favored by most folks, Alexander's landscaping resembled a patchwork quilt of sand, soil, mulch, and compost. A list of the fruits alone—pear, plum, blueberries, lemons, raspberries, grapes, and strawberries—gives a sense of the botanical cornucopia. The strawberries grew into intensely flavorful fruit but didn't travel well, according to Alexander, so agribusinesses avoided the varietal. Likewise, the grapes tasted so strong that you'd swear they were artificial—each one a tiny pitcher of juice spilling in your mouth.

Alexander's nemeses in the garden were the small animals of the North Carolina Piedmont. "I'm not a violent person," he said with a laugh, "but I want to kill every one of the birds and squirrels in my neighborhood." Instead, he carefully crafted wood and chicken-wire cages to place around his fruitful menagerie, protecting each tree, bush, and vine as it ripened into an urban harvest.

For his botany dissertation, Alexander researched vines native to Central America and, not coincidentally, found time to surf. He rode the best waves of his life on a research trip to Costa Rica, speaking wistfully about the board he rented. A wicked crack jagged across the nose, threatening to snap on every wave. Even though the tiny board barely floated him, it carved effortlessly through a series of epic rides at a mysto Costa Rican break.

For our North Carolina surf trip, Alexander took me out to the garage to show me the quiver of potential boards. I spied a Natural Art shortboard leaning in the corner with a familiar neon green and yellow decal. That board, one of the first that Alexander bought in the late 1980s, immediately brought back a flood of memories of our countless high school sessions. I had one just like it until I snapped a fin off in the sand at Wrightsville Beach.

Next to Alexander's Natural Art stood an even more ancient board. This board hadn't been dusted off in decades. Something about it struck me as familiar. Alexander hauled it out. Watermelon green arced across the pockmarked deck. Thick, rounded rails betrayed the board's 1970s origins. There it was, my first board, bought used for $100 in the 1980s. By the time I purchased the Surfboards Hawaii model, it was way past its prime. Decades later, it could have been a museum piece if it weren't so trashed. "I'm sorry that I didn't get a chance to patch it up for you," Alexander said. Patch it up?! I was amazed he kept the dinosaur. He flipped it over to reveal a huge gash in the belly of the beast. Then I remembered losing a beachside brawl with a rock jetty sometime around 1988. Alexander had adopted it with dreams of healing its wounds. He was still dreaming. Sentimental value aside, that board was a piece of junk.

Alexander's Natural Art shortboard made the cut for our traveling quiver, but we needed more beginner-friendly equipment for Sasha and Zinnia. Several years before, Alexander had bought his kids a Wavestorm, realizing that they'd never learn on his knife-like Natural Art. Wavestorms are the kookiest surfcraft imaginable. Costco sells them for $100 each amid the gallon-sized jugs of ketchup and the zombie-apocalypse-sized cases of juice boxes.

Costco's self-proclaimed "classic" Wavestorm is an eight-foot soft-top with blue stripes running up the deck like a landing strip. They say "classic," but which of our esteemed wave-riding ancestors first harnessed the graceful power of the Wavestorm? The history of the Wavestorm is shrouded in legend. A shallow dive into the internet unearthed an official Wavestorm website with suspiciously broken links to pages entitled "About" and "Sustainability." How old was this surf classic? Had the ancient Hawaiian kings and queens boasted of their decks' patented Graphic Film Technology (GFT) and Water Barrier Skin (WBS), their slick, high-density polyethylene

(HDPE) bottoms? Somewhere in a secure vault beneath Honolulu's Bishop Museum must lie the original Wavestorm and the archival answer to this historical mystery. Without access to that inner sanctum, I went back to the internet. The first Wavestorms probably rolled off the Taiwanese factory assembly line in the 2000s. As for sustainability, there ain't a damn thing sustainable about these boards.

When I asked Alexander to get Wavestorms, I specifically requested the Rasta-flavored model, painted red, gold, and green in honor of the Most High. I don't know which Costco vice president (and not-so-secret stoner) came up with the Rasta Wavestorm, but I tip a bong appreciatively to him or her. It seemed impossible to improve upon the kookish Costco classic. The original color scheme reminded one more of hospital waiting-room decor than eye-catching surfboard art. The one advantage of that design was its bland invisibility. The Rasta model doubled down on kookishness by announcing to everyone in the lineup, "I don't know shit about surfing, but I'm ready to party in the waves, mon." Neither Bob Marley nor the Conquering Lion of the Tribe of Judah himself, Haile Selassie, could have looked cool on a Rasta Wavestorm.

Alas, the local Costco had no Rasta models, so we settled for two classics. As with everything from Costco, thick, clear plastic encased these boards like an Egyptian sarcophagus unwilling to give up its secrets. Alexander cut his hand so badly on the plastic that he started bleeding. I told him to wipe the blood on the Wavestorm to make us look hardcore. With the boards assembled, we rolled to the Carolina Coast ready to rock steady.

Zinnia and I took I-40 to Wilmington, a road I knew well from surf missions when I was in grad school at UNC-Chapel Hill. Unfortunately, I knew the locations of several rural speed traps a little too well. One place I had never stopped was the tiny town of Rose Hill. When Zinnia and I pulled off the highway for lunch, we learned that Rose Hill is home to the World's Largest Frying Pan. Signs on every street lamp champion this massive cooking implement. We asked what all the fuss was about. "Yep, it's big," admitted the bored gas station clerk. "They cook on it once a year." With that ringing endorsement, we went searching for the pan. When we finally found it, sheltered in a shack, the frying pan turned out to be a rusty, circular, iron tub about seven feet in diameter. After about two minutes of reverent meditation, we got back in the truck and headed to Wrightsville Beach to conduct our first North Carolina interview.

Skipper Funderburg seemed very much at home at the Wrightsville Beach Museum of History. Based on his nickname, I expected a gruff, old sea captain with salt water in his veins. Skipper didn't look the type. He wore khakis and a polo shirt. His well-trimmed white hair suggested a retired salesman. He carried the slight paunch of someone who had worked hard and enjoyed life, but neither to excess. Skipper greeted us warmly with a native North Carolina accent and ushered us to the back of the tiny museum past one of his old surfboards on display in the permanent collection. Part of the first generation of wave riders in Eastern North Carolina, he wrote a personal history of *Surfing on the Cape Fear Coast*.

Joseph "Skipper" Funderburg comes from a long line of sailors and fishermen that traces its local lineage back to the eighteenth century. "Life by the sea is in my genetic makeup," Skipper explained. He and his brother grew up on Wrightsville Beach. Their mother struggled with mental-health issues in the 1950s, and Wilmington doctors prescribed the novel treatment of beach time. If his mom complained that he was spending too much time surfing, Skipper and his friends joked that they were following doctor's orders.

A historian in his own right, Skipper gave an impromptu lecture on the history of wave-riding and water sports in the Tar Heel State. North Carolinians raced canoes, boats, and rafts in the surf during the nineteenth century. By the twentieth century, some intrepid residents began to ride solid wood planks on their stomachs. In the late 1920s and early 1930s, a lifeguard in southern California named Tom Blake began experimenting with new designs for hollow surfboards with horizontal braces on the inside that allowed for more length and strength without the daunting weight of solid wooden boards. Blake also added fins beneath these boards to help with maneuverability. Blake's innovative design caught on with North Carolina lifeguards in the late 1930s and 1940s. Skipper found photographs from that era depicting locals "aquaplaning" the long, hollow boards.

Surfing, as we know it, didn't really arrive in North Carolina until the 1950s and early '60s. In 1964 Skipper and several of his buddies created the Wrightsville Beach Surf Club. Skipper's car—a massive, black hearse—ferried club members and their longboards up and down the coast in search of waves. The club often found itself on the run from Wrightsville Beach police chief Millard "Stinky" Williamson. Stinky Williamson and the town fathers debated banning surfing altogether but ultimately relegated the sport to the north end of town, away from most beachgoers. Before the era of leashes, longboards often became tourist-seeking missiles after wipe-outs, risking not only life and limb, but dollars and cents spent by visitors.

Skipper and his buddies chopped down their longboards and began to ride shorter equipment in the late 1960s and 1970s. In this era, Skipper's favorite break was Fort Fisher, near the mouth of the Cape Fear River. Dredging and construction debris had created a manmade cove and reef there. Big swells from the northeast pumped into the cove and broke in long lefts over the reef. The Fort Fisher break was so mystical that an honest-to-god hermit named Robert Harrill haunted the cove, dispensing wisdom in a crazy straw hat and bushy, white beard. Photos of the break on hurricane swells in the 1970s reveal surfers racing down the line of solid eight-foot peelers on new, lightning-fast shortboards. "It was the perfect wave," Skipper told me. "It broke just like Pipeline." Of course, by the time I got there the wave was "not like it used to be."

Skipper found a way to make a living on the water. He worked for the National Oceanic and Atmospheric Administration (NOAA) doing bathymetry charts and other measurements of the ocean floor off the Carolina Coast. Eventually, he left government service to captain his own boats, earning his nickname after a transatlantic voyage to the Mediterranean. Skipper also raced Hobie catamarans in the 1970s and '80s and introduced his kids to the ocean during the 1990s. By the 2010s, Skipper had lived long enough to see a new generation of watercraft—stand-up paddleboards, kiteboards, and Jet Skis—join the lineups along the Cape Fear Coast.

After the interview, Zinnia and I met Alexander and Sasha at Flaming Amy's Burrito Barn. Carrying Northern California chauvinism, I was glad that Flaming Amy didn't even pretend to be authentic—whatever that meant. Instead, Amy embraced fusion cuisine in the extreme. She wrapped an array of dishes in a tortilla. Jambalaya burrito? Check. Bacon cheeseburger burrito? Check. Philly cheesesteak burrito? Check. Greek salad burrito? Yep. Even though I can't recommend the wasabi avocado "salsa" that came with my shrimp burrito, I understood Alexander's love for the place, particularly once I found out that he ate there after surfing.

Before dark, we went to set up camp at Carolina Beach State Park, where we stayed for the first leg of our trip. Located on the back side of a barrier island, screened from the intracoastal waterway by a thin stand of new-growth pine, the campground resembled dozens of other sites where I had pitched tents in the Carolinas. If not for the occasional call of gulls flying overhead, you'd never know that you were a few miles from the Atlantic Ocean.

It rained just enough to flood Alexander and Sasha's tent. While the tent and gear dried out, we ate breakfast and Zinnia taught us card games like "spit" and "presidents" that she learned at Jewish summer camp. Zinnia and Sasha seemed really happy together. Only a year apart in age, they clicked. Sasha was quiet, like Alexander, but every so often, she'd bust out something precociously brilliant. After a debate about whether mosquitoes bite dogs, Sasha informed us—in a typically quirky non sequitur—that dogs outnumber people in Newfoundland. Point to Sasha.

Against Alexander's better judgement, we decided to squeeze in a surf session at low tide that first morning. A lone surfer sat on the beach with a shortboard, but no one else braved the waist-high cloud-break. I asked the lifeguard if there were any restrictions on surfing. Actually, I swallowed the word "surfing," embarrassed to call what I planned to do with the soft-top wave-riding. The teenager in the guard stand couldn't have cared less. He didn't even make eye contact, much less look down his nose at the kook-mobile I carried. "Nah," he said nonchalantly and went back to studiously ignoring the beach and everyone on it.

Alexander and I paddled the Wavestorms to the waist-high breakers on the outer bar while Sasha and Zinnia charged the knee-high shore break with boogie boards. Warm sunlight filtered through cool, clear water. Riding waves across the shallow sandbar, I could actually see the contours of the bottom for the first time on our trip. I couldn't tear my eyes away from the poetry of shadows playing on the sea floor punctuated by the play of tiny fish. Softball-sized jelly fish hunted with infinite patience closer to the surface.

The Wavestorms caught nearly everything that came through. They turned much more slowly than even the Bingo Board, despite being a foot and a half shorter. But the slick bottom and minimal rocker did carry speed down the line. Traction pads on the back of the board offered better grip than the rest of the deck. There would be no cross-stepping to the nose on these boards.

Good surfers know that you have to surf with the wave, not against it. Even for aerial contortionists or avid barrel hunters, some waves just beg to be carved. Some demand a soul arch. Slow rollers lend themselves to long cutbacks that allow the rider to remain near the wave's power source. Surfers also have to "listen" to their equipment. A Wavestorm wants to go straight. Stepping hard on the traction pad (or better yet, behind it) gave a bit of turning power, but setting a rail early for maximum length of ride seemed a better strategy. I eventually found that the best approach was to zen it out. Allow the board travel where it would. There was freedom in fatalism. A Zen master might advise letting go and then hanging on for the ride.

Zen is rarely a state that I can maintain for more than five minutes. I quickly tired of this approach. By some miracle, on a larger set wave, I managed to cut back and stick with the ride through the deeper water and connect to the shore break. On a back side, I jumped straight into a low crouch, grabbed the outside rail with my right hand, and let a few fingers of my left comb through the wall of the tiny wave. Since Alexander happened to be paddling out at that moment, I stuck my tongue out the side of a crazed grin.

Alexander and I traded waves just like the old days. I had forgotten his comical kickouts at the end of longer rides. He stood up rail straight and then timbered over as if felled by an invisible woodsman's axe. He slapped the water with mock frustration after losing his footing on takeoff. I had forgotten these funny mannerisms that gave surfing with a longtime friend such a joyful rhythm. I'd also forgotten how naturally gifted Alexander was as an athlete. A tennis player and runner, Alexander had powerful legs, a solid stance, and lithe footwork on the board. He made tiny adjustments in his footing while riding that gave his turns maximum strength and speed. The Wavestorm and several decades of living inland handicapped some of his rides, but every fourth or fifth wave, I could see the graceful power return as even the intractable Wavestorm bent to my friend's will.

The girls took their turns on the Wavestorms. Zinnia caught two good waves and then started complaining about the slipperiness of the deck. A lot of whining and scolding ensued. I told her that I didn't care if she fell off a hundred times, as long as she did her best and had fun, damn it! She paddled into a few waves by herself and snapped out of her teenage funk. Sasha struggled a bit more, but she rarely complained, even when Alexander pushed her into bigger waves that destroyed her. I'd see the board start to pearl in slow motion as Sasha face-planted into the flats. Then the lip came crashing down on her. Regardless of how badly she wiped out, Sasha invariably emerged with a smile on her face underneath a mop of mussed, brown hair. She was a warrior.

The jellyfish floated a little too close to Zinnia. She started to freak out. I convinced her that they didn't really go on the sandbar—a bald-faced lie which bought me time for a few more rides. Alexander and Sasha had already headed in, conscious of the fact that our time was short. Alexander put his arm around Sasha as they walked up the beach. I couldn't hear what he said. The hug alone told her how proud he was, making her glow with confidence. Zinnia and I fought when one more wave turned into three or four. It appeared that Alexander and I would be playing good Dad, bad Dad for this leg of the trip.

---

Skipper Funderburg told me that I should interview his friend Will Allison, a legendary surfer and shaper from Wilmington. The winner of a dozen East Coast championships and two U.S. championships, Will had gone on to judge professional contests, keeping a toe in the water of competitive surfing for decades. According to Skipper, his Eastern North Carolina neighbor rarely talked about all of that. "Will's a quiet icon," Skipper told me. Since he lived just down the road in the Middle Sound section of Wilmington, I drove to the shaper's house the next day.

Will Allison has long, brown hair and the permanently tanned skin of a dude who still gets into the water as much as he can. He favors Hawaiian shirts that hang loose over slightly hunched shoulders. I couldn't tell if his posture resulted from his work or from what I'd describe as a 1970s slouch, embodying the laidback attitude from his youth. Will divides his time between Wilmington, where he grew up, and Oahu, which has been a second home for decades. Skipper was right about Will's low-key demeanor, but the sixty-seven-year-old shaper also turned out to be a natural storyteller.

Will started surfing in Wrightsville Beach in 1963. His first board was an ugly Malibu Styrofoam pop-out coated with epoxy. Three aluminum rods ran the length of the board, giving it structural integrity, instead of the wood stringers that stabilized most boards. The Malibu's previous owner had tried (and failed) to shoot the pier, smashing into one of the pilings. An attempt to re-glass the nose dissolved the Styrofoam. The jousting match with the pier and failed chemistry experiment to fix the damage accounted for the bargain basement price of $12.50, which Will gladly paid. He melted paraffin wax to fix the Sphinx-like nose and then wrapped the front in electrical tape. "It looked horrible, but rode great," he told me.

It would be several years before Will tried his hand at shaping an actual board. In the mid-1970s, the North Carolinian took a job as a navigator for an oil company in southern Louisiana. He'd be on the Gulf for three weeks at a time helping to position oil platforms and doing exploratory work for new drill sites. Then he'd have two weeks off. He'd occasionally surf Grand

Isle, but more often than not, he'd drive back to the East Coast for better waves. Pete Dooley, a friend in Florida who founded Natural Art surfboards, encouraged Will to try shaping a board in his spare time. "Why not?" Will said. He brought a blank and the other materials that he'd need back to his place on Bayou Manchac, set up two sawhorses and went to work. "All I had was a saw, a block plane, a short form, and some sandpaper," he said. "I airbrushed it myself, glassed it myself, and made a fin. It rode pretty good, so I just kind of kept going."

Shaping a surfboard starts with a block of polyurethane foam called a blank. The shaper carves the roughly door-sized blank into a board with a nose, rails, tail, and the rocker curve of the board's underside. For each of these board sections, the shaper makes a number of decisions big and small. Should the nose taper into a needle-like point for maximum speed and maneuverability or blunt into a rounded edge for stability and potential nose-riding? Should the board's center of gravity shade toward the front or the rear? Should there be vee in the tail or subtle channels in the bottom for aquadynamics? Once shaped, the foam is covered with a fiberglass cloth and two or three coats of resin. Fin placement is an important part of these finishing steps, as the number, size, and location of fins dramatically influences the way a board turns (or doesn't). Shapers decorate their boards with artwork or bold colors. Some purists opt for unadorned, white boards that pop against the blue-green canvas of the ocean's surface. Many longtime surfers attempt to build a board at least once in their lives, but mastery of the arduous process requires time and dedication. As with other life choices, many surfers opt to hit the waves instead of spending time behind a ventilator mask in a dusty shaping bay.

With few waves on offer in Louisiana and a growing love of his new-found craft, Will sidled up to the sawhorses beneath his bayou house again and again. Before long, friends were asking Will to make them boards and those orders eventually turned a hobby into a profession. For a short while, Will served as a sales rep for Lightning Bolt, the preeminent surfboard manufacturer of the 1970s, but working for a company didn't fit his independent personality. An offhand conversation with Tim McKevlin, a surf shop owner in Charleston, South Carolina, led to Will's first store account. From there, he built a small but well-respected line of surfboards.

To talk about an artist's work as a "brand" seems tawdry, undervaluing the creativity and originality of the craft. Branding is necessary when the product doesn't sell itself. Will wasn't some starry-eyed idealist. Shaping wasn't altruism. It was his job. Will realized he needed a logo that helped distinguish his boards visually. A marine biology major in college, he designed an eye-catching seahorse logo with laser-cut mosaics of abalone shell. The logo shimmered in infinite variations depending on the direction and intensity of lighting. Schools of small fish followed Will around the lineup chasing the light reflecting from his logos. "I put them on the deck," he explained. "I don't put them on the bottom—you don't want to attract anything big down there."

Since my brother had a beautiful Allison longboard, I'd spent countless hours mesmerized by the shiny logo on trips back to South Carolina, but on this trip, I had the shameful Wavestorm quiver. When I pulled up to Will's house, I parked outside of the fence around his property and threw a towel over the Wavestorms, hiding the evidence of my kookish crimes against nature. In a conversation about the history of surfboard shaping, it was only a matter of time before the topic of Costco classics came up. In Will vs. the Wavestorm, I had to decide if I was going to come clean about my own complicity. "Nowadays, a lot of people would rather go to Costco and buy a Wavestorm for a hundred dollars instead of paying a thousand for a custom-made surfboard," Will complained. "I can't even buy a blank for a hundred."

As the old shaper observed, the Wavestorm was the logical conclusion of a race to the bottom in surfboard shaping that started back in the 1960s but accelerated in the 1990s with globalization. Companies realized that they could outsource the manufacturing to China and Thailand, where labor was much cheaper. Computer templates allowed these factories to produce exact replicas of boards that had been hand-shaped by masters. Will didn't upload his designs to the digital realm, but other shapers did. The Wavestorm undercut this mass-production market more than it hurt independent craftsmen like Will, but it didn't exactly help him either. I sheepishly admitted that I had bought Wavestorms for the trip. "Those kind of pop-outs are so cheap that you bought one, so hey. I mean . . ." He trailed off in disgust. I told him that I felt like coming to talk to Paul Revere in 1776 and admitting that I just purchased a British silver tea set. He shook his head.

If Wavestorms seemed harbingers of doom for custom shapers, other crosscurrents in the industry made Will more hopeful. In the 1990s, a longboard renaissance broke the dominance of the thruster (three-fin) shortboard that had reigned unchallenged since the early 1980s. By the 2000s, shapers and surfers were experimenting with all kinds of board styles. Funboards mashed up qualities of classic longboards and thrusters.

Five-foot-long fish with twin fins or quads reached back to the 1970s for inspiration. Asymmetrical shapes, future fins, finless boards, hydrofoils, and other sci-fi innovations pushed the boundaries of the craft.

Will's boards hewed closer to classic shapes, but he appreciated the freedom of modern shaping. He was always tinkering with his designs, always trying to build a better mousetrap. Will traced the arc of surf history in his workshop to shape the future from the boards of the past. "I've got a bunch of templates from those boards, and I still use them," he said. "You mix and match and use the curves for everything. All the old longboards and all the old single-fins and guns. Like, Dick Brewer guns have great templates, just great curves. I use them every day. They're old, but they're valuable things to have."

Will gave me a guided tour through the quiver of boards hanging on the walls of his house. A gorgeous balsa-wood number hung in a place of honor, the last of a series of boards that Will had shaped from Ecuadorean timber. The natural grains of wood eddied in stunning patterns under a high gloss. According to Will, the balsa didn't flex as much as fiberglass, allowing the board to cut through chop. Opposite the balsa board hung a psychedelic masterpiece. The stylized gun depicted the aurora borealis on one side and an equally spaced out geometric pattern on the other—a collaboration between Will and an artist friend. There were also classics representing every era of surfing's history from a roster of legendary shapers: Hansen, Brewer, and a sentimental favorite, the used Lightning Bolt that the North Carolinian surfed during his first sojourns to Hawaii in the mid-1970s. We passed by a crowded trophy case without discussion.

The shaping shed was a workshop, but also a work of art in itself. In 1982 a lightning bolt struck the pine tree just outside. Thousands of volts of electrical current jumped from the tree into his phone line, exploding out of the wall in his shed and bursting into a fireball that burned nearly everything inside. A few tools survived with wicked scars from the fire, but much of the shed had been refurbished in simple, functional lines not dissimilar from Will's boards. Two lights equidistant from the far wall on either side of the shaping bay threw shadows along the perfectly symmetrical curves of a blank Will had been carving in the middle of the room. Standing in the workshop, I realized how much surfboard shapers really are the heirs of Renaissance sculptors, with their dedication to balance between mathematical precision and creative artistry.

Near the conclusion of our conversation, Will spoke about the future of his profession. The Wilmington native mentored kids from local high schools in an internship program. The kids collaborated with the master to shape their own watercraft, while researching the history of surfing. "But hardly any of them have continued making surfboards," he said. Will worried that he and his peers in the informal guild of shaping masters were a dying breed. They all planned to work as long as they could. "We egg each other on," he explained. "There's not a whole lot of us left, and the people that I do work with are real characters. It's neat to hang out with them because we all have that common thread of making stuff, and we're okay at it." With understated pride, he corrected himself: "We're pretty good at it."

Leaving Wilmington, we decided to stop at the North Carolina Maritime Museum to check out a small exhibit on the history of surfing in the Tar Heel State, before heading on to the Outer Banks. Located in Beaufort, the North Carolina Maritime Museum stands across the street from a marina. The music of sailboat rigging clanging against masts plays as a constant wind-chime soundtrack in the waterfront town. The museum itself is sheathed in roughhewn shingles. A small room rises above the second floor, reminiscent of a lighthouse. The tower is surrounded by a narrow balcony or widow's walk—so called because wives in coastal towns would climb their balconies to peer out to sea in search of husbands who might never return.

The inside of the museum has beautiful, exposed wooden beams and similarly wood-paneled walls that complement the shingled exterior. The wood also gives the feel of being in an eighteenth-century ship's hold, a vibe accentuated by innumerable models of sailing ships and hulls of coastal skiffs that require a circuitous route through the museum's exhibits. A surfing exhibit with a Day-Glo shortboard and spring suit seemed out of place among the other seafaring artifacts. Yet the juxtaposition reminds visitors that life on the coast of North Carolina continues to revolve around maritime pursuits. Small bios of surfers and shapers, along with photos of riders on heavy winter swells, offer non-surfing visitors a sense of the ways that fishermen, sailors, and wave riders enjoy the sea's bounty even as they also risk its wrath.

I climbed to the second-floor administrative offices to interview Ben Wunderly, the exhibit's curator, while Alexander, Sasha, and Zinnia waited in the museum. A "brief chat" stretched to more than an hour, filled with tales of misadventures in the Outer Banks—our next destination.

Alexander and Sasha hit the road, fearing that they might miss the last ferry to Ocracoke. Zinnia texted with increasing alarm.

"Dad!"

"Where ARE you!!

"WE HAVE TO GOOOOOO!!!

"NOW!!!!!!!!!!!!!! [angry emoji]"

Finally, I looked at my phone. Shit, we were going to miss the ferry. I drove over ninety miles per hour on the two-lane blacktop that snakes from Beaufort to the Cedar Island Ferry landing. We were the last car to make it onto the boat. As we lost sight of land, Zinnia and Sasha played their 500th game of Spit. Alexander meditated on the beauty of nature on the top deck of the ferry. Eventually, we joined him, the view at sunset too beautiful to miss, as we motored over the horizon to the edge of America.

# 10

# The Edge of America
## Outer Banks, North Carolina

The National Seashore campground on Ocracoke sat a few miles outside of the seaside village that housed the permanent residents on an island reachable only by boat. Fifteen-foot-high sand dunes defended the campground from the ocean. Surfers made up about a quarter of the other campers. Soft-tops lay discarded in the dunes and longboards lounged on top of a few cars. The requisite number of RV-driving retirees and German tourists rounded out the campground residents.

We chose where to camp based on the sighting of a bunny in a vacant site. Zinnia dubbed him David. He had the thin, wiry build of a wild rabbit. Unafraid of humans, David was perhaps not as wild as I suspected. Neon-green frogs the size of nickels and dimes hung around the showers and water fountain, but insects dominated Ocracoke fauna. The mosquito reined as the undisputed king of the campground.

We strolled over the dunes to the beach. A bit of swell roiled the water, but the high tide was killing it. As night fell, the mosquitoes sprang their ambush. Five bit me in the few seconds it took to descend the leeward side of the dunes. Welts erupted on my uncovered legs. We dove into the tents, trailing a dozen bloodsuckers. Zinnia shined the flashlight as I smashed the stowaways into red-and-black streaks on the inside of the tent's netting. I must have gotten them all. Miraculously, we slept without the incessant whine in our ears.

A downpour began at dawn. Zinnia and I lay on our backs as bullets of rain sprayed down on us. Alexander and Sasha's tent leaked. Ours proved water tight. A warm, dry tent in a cool rain is its own little universe. I read a history book—Theodore White's classic account of John F. Kennedy's nail-biting victory over Richard Nixon in *The Making of the President 1960*. The triumphal optimism of a book written in 1962 stood in stark contrast to the tragic wisdom that would come of the Kennedy assassination and Watergate. It felt like the rain had washed away the sins of history.

After about a half hour, the rain let up. Alexander and Sasha emerged first. Zinnia and I cautiously followed when we saw that the mosquitoes didn't devour them. While the other three ate breakfast, I snuck off to check the surf. I climbed over the dunes and let out a whoop as glassy, waist-high peelers met my hungry eyes. Suddenly, I didn't need breakfast. Alexander joked that I could subsist on "tasty" waves. I harassed the rest of the gang as they wolfed down cereal. Two Wavestorms and two boogie boards later, we made it to the break.

With the other surfers at the campground snug in their sleeping bags, the lineup stood absolutely empty. Rights and lefts reeled off the sandbars, free for the taking. At first, I let the Wavestorm do its thing. I tried a few turns, resulting in several wipeouts before I figured out the board's limited turning radius. Finally, I caught a few waves that gave me room to move. A back-side rail grab led into a sweet little suicide tube. As the tiny cylinder closed around me, I laughed, gulping in seawater. It was worth a rinse cycle for that split-second vision from within the eye of the wave's tiny vortex. On the front side, I actually had a few little roller-coaster rides up and down the peeling faces. Alexander, as usual, had more soul, styling his way from the sandbar to the shore break. A worsening cold and a poor night's sleep tempered his joy but couldn't dampen his spirits completely.

The girls came out and took the boards. Zinnia caught lots of shore-break rides by herself, beaching the board nearly every time. She survived a harrowing one-foot elevator drop. On her way back out, she gesticulated wildly, narrating the entire ride with her hands before I could hear the story over the noise of surf. Sasha struggled a bit more. Alexander shivered with a fever, mustering every ounce of his waning energy to coach his daughter.

When the girls got tired, I took Zinnia's board and headed back out. Alexander stayed on the beach, increasingly miserable. I felt awful for him, but not bad enough to go back to the campground before "one more wave." The girls went on a seashell safari and then buried themselves up to their knees in sand to create the illusion of mermaid flippers.

With fewer than a thousand permanent residents, Ocracoke often gives the illusion of solitude nestled in unspoiled nature. Zinnia and Sasha could have been actual mermaids, for all the rest of the world knew. As I sat on my board, alone in the lineup, my mind drifted to a time before human surfers, before crowded lineups and hassles for waves. Ocracoke offered a glimpse of that time, a brief vision within a collapsing tube.

~~~~~~~~~~~~~~~~~~~~~~~~~~~~~~~~~~~~~~~~~~~~~~~

Scott Busbey first surfed the Outer Banks in the 1970s. Though his family had moved around a lot when he was young, Scott called Cocoa Beach home. He surfed his first wave in the Space Coast town. As his brothers gravitated toward basketball, Scott stayed the course with surfing. His quest for better, more consistent waves pulled him northward. On a trip to spend the summer surfing and shaping boards in New Jersey, Scott's friend took him on a slight detour to check out Cape Hatteras.

"It was kind of a ritual for most of the guys from up north to stop at Hatteras on their way to Florida," Scott told me. He and his friends reversed the flow, camping for a few days near the iconic lighthouse and catching a pretty good swell with only one other guy out. Scott deposited the images of those uncrowded, fun sessions in his memory bank, where they sat, gaining interest.

After a few years back in Cocoa Beach and an aborted attempt at community college, Scott got a call from a friend who had relocated to the Outer Banks. His friend worked on a garbage truck. "That was easily one of the best surfer jobs to get in this area in the early seventies," Scott explained, "because you started out at three or four in the morning and you're done as the sun was coming up and you could surf all day." Unable to resist the promise of cheap housing, uncrowded waves, and possible employment as garbage men, Scott and a bunch of his buddies relocated to North Carolina.

The crew had founded the Natural Art surfboard company in Cocoa Beach one year earlier. When they moved to North Carolina, Scott, Richard Price, Greg Loehr, and Tommy Moss to continued making Natural Art boards whenever they weren't surfing. They sold some of their boards to locals and traveling surfers, but they were also well positioned to sell boards up and down the East Coast. The relatively young Eastern Surfing Association had also begun holding regular contests at Cape Hatteras.

By the mid-1970s, Scott's local break was quickly becoming known for the best waves on the Atlantic Seaboard. Thrusting deep into the Atlantic like the prow of a ship, the Outer Banks bear the brunt of the ocean's fearsome storms and the swells they generate. The islands form a V, with Cape Hatteras at the point. The uncrowded, wave-rich breaks along the Outer Banks seemed like heaven. Scott looked back on the 1970s with great fondness. Epic sessions and hurricane swells blurred together. He recalled massive waves breaking in triple-overhead chaos on Diamond Shoals, just off Cape Hatteras. No one surfed out there. It was enough just to witness the power of the ocean.

The best view of Diamond Shoals and in fact much of Hatteras could be found at the top of the cape's iconic lighthouse. The black-and-white barbershop pole of a tower reached nearly two hundred feet into the air. In the 1970s, the lighthouse was rarely locked. Scott had friends who climbed it at night and slept on the deck, where they found cool breezes and a rare no-fly zone for the island's notorious mosquitoes. Another daredevil would hang upside down out of the window of the lighthouse with only his feet holding him in place. Scott remembered a "surf sacrifice" that he and his friend filmed on Super 8 camera. The footage captured a bunch of guys wrestling Scott to the ground before dragging him and his board to the door of the lighthouse. The film then cuts to a shot of the tower, where a surfboard sails out of the highest window followed by a body that drops hundreds of feet on the ground below. Scott survived the fall, because he had helped stuff newspaper into the dummy and sacrificed his clothes for the stunt. The grainy footage and gauzy memories of surf in the Outer Banks of that era still bring a smile to his face.

If Cape Hatteras was becoming the center of the southern surfing world, it remained on the periphery of mainstream society. The tiny hamlet of Buxton, North Carolina, near the cape, was a cold, windblown ghost town in the winter months. Accessible by bridge only to the north and twenty miles out from the North Carolina mainland, there was little to do but hunker down. Life on the isolated islands could get claustrophobic. Scott's buddies and their wives lasted less than a year before fleeing back to Cocoa Beach and the old Natural Art headquarters. Scott and his wife tried Hawaii. The crowded lineups and high cost of living drove them back to the Outer Banks in 1977.

The Busbeys set up their Natural Art outpost with a grand total of a thousand bucks—$200 of which went to replace the shop's busted front door. The rest paid for leashes, board shorts, and T-shirts to sell along with what would eventually become Scott's line of "In the Eye" custom boards. Scott took another job cleaning fish at night, and his wife sewed clothes to help them make ends meet. "At first most all my business was from traveling surfers and a little bit from the few people that lived here," Scott recalled. Then came a wave of development in the 1980s.

Geographer Stephen Strader estimated that over 600,000 new homes were built within fifty miles of the Carolina coastline from the 1980s to the 2010s. Much of this development took the form of beach-house rentals and condominiums that filled up every summer and emptied out in the off-season. By the 2010s, the population of Dare County in the Outer Banks would jump from an off-season total of 35,000 permanent residents to over 200,000 sunscreen-slathered visitors in the summer months. Park rangers at the National Seashore counted nearly 2.5 million visitors each year when we visited. By then, most of Scott Busbey's business came "from the people that are staying for the week."

After talking about this development boom, I wondered whether surfing influenced Scott's politics or his views of the environment. It turned out that being a business owner influenced his views as much or more than surfing. Forty years of running a small shop had given him conservative views on taxes and government spending. This fiscal conservatism dovetailed with a skepticism of environmental regulation and even activism. Scott valued efforts to limit runoff and overdevelopment, but he was just as critical of tree huggers as he was of rapacious real estate developers. He had seen the "ugly side" of the environmental movement. He bemoaned the use of court challenges and environmental impact studies to forestall bridge and road construction that connected the barrier islands to the wider world. Scott similarly had no patience for national environmental groups (including Surfrider) that utilized the Endangered Species Act to restrict access to the coast. "They're trying to close Hatteras Island off to the public. They're trying to chase people out of here," the surf shop owner said. "I don't want to see the ocean polluted. I don't want to see the dunes trampled, but at the same time, keeping the people out is not the answer either."

As Alexander, Sasha, Zinnia, and I crossed the channel on the ferry from Ocracoke, I read signs and portents to determine whether Hatteras hid favorable conditions. Waves broke on shoals between the islands. These shifting hazards looked dangerous even on a clear day. I imagined sailing through those same waters on a stormy day or, God forbid, at night without a depth sounder. Surf fantasies quickly replaced these worries. The ferry's wake curled over unseen sandbars. It looked totally rippable.

The Cape Hatteras National Seashore contains two campgrounds. For both sentimental and practical reasons, I chose the more sheltered Frisco campground a bit south of the lighthouse. The ranger handed us a pamphlet that recommended long tent stakes due to windy conditions. It concluded with the sadistic understatement: "Mosquitoes can be a problem." The ranger told us we could have our pick of the many vacant sites. We set up camp at the crest of a hill—a lone tree standing sentinel over the site. Thunder rumbled in the distance. I wondered whether we should weigh down the tent more. Nah, the stakes would hold.

The Park Service closed the old lighthouse due to lightning strikes just as we arrived. We sought shelter from the storm in a museum at the lighthouse keeper's old quarters. Maps of the seafloor around the Cape documented a fearsome number of shipwrecks in the "graveyard of the Atlantic." Diamond Shoals and other underwater hazards clawed at the underbellies of passing vessels, when the lighthouse proved unequal to its mission or captains proved unequal to theirs. The charts offered a stark reminder that the same powerful forces drawing surfers, pirates, and fishermen to the Outer Banks kept most sane mariners far away.

I dragged the crew to Natural Art Surf Shop to meet Scott Busbey and buy some swag. Scott's wife, Carol, directed us to his surfboard factory, an unmarked Quonset hut on stilts nearby. We let ourselves in the big steel door. There stood Scott in shorts and a T-shirt, carving a board from a foam blank. He turned around to reveal thinning blond hair, framing a friendly, tanned face. His arms and legs were covered in foam dust. Scott gave us a tour of his factory—an impressive operation, more a craftsman's workshop than the word "factory" implies, but larger than Will Allison's cozy shaping room down in Wilmington. Boards in various stages of completion revealed an assembly-line process, each stage requiring specific skills. Not wanting to impose, we left the factory and let Scott return to his art.

Reluctantly, we headed back to a sodden campground. When we drove up the hill to the site in the growing darkness, our tent was gone. "Oh, that's bad," I managed to say as my eyes scanned the area for the tent. Zinnia and Sasha spied it first. "There it is," they screamed in unison. "It's in the tree!" Sure enough, the squall had made short work of feeble aluminum stakes with only a tenuous grip on Hatteras's sandy soil. The tent hung suspended like an avant-garde sculpture, canted on one corner about three or four feet off the ground. Alexander thought we should just leave it until morning, but I didn't feel like sleeping in the truck. We unhooked the tent from various limbs as a few gallons of water poured from the bottom.

The girls got the job of running down the road with the drop cloth and fly to dry them off in the stiff breeze that still blew across our cursed hilltop home. They looked like twin superheroes with an olive-drab cape billowing behind them. Doubting the wisdom of their assigned task, the girls alternated between complaints and giggles. "How much longer do we have to do this?" they whined, even as they sprinted down the hill in a footrace that ended in unbridled laughter. I ran behind them, holding the tent high and letting the wind carry it like a box kite at the length of my outstretched arms. Miraculously, it dried enough for us to set up camp before nightfall. We killed more mosquitoes and bedded down, hoping for better weather and surf the next day.

We woke at dawn after another soaking. Sasha, Zinnia, and I took bikes to check the surf. Alexander brought four of them. My assigned vehicle was an old BMX frame repurposed into a sweet lowrider with a banana seat and ape-hanger handlebars. Our little bike gang screamed down the hill as if we were starring in a teen movie from the 1980s. All we needed was E.T. in a handlebar basket.

The boardwalk path to the beach cut through scrub pines that grew out of black-water wetlands. Mosquitoes buzzed angrily as we entered their kingdom. We flew through on our bikes before they could mount an assault. Then the boardwalk emerged into an open marshland covered with what Sasha told us was black needle grass. Alexander had regaled her with a botanist's lecture about how the grass filtered impurities from the water. Sasha remembered way more of this lecture than I ever could. The *Malus pumila* didn't fall far from the tree.

Whitetail deer grazed in the marsh. We stopped on the edge of the needle-grass sea to watch them. As they ate, the deer bowed their heads low, as if in prayer. Suffused by early morning light, the serene wetlands resembled an old naturalist painting. I felt the stillness of the world newly awoken. The kids and I mounted our bikes. We rumbled over the boardwalk, breaking the morning's quiet magic. The deer leapt away.

Sea oats perched at the summits of the sand dunes waved gently. Our first vision of the surf brought immediate joy and relief. Stomach-high sets rolled toward shore. Ghost crabs scampered in and out of holes in the dunes. The kids wanted to play hide-and-seek with the translucent white creatures, but I scooted them along. We raced back to the campsite. I threw on my board shorts and a rash guard to fend off the slight morning chill. Alexander and Sasha shimmied into neoprene spring suits. Zinnia borrowed Alexander's ancient Body Glove vest.

Even though he was still under the weather, Alexander paddled directly to the outside and immediately took a beautiful, stylish back-side ride.

Favoring front sides into the subtle side-shore wind, I didn't get pulled down the beach by the rip as fast as Alexander. We ended up far from each other—the only two guys out as far as the eye could see. The Wavestorms got the job done. The girls took their turns, with some beatings on the inside due to the more powerful Hatteras surf. At the end of the session, both girls had torn up their knees on the Wavestorms' unforgiving, industrial-strength traction pads and patented "soft" tops.

As we got out of the water, a large group of North Carolina Mennonites were walking down to the beach. The stair-step children walked in a line of ascending age and height. The girls wore ankle-length homespun dresses in indigo hues. White lace hair coverings accented the cool blue and lavender against the backdrop of beach sand and slate-grey sky. Zinnia asked me about the group, complaining that one of the girls stared at her in the campground. I explained that they were probably just as interested in her as she was in them—because of difference. The Outer Banks attracted all kinds of people from all over.

Ben Wunderly would deny it, but his story captures the history of the last few decades in the Outer Banks as well as surfers twice his age or skill level. I met Ben back at the North Carolina Maritime Museum, where he co-curated an exhibit on the history of surfing. Why would I want to interview him? Ben had never surfed a contest, never been sponsored, never worked in a surf shop, and never traveled to California or Hawaii. He wasn't even from North Carolina originally. A new father in his early forties, the Virginia transplant had lived on the Outer Banks for a relatively short time.

Raised in the Richmond suburb of Colonial Heights during the 1970s and '80s, Ben and his family joined the throngs of weekend warriors and weekly renters who descended on the Outer Banks from late spring to early fall. The Wunderlys packed towels, chairs, and rafts into their Gran Torino for the two-hour drive to the ocean. Ben bought his first beater board at the now-defunct Vitamin Sea Surf Shop, but he didn't get much chance to ride it. During the long, landlocked stretches between beach trips, he and his twin brother practiced their moves on skateboards, carving long lines into the smooth suburban streets of Northern Virginia.

Ben had an epiphany after his first year of college at Virginia Tech. "I've spent all winter here in the mountains," he thought. "I need to spend some time at the beach." As he told me about his crew's move to Nags Head after finals, he lapsed into a familiar dialect. "I wasn't going to go back to Colonial Heights. That would totally kill my buzz, be harshing on my scene."

That first summer on the Outer Banks, Ben and three other dudes lived in a one-room "apartment" that had been part of the Pink Shell Motel before the owner realized he could do less maintenance and work fewer hours renting the rooms by the month. The Pink Shell didn't even have air-conditioning. A group of roughneck construction workers squatted rent free in the room next door. The construction guys worked hard all day, drank harder most of the night, slept a few hours, and then repeated the cycle. The college kids kept a similarly rigorous schedule. They got slacker jobs in the evenings at Pizza Hut, Golden Corral, and Food Lion. That left the days free for surfing. They hit the nearby breaks when the surf was small and headed south to Buxton or Rodanthe when swells hit.

One of Ben's other neighbors at the Pink Shell invited him on a Hatteras strike mission for just such a swell. Since Ben's board was busted at the time, his neighbor offered to lend him one. Sponsored by Wave Riding Vehicles, she had an impressive quiver of more than one. A free ride, nice board, and the promise of good waves? How could Ben say no? The car pulled up. A cloud of skunky smoke billowed from the open windows. "On the Outer Banks, if you're into dope," he explained, "then you're pretty religiously into dope. I smoked a lot, but I wasn't into it like some people. We smoked all the way down there." The crew arrived in Buxton to the welcome sight of chest-high waves. By then, Ben was higher than a Kitty Hawk kite. Stoke and paranoia warred in his brain. Stoke won. He paddled out. Why had the waves just tripled in size? Why was everyone in the lineup staring him? "Here I am cruising down the line as fast as I can, because I'm worried that I'm going to wipe out and drown and die, just snaking all these people." He apologized profusely to everyone. They all just laughed. Ben had been nowhere near them. He cut back on the weed.

After a few slacker summers on the Outer Banks, the Virginia native was hooked. Majoring in forestry and wildlife, Ben landed a seasonal gig at Jockey's Ridge State Park—home to some of the largest sand dunes on the East Coast. He stayed on at the park after graduation and also led private kayak tours in Nags Head. Ben eventually became a state park ranger at a barrier island south of the Outer Banks. The waves weren't as good, but he could surf every day before and after work, and even on his lunch breaks. In the winter months, he had the place to himself. He'd shimmy into his wetsuit, lock his gun belt in the car, hide the key, and surf until he could barely feel his fingers to fire up the truck.

Ben and I talked about different styles of boards, strategies for riding certain types of waves, and the long history of surfing in North Carolina. He even divulged a few secret spots that he learned about from hardened locals, the kind who would kill you if you divulged their favorite breaks. (Turn to page 521 for maps and directions.) The conversation flowed easily. I recognized more than a little of myself in Ben's stories. We talked so long that after a series of angry, unanswered texts, Zinnia wandered back to Ben's office, demanding that we leave. Just a few more questions, I promised.

I wanted to hear about how fatherhood had affected Ben's surfing life. He admitted that he had started fishing more and surfing less. With a job at the North Carolina Maritime Museum, he hung up the ranger's gun and badge. Curating the exhibit on surfing in the Tar Heel State had inspired him to get wet again. He bought a used soft-top and started counting the days until he could teach his young son. I asked Ben if he ever traveled for surf. "When it's not good, I dream of going to all these places that are better," he said, "but I've never traveled out of the country. I don't even have a passport." Ben sighed contentedly, "The focus for me has always been North Carolina."

A few days into our stay on Hatteras, the storms let up enough for a climb to the top of the historic lighthouse. On the drive there, I spied an old campaign sign for President Donald Trump in one of the yards we passed. Made out of plywood, the seemingly permanent installation featured a Confederate battle flag emblazoned with TRUMP in all caps above the stars and bars and "2016" below them. I did a double-take, scratching my head at the historical irony of a businessman from New York City (a Yankee personified) as the standard-bearer for unreconstructed southerners.

The Trump sign was a temporary diversion. Our main mission was to climb the iconic Hatteras lighthouse. Alexander, Sasha, Zinnia, and I hiked to the top on what turned out to be a mercifully cool day. I got winded around three-quarters of the way up. Like many a middle-aged dude forever worried about his vitality and virility, I refused to rest at any of the window landings for fear of showing weakness. One glance down from two hundred feet above the ground, and my courage evaporated. Mortally afraid of heights, I didn't even want to go out on the iron balcony that circles the tower just below the glass cylinder housing the lamp. I worried about the age of the lighthouse and the rickety construction of the balcony. I thought about how a team of engineers had actually moved the lighthouse 3,000 feet from its original location less than two decades before. Surely, such a move had undermined the tower's structural integrity. I was going to be the straw that broke its brick back.

Zinnia literally dragged me through the door toward the railing/precipice. Then she called me a hypocrite for making her face her fears by surfing big waves, near jellyfish, or in stormy conditions, when I wouldn't overcome my own irrational phobia. On the one hand, she was right. On the other, I had no patience for the teenage self-righteousness that sees hypocrisy in every seemingly black-and-white scenario. I was the parent here, one step closer to death than this pip-squeak. I had every right to be a scaredy cat! Still, I circled the balcony as demanded, arms hugging the circular structure. Fears faced, I ran down the 257 steps to terra firma.

As night fell back at the campsite, we finally agreed to play charades, which Sasha had been lobbying for since the start of the trip. Dusk turned out to be prime feeding time for the mosquitoes. We couldn't distinguish between gestures for the number of syllables and slaps at bugs feasting on our arms. Alexander pointed to a tree with the thickest swarm of insects any of us had seen in our lives. Ever the scientist, Alexander hypothesized that they were mating, because the swarm remained in one place for nearly twenty minutes. Dragonflies showed up and feasted on them. Still, the orgy raged. We retreated to the tents, before the insects' carnal appetites morphed into bloodlust.

The morning surf check our last day in the Outer Banks revealed onshore wind and mushy, thigh-high surf. I headed out alone to try Alexander's six-foot, four-inch Natural Art shortboard. Cocoa Beach shaper Richard Price, an old buddy of Scott Busbey's, designed the board. Alexander had owned it since the late 1980s. The green-and-yellow airbrushing of the logo glowed with the aesthetic of a different era. Alexander apologized for the lack of fresh wax on the board. I assured him that this wouldn't affect my performance.

The shortboard moved so differently from the longer boards that I had been riding. Think about the relationship between baseball and softball or sprinting and jogging. With the shortboard, I could duck dive beneath incoming sets. Sitting up just beyond the break, I was so unused to the lack of buoyancy that I almost fell off. Turning to take the first wave, I remembered how frustrating shortboards could be in weak southern wind swell. There was no rolling into little ripples with this board. I had to catch waves at the peak and crank off a quick turn before the board lost momentum. In my imagination, I pulled rodeo flips, back-side punts, and any number of other aerial maneuvers above the lip. Alas, flyaway kick-outs were the apex of my air game. On that last morning in Hatteras, there wasn't enough speed, but I snapped off turns that would have been inconceivable on either the Bingo Board or a Wavestorm. The shortboard responded to the torque of my body. With better surf, that Natural Art board would have really performed.

We broke down the tents and found an army of frogs hiding beneath the rain flies. Alexander had observed them gathering the night before, ready to feast on the insects that were feasting on us. Zinnia and Sasha caught the frogs by cupping their hands over them. The critters proved naturals at selfies, sitting stock still as the girls snapped a million photos. Zinnia named each George or Georgina, based on some mysterious divination of sex beyond my zoological knowledge. Georges and Georginas happily hopped around until it was time to say goodbye.

One intrepid frog stowed away underneath the hood of our truck, emerging about twenty minutes up the road. One look at the landscape flying by at sixty miles an hour convinced George (or was it Georgina?) that the increasingly sweltering area under the hood was preferable to splattering on the windshield or asphalt. Zinnia rescued him when at our next stop. "He's going to have a story to tell the kids!" Alexander joked. He's probably writing about it now, exaggerating the size of the truck and speed of the wind.

~~~~~~~~~~~~~~~~~~~~~~~~~~~~~~~~~~~~~~~~~~~~~~~~~~~~

Driving on Highway 12 gives you a sense of the impermanence of the Outer Banks. Seawater and sand constantly threaten to reclaim the islands' main road. Many beach communities in the South lie on barrier islands that are, for all intents and purposes, just large dunes or shoals which have become permanent home to seeds floating on wind currents from the mainland. Those seeds take root and stubbornly hang on until more seeds join them, interweaving roots to create stability where nature has all but decreed that instability and chaos will reign. Hurricanes, gales, flood tides, and massive storm surges shake the organic foundations of these islands in cataclysmic cycles. Similar forces exert constant, less dramatic pressure. Whether through slow erosion or sudden explosions of fury, nature shapes the islands and life upon them. For long, narrow stretches of Highway 12, you can see both shores of the Outer Banks, just as you could see both the wetlands and Gulf on either side of Louisiana 1 in parts of Grand Isle. The sands from the dunes in these stretches blows over the highway, spilling across the asphalt, blurring the lines that humans have drawn on these shifting landscapes.

Perhaps the best example of this challenging endeavor to construct permanence on the Outer Banks is the attempt to link the islands to one another and to the mainland through bridges. Ferries have remained necessities even in an age when we have given ourselves over to automobiles. The ferries suggest that the gods of the sea will not bow to the gods of the earth, no matter how much General Motors, Ford, and Toyota wish they would. The North Carolina Department of Transportation fights this battle annually at the Oregon Inlet where a massive public-works project is attempting to replace an aging causeway with a modern concrete span that soars above the sound. Alexander explained that the project has been going on for years with annual interruption by hurricane season.

Driving over the old causeway that skims just above the surface of the inlet, it's clear why the government wants to build a better bridge here. Even a minor hurricane would swamp the current causeway, isolating thousands of people on Hatteras. The bones of the new bridge appear stronger than nearly any other structure built on the Outer Banks. Their permanence seems self-evident. Self-evident to everyone but Neptune.

We continued north until we reached Jockey's Ridge State Park, where Ben Wunderly had once worked. Alexander and I had both visited the park before. The place is named for horse races that once ran through the valleys between massive sand dunes. Spectators could sit on the natural amphitheaters, sipping lemonade or perhaps something stronger, and watch the races. In the jockeys' heyday a hundred years earlier, the dunes stood 140 feet high, but today, they squat diminished at just half that height. Alexander's colleagues at NC State suggest that prevailing winds are pushing the dunes southward, despite the state's best efforts to bulldoze their southern boundary to protect homes from the slow-motion avalanche. Marching up the dunes with the kids, one could tell that corralling these sand behemoths was a losing proposition.

Zinnia and Sasha didn't care about that history. They did exactly what kids have done for decades—laid down at ridgetops and rolled. Howls of laughter and pain played counterpoint against the beat of their flailing limbs. Small sandstorms flew from their hands and feet as they struggled to control unbridled descents. The childish joy in that chaos was wondrous to behold, eclipsed only by the preteen preening and complaining at the bottom. They seemed almost ashamed of the childhood abandon that had momentarily possessed their bodies and minds.

Near the spigots that washed away the sand and shame, Alexander pointed out the trip's 542nd interesting plant species. The vine growing just beyond the path's guardrail looked like a honeysuckle on steroids. After giving a name that I immediately forgot, Alexander enthused, "They're delicious!" He snapped off the end of one and popped it in his mouth. Before I could reach for a sample, my friend concluded, "Just like asparagus." I pulled my hand back as if fearing a burn. Alexander spit out the plant. "Too ripe," he asserted. You mean too asparagus-y!

We said a sad goodbye to Alexander and Sasha after Jockey's Ridge. Alexander had to get back to Raleigh to celebrate his wedding anniversary, and we were headed farther north. Alexander encouraged us to take one of the Wavestorms. I told him to keep the boards, leaving him with the most impressive quiver in Raleigh. "I have to admit," he texted me once he got home, "it's pretty cool to look at all the boards leaning against the corner of the garage." They were a promissory note on future surf trips to the Outer Banks.

*The Edge of America*

# 11

## Surf Local, Sell Global
### Virginia Beach, Virginia

After we said goodbye to Alexander and Sasha, Zinnia and I drove to the Outer Banks Boarding Company in Nags Head. We had an appointment to meet the proprietor, Lynn Shell. Even though Lynn was born in North Carolina and had run a business in Nags Head for nearly twenty years, he grew up in and learned to surf in Virginia, specifically the tiny hamlet of Sandbridge near Virginia Beach. Since Virginia Beach was our next destination, I wanted to talk with Lynn about growing up there.

Lynn sat behind the counter at his shop working on merchandise orders when we arrived. He stuck his strong shaper's hands out in greeting. A flower-print Hawaiian shirt betrayed his time on the islands and in the industry. We sat at a picnic table next to the shop. Zinnia played with her phone. Her grandmother called in the middle of the interview. Zinnia will usually only chat with her grandma for five or ten minutes on the phone. This time, the half-hour call rescued her from the purgatory of another surf interview. I could hear her interviewing her grandma while I interviewed Lynn.

Lynn's family ran a beach concession in Sandbridge, in the 1960s and '70s. Their surname seemed to shape the family's destiny. The younger Shells worked as beach lifeguards and parking attendants. They rented beach chairs, umbrellas, and the canvas rafts that served as the first watercraft for so many southern surfers.

More than any other coastal town that I visited, except perhaps Pensacola, Virginia Beach was dominated by the military. World War II and Cold War mobilizations in nearby Hampton Roads, Virginia, led to a proliferation of bases. This included the Naval Station Norfolk, the largest navy base in the world, with nearly 150,000 service personnel, dependents, and civilian contractors. Seventy-five ships were berthed there. Nearly twice that many naval aircraft called Norfolk their home base. At the shipyard across the James River in Newport News, over 800 boats had been constructed in a century and a half of operations. The Langley Air Force Base employed almost 10,000 more military personnel just up the road. When President Franklin Roosevelt vowed that America would become the arsenal of democracy, Hampton Roads fulfilled that promise.

Virginia Beach became home to many of these military personnel and their families as well as the recreational arm of this sprawling military complex. Like many of the kids Lynn grew up with, Lynn Shell's dad worked for decades at a local base. This was only one way that the military influenced Lynn's life. As in other southern coastal towns, military personnel from California served as a vector to spread the contagion of surfing. Once the Shell boys saw folks riding the waves, they were hooked. Lynn quickly graduated from the Sandbridge shore break to heavier waves on the Outer Banks.

When Lynn offhandedly mentioned that one of his first shortboards was a Surfboards Hawaii model, I committed a cardinal sin of interviewing. I interrupted him and launched into the story about the recent rediscovery of my first Surfboards Hawaii twin fin in Alexander's garage. Finishing up this longwinded aside, I realized my mistake. I fumbled with my question list, trying to recover the flow of the interview. Lynn saved the day. His eyes were on fire with a glimpse of the past, a vision of paradise lost and found. He launched into his own story.

"My first winter on the North Shore of Oahu in Hawaii was the winter of '75–'76," Lynn began. It was a heavy winter to arrive at surfing's mecca. Bad vibes roiled the water. As Lynn remembered, a brash young crew of Australian pros came "bustin' down the door" to battle Hawaiians for supremacy on the North Shore. Lynn avoided most of the drama by keeping his head down and staying out of the fray.

Flat broke after spending most of his savings on the airline ticket, Lynn was subsisting on peanut butter when he lucked into a busboy job at the Kuilima, the major resort hotel on the North Shore that later became the Turtle Bay Hilton. He eventually worked his way into a lifeguarding gig at the resort. Meanwhile, he and his buddies had started to investigate the famous North Shore breaks that they'd only read about in surf magazines. Lynn surfed these fearsome breaks tentatively at first. Then he found a magic board.

Lynn and a roommate saw the new Ben Aipa model in a North Shore shop. The futuristic Sting shortboard had two rail lines. The front rail gracefully arced from the nose and then cut in a few inches about three-quarters

*Surf Local, Sell Global*

Lynn Shell shows off the magic board that he rode on
the North Shore of Oahu in the 1970s.
*Courtesy of the author.*

of the way back tapering into a beautiful swallow tail. The Sting could perform radical maneuvers but also handle the size and power of the North Shore. Lynn and his roommate bought an Aipa-shaped blank and finished the glassing themselves. "I surfed that board at Velzyland, Rocky Point, at Gas Chambers, at Camyland—all those places," Lynn recalled, staring off into the distance as if he could see each of the breaks on their best days. But Lynn's favorite place to ride that magic board was the world famous Sunset Beach. "There's such an arena at Sunset. It's a huge play-ing field," he said. "It's like a gladiator pit." The break truly tested Lynn as a young man, and he proudly remembered rising to the challenge on his Sting. He surfed the board without a leash, and it had met its match in the boulders at Rocky Point more than a few times. Lynn brought the board back to Virginia when he came home, but it was so beat-up he sold it to a cousin and moved on to newer surfcraft.

Two decades later, Lynn was talking to his cousin's daughter, a surfer in her own right. She casually mentioned that she had an old board with his name on it. It was the Aipa Sting in all its faded glory. Lynn promised to shape her a new board if she'd return the Sting. She agreed. Lynn painstak-ingly refurbished the Sting and displayed it in a place of honor in his shop.

That story animated the rest of our interview, as memories of a long career in the surf industry unspooled from Lynn. It's quite possible that our conversation would have flowed this way even if I'd never interrupted him with my lost-board story. The former sales rep was an avowed extro-vert. But while I'm sure Lynn would have told me many of the same stories eventually, they wouldn't have had the passion that the memory of that old board had elicited.

I worried about taking up too much of the busy shop owner's time, but he wasn't finished with me. As Zinnia shopped for a T-shirt, Lynn beck-oned me over to see the Sting. His eyes twinkled like a proud parent as he showed me the bright-yellow board. Was it my imagination or was it the same yellow as the Bingo Board?

Within fifteen minutes of leaving the surf shops and beach stores of Nags Head, we were passing through tobacco fields of Eastern North Carolina and southern Virginia. The culture shock gave me whiplash. It felt just as surreal to get onto the massive interstate loop around Norfolk an hour or so later. Traffic accidents and road rage signaled the end of the wondrous Outer Banks phase of our surf trip.

We were in striking distance of the Jamestown settlement, so I had to drag Zinnia there. A pilgrimage to Jamestown seemed warranted if only because Zinnia had read (and enjoyed!) a historical novel called *Blood on the River* about a boy living in the earliest days of the Virginia Colony. Though she said that she was only going to Jamestown to eat and check out the gift shop, I think she actually *wanted* to see the early colonial settlement.

When I teach my southern history class about Jamestown, one of the lecture sections is called "Up Shit Creek." The Virginia colonists wisely chose the James River for its navigability and then sailed upriver to found their settlement far enough inland to avoid conflict with the Spanish. Unfortunately, they also misjudged (or perhaps were simply unaware) of the awful water quality at their chosen site. As a brackish waterway with salt levels that change from season to season, the James River tainted the water table around the settlement with high salinity levels. Salt poisoning probably did not kill the colonists outright, but it may have made them lethargic and sickly, susceptible to other health problems. The tidal nature of the river also may have hurt the colonists who used the waterway and nearby privies to relieve themselves. While the river appeared to wash away this waste, its tidal swings may have in fact brought human and animal excrement floating right back to the settlement. Dysentery was just one reason for high mortality rates in Jamestown, but it was the most colorful one. As I explained to Zinnia, the colonists found themselves literally up shit creek. "Gross, Dad!" she said. But I heard, "Thanks for dropping such cool historical knowledge on me."

Zinnia appreciated the history lesson at Jamestown so much that she waited for an hour before demanding that we go to the Virginia Beach water park advertised in our hotel's lobby. Ever since the trip started, Zinnia had been begging to go to a water park. We passed one several times in Wilmington, and each glimpse of chlorinated fun further stoked her desire. The begging morphed into demands as the rain and mosquitoes plagued the camping in the Outer Banks. Add to that a forced march through the history of public sanitation in Jamestown, and the water park visit became mandatory.

Ocean Breeze, as its name implies, lies within a few miles of one of the largest natural "water parks" in the world—the Atlantic Ocean. Look, I'll admit it. As a kid, I loved water parks. Who doesn't love tall, twisted tubes of plastic sluicing with water and screaming kids? But now that I'd fallen in love with playing in the real ocean, Ocean Breeze ranked a distant second on my list of aquatic recreation priorities. Every time Zinnia begged to go to the water park, I'd respond with the classic parental parry: "We'll see." Secretly, I knew that Zinnia deserved it. She'd gamely circumnavigated a quarter of the United States with her crazy father, venturing to places that most Americans will never see, much less surf. It was payback time.

Even so, I lied. I told Zinnia we had to visit a surf shop, rent a board, and surf Virginia Beach before I'd even consider the water park excursion. Ripping her away from a Disney Channel show that she professed not to like anymore, I told her to throw on her bathing suit and rash guard to get ready for another epic southern surf session, Virginia-style. We drove south on Atlantic Avenue, passing not one but two surf shops. I thought the jig was up. Inane Dad patter distracted her. "Did you know that Virginia Beach is one of the oldest . . . ?" Then, we got to the water park entrance. She complained that it was cruel to drive so close to heaven only to enter hell. "I know," I responded, "but the best surf shop happens to be down this road." When we finally parked next to all of the other families with kids frothing at the nirvana of funnel cakes, Dippin' Dots, and nautically themed rides, joy spread across Zinnia's face. "I won!" she exclaimed.

Neptune's Revenge isn't just a water slide; it's a cosmic joke on parents that comes with a wicked case of athlete's foot, an ear infection, and a massive hole in the wallet. Like most water parks, Ocean Breeze has a wave pool. This million-gallon monstrosity periodically pulses with the most anemic of swells. Their impotence offers only a maddening simulacrum of the real thing, resulting in the surfer's worst nightmare: a supercrowded lineup without rideable waves. Catching my disdain, Zinnia said she "hated" wave pools, although she exhibited the lemming-like response to enter the pool when the first notes of Queen's "We Will Rock You" blared over the loudspeakers, signaling the start of the ocean motion.

As we bobbed up and down, Zinnia and I had a surprisingly frank discussion of the pros and cons of Kelly Slater's Surf Ranch, which is one of the first modern wave pools to produce not just rideable, but perfectly rippable surf more than 100 miles from the ocean in the town of Lemoore, California. The wave ranch cost $30 million to design and build. The 2,000-foot-long-by-500-foot-wide pool uses a massive hydrofoil machine to generate waves that break about head high. By altering the pool's bathymetry, Slater and his team were able to sculpt waves that offered carvable sections, hollow tubes, and steep ramps for aerial maneuvers. In short, Slater's artificial wave was a miracle of modern hydrodynamic engineering.

The wave ranch, and wave pools in general, intrigued Zinnia. With youthful enthusiasm, she fully embraced new technological innovations.

As we bodysurfed the manufactured chop at the Ocean Breeze water park, Zinnia ticked off the advantages of waves pools. "You can see the bottom," she said. "There are no crabs, jelly fish, sting rays, or sharks." Best of all, she liked the idea that the folks that run the pool "can make the waves whatever size and shape you want." In other words, Zinnia liked the control that wave pools offered. They limited the scary variables that had daunted her from our first outing in the ocean.

The coach at a surf camp that Zinnia attended in the summers had actually surfed Slater's wave ranch. Ian "Big Dog" Glover was an Ocean Beach regular in San Francisco, a man-child as happy in the company of forty-five stoked groms in the summer as with a crew of heavies charging winter swells. How Big Dog got a golden ticket to the wave ranch (rumored to cost thousands of dollars *per hour*) on a middle-school teacher's salary, I'll never know. He had friends in high places, evidently. Big Dog's social media posts about surfing the wave ranch (that is, influencer advertising) further fueled Zinnia's belief that Kelly Slater's team had built a surfer's paradise. I still had my doubts.

One year younger than Kelly Slater, I'm on the cusp of becoming a cranky old man. Okay, I may be a wee bit past the cusp. I initially reacted to the stories about Kelly's pool with dismissive skepticism. I've been reading surf magazines and websites long enough to realize that rumors of the "perfect" artificial wave have long been greatly exaggerated. Then Slater started to release videos of himself tearing the wave to shreds and getting barreled. Sure, the wave looked cool, but it was Kelly riding it. He could probably make the Ocean Breeze wave pool look epic. The more videos that came out, the more I reconsidered my gut reaction. Could this be a solution to all of those flat, gutless days when we wait for the ocean to awake? As kids, surfers create thousands of perfect artificial waves, doodling in the margins of their school notebooks. Slater, whose surfing wizardry had already earned eleven world titles, had conjured real waves from the doodles.

Professional contests held at the wave ranch revealed both the possibilities and limitations of the artificial wave. Standardization of each wave meant that surfers could plan "routines" like gymnasts, skaters, or snow boarders. This made for impressive tricks that grew more awe-inspiring as the world's best got the feel for the wave. Twelve-second tube rides—nearly unimaginable at most ocean breaks—became the norm as surfers could time exactly when the wave would bowl up and schedule their entry into the barrel. The suspense lay in whether a surfer would execute the move or barrel as well as the heat leader. Yet taking the chance out of when waves came and how they broke made for surprisingly humdrum viewing. If the wave pool allowed surfers to take fate into their own hands, the loss of serendipity dramatically undermined, well, the drama. Much of Kelly Slater's own professional career had been driven by a seemingly magical connection to the ocean. He won innumerable heats at the final horn as the perfect set wave rose up from nowhere, allowing the champ to execute the surfing equivalent of a Hail Mary pass.

As the debate about the merits and demerits of the wave ranch raged in the media, it became a blood sport online—the way controversies big and small devolved into digital shouting matches within seconds. To some, Slater's pool could save the sport, making it advertising-friendly for broadcasts and syphoning off the hoards of inland residents who invaded breaks every weekend. To others, a "perfect" artificial wave represented the logical conclusion to the commercialization of surfing that had been selling off portions of its soul year after year to multinational corporations. After debating the merits of the wave ranch with Zinnia, I remained unconvinced that it was the answer to surfers' prayers. But I had to admit that it was no sign of the apocalypse. I decided to remain agnostic on the Surf Ranch until Kelly invited me down for a session.

Two overpriced hamburgers, a sunburned scalp, and 342 rides later, Zinnia had finally had her fill of Ocean Breeze. If I'm being honest, I had fun too. I worried that the slides would tweak my back. They didn't. I feared the lines would stretch miles long. They didn't. I was sure that the other kids and parents would be pushy and aggressive. They weren't. In fact, everybody at the park was nice and laid-back. We waited only a few minutes for each ride that weekday morning. The slides felt awesome. It was a blast. Maybe teenagers aren't the only ones who need to get back in touch with their inner child.

In addition to the usual nautical themed decorations that festooned the fences and walls of the Ocean Breeze, the park's designers had nailed up real surfboards—some painted garish colors and others with shark bites cut out of the rails. The one thing that these boards had in common—they were all shaped by the folks at Virginia Beach's own Wave Riding Vehicles. The largest manufacturer of surfboards on the East Coast, Wave Riding Vehicles (or WRV) had just celebrated its fiftieth anniversary before Zinnia and I arrived. An interview with Virginia Beach shaper Bill Frierson turned into a primer on WRV.

This 1963 movie poster suggests that the surfing community in
Virginia Beach was well-established by the time Bill Frierson and
Les Shaw took over Wave Riding Vehicles in the mid-1970s.
*Courtesy of the author.*

Bill Frierson and his future WRV partner, Les Shaw, were both navy brats. Frierson had picked up surfing when his dad was stationed at Coronado in Southern California. By the time his dad retired from the service and settled in Virginia Beach in the mid-1960s, Frierson was good enough that he easily worked his way into the lineup at the old Steel Pier. Although the city tore down the storm-damaged pier in the 1970s, that break at First Street remained the proving ground for young hotshots.

Founded in 1967 just a few years after the Friersons moved to Virginia Beach, Wave Riding Vehicles hired the California kid to fix dings and eventually to shape boards designed by the company founder, Bob White. Frierson threw himself into the work, shaping twenty-five boards a week at a breakneck speed. One day, he had enough. "I was sitting there on my little stool in the shaping room," he said. "I'd pulled an all-nighter and had number twenty-four on the rack. It was just about finished when the boys started coming in for work that morning." That was it, Frierson told the boss, "I'm not going to be doing twenty-five again; I'm going to do what I can do." Looking back, he realized, "That was the beginning of my shaping with my own design thoughts."

Young enough to embrace the shortboard revolution, Frierson chafed at his mentor's allegiance to older designs that had inaugurated the Wave Riding Vehicle line. Frierson continued to shape for WRV and other shops on and off, but he eventually moved down to the Outer Banks to open his own business. His wife, Grace, ran the books, and they started a family. Kitty Hawk waves beat Virginia Beach almost any day of the week, and even though the Friersons didn't make much money, life was good.

Frierson heard that WRV wasn't doing well financially. Then, one day in 1974, the Friersons were driving up to deliver some boards in their old Ford pickup with the camper shell. Bill saw his buddy Les Shaw driving the opposite direction and pulled over to chat. "They're selling WRV!" Les shouted. Bill and Les immediately offered to buy the business. Frierson's share cost $1,500 (minus $750 they owed him for boards that he had shaped). For $750 he bought half of a company that a few decades later would be worth millions. Not a bad investment.

At WRV, Frierson ran surfboard manufacturing, while Shaw handled retail. Grace Frierson continued to do the books. During the slow, early years, Frierson recalled sitting at the counter playing guitar to pass the time in their hole-in-the-wall shop at the corner of Norfolk and Cypress Avenues. Business wasn't slow for long. Located right on the route that surfers took to get to the main break at First Street, WRV became *the* surf shop in Virginia

Beach. They built a surfboard factory in a cheap industrial neighborhood, where Frierson once dodged a bullet fired by their biker gang neighbors. The budget was so tight in the 1970s, they joked at the surfboard factory, "Would you rather buy resin or groceries?" I imagine Grace Frierson didn't find that one so funny.

As the retail side of WRV took off in the 1980s, so did board manufacturing. Frierson took pride in his designs, but he had no problem giving up control to other shapers in order to grow the business. He hired folks like Lynn Shell to shape for him. Eventually, Frierson (and Shell) would embrace new technologies shunned by many of their peers. By the 1990s, Frierson struggled to keep up with orders for nearly 3,000 WRV boards a year. When two Southern California entrepreneurs came to WRV to pitch a surfboard shaping machine, Frierson saw the hours of labor that automation could save. He'd upload his designs into the machine, and finish the rough shape by hand. As computer technology advanced, those machine shapes got better and better. Bill Frierson was no John Henry. He wouldn't fight the future. Using a shaping machine seemed like a no-brainer to Bill. Not everyone agreed.

The debate about machine shapes mirrored the wave pool wars. When both shaping machines and wave pools were in their infancy in the 1970s, the boards and swells they produced were so much lower quality that it was relatively easy to be a purist and reject artificiality. As the technology caught up with the engineers' visions, however, arguments about the quality of machine-shaped boards and wave pools became moot. The purists took their last stand on authenticity, spirituality, and "soul"—decidedly slippery concepts. This metaphysical crisis over automation and authenticity in surfing paralleled larger cultural concerns about our relationship with technology in an increasingly digital age. Was technology making humans irrelevant? How would the real world compete with virtual ones? Could we find God in our machines?

When he was at Wave Riding Vehicles, Bill Frierson made peace with shaping machines. He had to. His hole-in-the-wall surf shop had become a huge company by the mid-1990s with a second surfboard factory in the Outer Banks and retail stores in Virginia, North Carolina, and Hawaii. Ultimately, the WRV brand went global, adding stores in Puerto Rico, Japan, and even a tiny outpost in South Africa. By then, Frierson was gone. He sold his half of the business to his partner Les Shaw in 1997. Frierson used the proceeds of that sale to set himself up as a sole (soul?) proprietor, making a much smaller number of hand-crafted boards once again. "I think I was the first guy on the East Coast to use a machine," he told me. "And now I puff up my chest and say, 'I don't use the machine!'" Bill laughed at his newfound self-righteousness.

~~~~~~~~~~~~~~~~~~~~~~~~~~~~~~~~~~~~~~~~~~~~~~~~~~~

Zinnia and I went to rent a board at the 17th Street Surf Shop. I asked for a fiberglass board. The guy at the counter told me that they only rented soft-tops. It just didn't make sense to rent ding-able boards to beginners. (He studiously avoided the word "kook," but we both knew what he was thinking.) At the beginning of summer, the rental quiver was brand spanking new. Even thought they were soft-tops, the rentals were a step up from the Wavestorm in terms of both shape and maneuverability. They were perfect for the "poor" surf that the forecasting website predicted.

I had learned something surprising about the relationship between surf shops and internet forecasting on this trip. Natural Art owner Scott Busbey told me that forecasting sites hurt his Outer Banks shop worse than competition from online retailers like Amazon. Sites like Surfline and Magicseaweed actually limited inland surfers' trips to the beach and even kept locals on the couch when they once trusted only their own eyes.

Hunting for waves once made surfers weather nerds. Coast Guard storm reports, NOAA buoy readings, even the local weatherman or woman dancing to a strange, herky-jerky rhythm in front of a green-screen map helped predict incoming swells. A phone call to the local shop early in the morning would confirm such prognostications or prove them wrong. When surfers returning from the beach saw boards on top of a car driving the opposite direction, they gave a thumbs-up (or down) as a final judgement. If you planned a surf trip, you packed musical instruments, books, and hope along with a quiver of boards, embracing the inherent fickleness of fate and the ocean. No longer.

Once a dark, mysterious art, surf forecasting in the twenty-first century swung decidedly in the direction of science. Isobars and intervals replaced the finger in the wind. Forecasters tracked storms as large purple blobs of intense weather patterns marching across the open ocean. Computer models predicted with impressive precision how big the waves would be on a certain day, or even hour, a week into the future. They could also foretell the direction and intensity of the wind at your local break. Such predictive power meant big business, as thousands of surfers eyeballed these websites and their accompanying ads for beer, trucks, board shorts, wetsuits, and the like. That business bled some surf shops nearly dry.

Back in the day, Scott Busbey explained, "You were just getting in the car and you were going. If the surf was one foot, you surfed one-foot surf. And you'd probably have fun. Maybe if it was four-foot, you surfed all day, but if it was one foot, you'd surf for two or three hours and you came in and then you went to the shop and maybe you bought a T-shirt or maybe you bought a bar of wax or whatever." The surf forecasting sites let you "know before you go," but often times, you no longer went. "Until they forecast a really good surf, nobody moves," Busbey concluded. Surfers had traded away serendipity for certainty. We responded to the website forecasts like Pavlov's dogs. We salivated (and surfed) only when they whistled.

The websites hadn't whistled, but Zinnia and I were going to get wet regardless. We could have gone to the main break at First Street. Instead, we opted for the random spot a block from our hotel. The waves weren't exactly firing, but gentle rollers broke on a sandbar far enough out from the bobbing tourists that I could give Zinnia free rein with the rental board. In fact, she demanded that I *not* push her into any waves. She was going to paddle for all of these by herself. She caught ten to twelve waves alone as I shivered on the sandbar, cheering every time she caught one. You could see the envy on the faces of tourists who didn't surf every time my daughter popped up. "Oh, that kid's cool!" Their eyes seemed to say. I agreed.

The waves were too small to carry me more than a few feet, so after two or three attempts, I handed the board back to its new master and continued my role as cheerleader from the sandbar sideline. Zinnia paddled for one particularly promising wave that was around thigh high, one of the biggest of the afternoon. She stayed on her belly until it broke, before popping up and connecting the ride all the way to the shore, beaching it triumphantly. It was her best ride by far. Paddling back out, she was hard on herself, disappointed that she hadn't popped up sooner. "Dad, that wave actually had a pretty good face, and I blew it." She hadn't, *and* she sounded like a real surfer.

As we carried the board back to the hotel, we didn't see any other surfers heading out for a session in the tiny evening glass. If we had, I would have shot them a thumbs-up for sure. It was far from "poor," despite the forecasters' predictions.

~~~~~~~~~~~~~~

When Zinnia and I went to rent a board at the 17th Street Surf Shop, we got a lead on one last Virginia Beach interview. I told the shop manager about our trip and my project to interview southern surfers. He handed me a flier for the local surf camp run by a former Quiksilver Team rider named Jason Borte. The ad included Jason's cell number. "Call him," the manager said. Five hours later, I set up my recorder on the porch outside Jason's girlfriend's house. Low-flying military jets frequently interrupted our conversation. "That's the sound of freedom," the Virginia Beach local joked after a particularly deafening, *Top Gun*–style flyover.

Jason Borte's name rang a bell, but I couldn't remember why. Then it came to me. Just before I left on the trip, I bought Kelly Slater's autobiography, *Pipe Dreams*. Jason cowrote the book based on hours of interviews with the world champ. This was as close as I was ever going to get to an interview with Slater, and it wasn't *that* close. No matter, the Virginia Beach pro had a damn impressive career in his own right.

Like Kelly Slater, Jason Borte came of age in the hypercompetitive surfing world of the 1980s. Yet Jason's first forays into the water gave little inkling that he would have a long professional career. "I feel like for at least a year I was a total kook," he admitted. Even though his older brother and some of his friends surfed, Jason bemoaned that fact that "no one was teaching me anything. It was just trial and error." He wore out VHS tapes of surfing videos like the *Off the Wall* series. For surfers growing up in the eighties, these videos served as tutorials on the stylish moves of pros like Santa Barbara champ Tom Curren, who achieved godlike status during that era.

Aspiring to an unlikely professional career of his own, Jason bought his first custom surfboard from the town drunk, Ronnie Mellott. When he was sober, Mellott was a solid surfer and shaper. Unfortunately, sobriety was not his natural state. A profile in the local paper noted that the colorful character was known for two things—his "party lifestyle" and skill with a board. Riding Mellott's custom five-foot, four-inch twin fin, Jason Borte graduated from kook to surfer. He quickly ascended the First Street pecking order. Within just a few years, Jason turned pro, riding boards shaped by local luminaries like Lynn Shell, Bill Frierson, and others. In 1985, Borte placed third in the East Coast Championships, behind a rising star from Cocoa Beach named Kelly Slater. The young surfers won spots on an East Coast All-Star team and would eventually both earn sponsorships from Quiksilver.

While other friends surfed just for fun, Jason threw himself wholeheartedly into competing. "In the eighties," he explained, "if you wanted to surf and make it your life, you did contests. I knew if I didn't succeed competitively I was going to have to get a real job." Competition consumed him. Every session became a heat whether he had a jersey on or not. "I could really never go out without there being some kind of competition," he said. "Someone would paddle out that was doing pretty well, getting some waves, and all of a sudden I would snap into this other mode where I'm like, 'Okay, now it's on.' I couldn't help it. I had to get competitive and feel like I got the best of that person."

Jason surfed competitively for decades. He was affiliated with Quiksilver from age fifteen until he turned thirty-five, an impressive run by any standard. When I asked Jason about his pro career, however, he downplayed his accomplishments. With mock bravado, Jason joked that he won the championship of the East Coast Pro Tour the year before it folded. In other words, he remained the reigning East Coast champ.

As his competitive career wound down, Jason shifted focus to surf journalism, becoming the East Coast editor for *Surfer* and the short-lived swell.com. A feature on Kelly Slater in *Surfer* won him the gig to cowrite the champ's autobiography. Although the book did give Kelly's backstory, it largely chronicled his competitive career, reflecting both the era in which it was written and Kelly's own laser-like focus on winning world championships.

Jason continued to surf and win contests into his forties, but trophies lost their luster for him. After reading an article in *The Surfer's Journal* about how lifelong wave riders rarely let go of the sport completely, Jason decided to quit cold turkey for an entire year. He wrote a blog describing his self-imposed exile from the ocean and how it forced him to reflect on the meaning of surfing in his life. As he told me about the challenges completing this experiment, I said it sounded like another contest—a heat against time itself. "Yeah, he said, "you're probably right. It's probably the last competitive thing I do."

# 12

## Castles Made of Sand
### Ocean City, Maryland

Due north of Virginia Beach and across the Chesapeake Bay from Washington, D.C., the Delmarva Peninsula hides in plain sight from most Americans. The fat finger of land includes jurisdictions of Delaware, Maryland, and Virginia. A mashup of these states gave the peninsula its distinctive name: Del-Mar-Va. Marylanders call it the "Eastern Shore" because of its orientation to the Chesapeake Bay. I always preferred Delmarva, which sounded like a forgotten Greek goddess.

The first settlements in Delmarva were some of the oldest in British North America. With fertile land and access to water transportation, many of the farms and plantations on the peninsula relied on slave labor. Frederick Douglass and Harriet Tubman were born into slavery in Delmarva, but fled to secure their freedom. Douglass forged the stories of his time there into powerful weapons for the abolitionist cause. Tubman returned many times to spirit away fellow slaves. Even though Delaware and Maryland did not side with the South during the Civil War, Confederate flags still flutter atop poles throughout Delmarva. The peninsula's history, culture, and geography point southward.

The coastal capital of Delmarva is Ocean City, Maryland. More than the rural hamlets on the peninsula, Ocean City represents a true hybrid of northern and southern cultures. In the summers, the resort town attracts vacationers from Baltimore and Washington as well as Ohio, Pennsylvania, and West Virginia. The Ocean City boardwalk resembles Atlantic City, New Jersey, more than the less populous beach communities further south. The water is also relatively cold throughout the year, since the Gulf Stream veers away from North America far below Maryland.

If Delmarva isn't exactly known for its surf, the region does boast miles of beach breaks that catch occasional swells from hurricanes and nor'easters. Unfortunately, most of the year sees small, disorganized wind swell up and down the peninsula's Atlantic Coast. In other words, Delmarva waves break as inconsistently as everywhere else Zinnia and I had visited along our trip. As an added bonus, the water felt about ten degrees colder. I rubbed my hands together in gleeful anticipation—and also to warm up.

Zinnia and I went through the Maryland suburbs just north of Washington to pick up my wife and her mom for this final leg of the trip. Grandma Ruthie had been going to Ocean City for decades. My in-laws grew loyal to an imposing hotel at the north end of the boardwalk called the Dunes Manor. Although the hotel prided itself on its "Victorian style," the pink high-rise reflected more the architectural aesthetics of Ronald Reagan's presidency in the 1980s than the reign of Queen Victoria a century earlier. The founder of the place, Thelma Conner, infused her boxy modern structure with hints of historical charm—tea time in the afternoon, sing-along piano performances in the evenings, and Eastern European bellhops to welcome the guests. Okay, the Transylvanian accents of the seasonal workers brought in every summer seemed a little incongruous with the 1880s/1980s posh Victoriana, but they brought their own Old World charm.

By the time Grandma Ruthie accompanied us to Ocean City on the surf trip, she struggled to walk the boards with a bum knee. Even the Dunes, which held so many happy family memories for Ruthie, had lost its luster. The decades since the 1980s had seen the once chic establishment fade into slightly shabby disrepair. In a way, the wear and tear did what a decorator with oversized shoulder pads in the 1980s had been unable to accomplish—created a real, historic feel to the place. Best of all, the Dunes Manor was close to Chauncey's Surf Shop, where we could rent a board to ride the rebel swell one last time.

Before I began interviewing folks, I assumed that I would be excavating long-buried stories of southern surfing. Instead, I found that many of the surfers had already chronicled their own history. They wrote books, made films, and curated museum exhibits to document surfing in their communities.

No one was more dedicated to this task than Will Lucas. Growing up in the D.C. area, Will learned to surf in Ocean City. By the time I contacted him, Will had retired to Melbourne Beach, Florida, where he made surf documentaries. Will's wife, Karen, answered the phone with more than the usual skepticism of calls from strangers. "Will got some bad news today," Karen said. I recognized the solemn tone. Will's doctors had just given him a devastating prognosis for the cancer that he had been fighting. He agreed to talk, but the diagnosis weighed heavily on him.

Will and Karen's well-appointed house stood just a few blocks from the Atlantic Ocean. I would never have guessed that the bear of a man who met me at the front door was sick. He reached out to shake my hand with a strong grip. The sun gleamed off Will's bald head, a bushy mustache all that remained of the freak flag he proudly flew in the 1970s. Will motioned for me to follow him out to an island-style lanai next to a small pool.

We started with the life of a happy-go-lucky teenager who fell in love with the ocean in the 1960s. After high school, Will surfed and gigged with rock bands. The Vietnam War interrupted that carefree life. Sleeping in one Saturday, Will awoke to a knock from his older sister. "Go away. I want to sleep!" he shouted, burying his head beneath the pillow. "No, get up," she insisted. "I've got a piece of mail here for you." Will's sister had a letter in one hand and a shot of whiskey in the other. "Drink this," she said, extending the shot glass. "I'm not drinking at eleven in the morning," he protested. It was an order. Will downed the whiskey. Then, he opened the draft notice.

Will waxed nostalgic about his trip along the Pacific Coast before heading to Vietnam. From the deck of the transport ship, Will watched swells roll by and fantasized about riding them as they broke along the mythical California coastline. When he arrived in Vietnam, Will quipped that the only resistance facing his unit was a platoon of prostitutes. An abortive trip to surf at Vung Tau ended when Will and a buddy lost all of their money to a couple of local con artists. He surfed in Hawaii for the first time on leave. His sister even met him in Oahu and snapped pictures of him.

Will sugarcoated his wartime experiences in letters home to his parents, and I realized that he was also doing this during our conversation. Without too much prodding, however, he spoke of his work as a radio man in an engineering unit that spent months doing the dangerous, dirty work of constructing an infantry base. He spent the rest of his tour operating around an abandoned French rubber plantation. Land mines littered the grounds, and insurgents from the National Liberation Front (commonly called the Vietcong) ambushed the American soldiers when they ventured far from the plantation house. Will remarked on the surreal dichotomy of the place. "You've got combat all around you, and you've got this beautiful mansion with a swimming pool."

The Maryland surfer eventually circled back to the story of his leave in Hawaii. This time, it wasn't a tale of fun in the sun. A week before Will went to Hawaii, a buddy in his unit traveled there on the way to see his newborn son. Will wanted to ask all about Hawaii, but he bit his tongue. His friend talked for hours about becoming a father and holding his son in his arms for the first time. Will flew to Hawaii a few days later. While he was surfing, his unit came under attack. Three of his buddies didn't make it. One was the new father. Years later, Will tried to track down the son, but the kid had disappeared into a life on the streets. Will saw both the father and son as casualties of Vietnam. Exposure to Agent Orange meant that Will might one day join them.

After the war, Will worked his way up from warehouse stocker to vice president of a Maryland company, while raising a family and taking weekend surf trips. With his kids grown and retirement on the horizon, surfing took center stage in Will's life again. He moved to Florida so he could surf more. "Although I'm not surfing much this year because of my cancer," he told me, "up till a year ago I was in the water three, four days a week." With his diagnosis, days in the water became more precious. "I hate to use the word 'escape,' but you just kind of get lost in [it]. When you're out surfing, you're not worrying about . . . anything else. You're in the moment and that's how it is for me. It's therapeutic."

Will started interviewing fellow surfers in Maryland in the late 1990s. It became a labor of love. Will interviewed nearly 200 people. I asked him why. "Just out of curiosity," he said. "Being drafted and being away in '66 and part of '67, so much went on during that period that I didn't know about. And so, it was really curiosity. Who were these people who were surfing in Ocean City? What were their names? What were their stories?" His wife asked him why he kept doing it when he was barely breaking even on documentary sales. "It was never my intention [to make money]. I just wanted to get this stuff out there before these people die, before their stories go away. It's a passion for me."

I felt an instant connection to Will Lucas. Here was a surfer, musician, and historian who had led a strangely parallel life to my own, just a generation removed. This made his devastating prognosis strangely personal for me, even though we had just met. Will Lucas paddled out for the last time

Will Lucas leans into a bottom turn in Florida during the 2010s.
*Photo by and courtesy of Walker Fischer.*

about six months after our interview. Will was wheelchair-bound near the end, and his wife, Karen, rolled him to the beach to watch surfers riding waves. Being a spectator wasn't as good as surfing, but it was a hell of a lot better than the other alternative. Will died a year after we spoke. I hope my project honors his legacy in some small way.

One year younger than Will Lucas and twenty-five years older than me, Randy Dodgen had always been one of the hardest chargers I knew. The near-drowning at Ocean Beach forced him to face his own mortality, but it hadn't really slowed him down. In the years immediately following the incident, I'd still get calls at dawn to surf. "Raaaaaandy!" my wife and daughter would sing in a mocking chorus when the phone rang at that hour.

Then, a few years before Zinnia and I took our southern surf trips, I noticed something strange during these early morning sessions. Randy and

*Castles Made of Sand*

I would hit the shore break together, but then he would lag behind. When he made it out to the lineup, he'd be huffing and puffing. The change happened so gradually that it didn't register at first. "I must have gotten lucky to get out before that set," I rationalized. After Randy caught his breath things would return to normal. He'd turn on the bigger waves, make the drop, lean into a deep bottom turn, carve up onto the open face, and then head down the line. All was right with the world. But paddling back out would leave him winded again.

Just as Randy began to lose paddling power, he also struggled biking up San Francisco's infamous hills. One day, on a road ride with another friend, he felt more winded than usual. His chest tightened. He waited a minute, caught his breath, and rode home. Then, he went to the hospital. The doctor told Randy that he was lucky to be alive and scheduled emergency heart surgery the next day. Had Randy been surfing, he could have suffered a heart attack and drowned.

Within three or four months of the surgery, Randy returned to the water. He regained strength and stamina. Paddling left him less winded. Now, however, his takeoffs were shaky. He became tentative, letting larger sets roll through and passing up waves that he would have sailed into a few years earlier. When he made the drop, he could still execute a graceful bottom turn, but it was not nearly as deep. He was just as happy to straighten out and ride to the beach. Our sessions together grew less frequent. If the surf broke over five feet, Randy had errands or other plans. I missed surfing together, crowing about the best rides, and sharing a laugh at the worst wipeouts. On a rational level, I understood Randy's growing reluctance to surf OB. We chatted briefly about his declining interest in bigger waves, but much went unsaid.

After charging so hard through his fifties and sixties, Randy came to terms with his limits. He dialed back the surfing quite naturally, offering self-deprecating jokes about his ability on the smaller days when we paddled out together. He found pleasure in catching a single wave in particularly difficult sessions or treasuring the beauty of the rare, warm days with gentle two-to-three-foot longboard waves. Maybe his takeoffs weren't as critical. Maybe his bottom turns weren't as deep. He didn't care. As I entered my own midlife crisis, Randy taught me that aging gracefully meant embracing a new relationship with the ocean and with life.

The dawn patrol calls came less often. The "Raaaaaandy!" chorus in my house stopped almost entirely. Instead, I was always the one to reach out, goading Randy into an early-morning session. "It's pretty small," my texts began, regardless of the swell size. When Randy's phone buzzed at dawn with an incoming text from me, his wife probably sang out, "Steeeeeeeeeve!"

~~~~~~~~~~~~~~~~~~~~~~~~~~~~~~~~

Skip Savage reminded me of the *Star Wars* character Yoda. I don't mean that Skip was three feet tall and green. But talking to him, I felt the same impatience that Luke Skywalker exhibited when training under the wizened Jedi master. Skip rocked a classic Vandyke beard that he stroked pensively. He drank coffee and chain-smoked throughout our interview. I knew that I was in trouble when he grilled me for fifteen minutes before I turned on the recorder. The Delaware native started the interrogation by asking how I felt about southern cities taking down confederate monuments. (I supported it. He did not.) When I asked Skip questions, he paused for a good fifteen to twenty seconds to consider his answer, all the while stroking that goatee and pulling long drags from his coffee mug or cigarette. Sometimes, he'd answer the question; other times, he'd toy with it like a cat with a blind mouse. The interview frustrated the hell out of me. It was also one of the most enlightening conversations from the entire trip.

In response to my standard first question about when he was born, Skip deadpanned, "I was born at a very young age." Thanks, Groucho. Eventually, he admitted that he was born in Rehoboth Beach, Delaware, at the end of World War II. Even though he grew up at the beach, Skip didn't learn to surf until his early twenties, when the Air Force stationed him in Florida. After the service, he headed back to Delaware to open a surf shop in the late 1960s. He ran Surf Shop East for about four years, but chafed at the responsibilities of being a sole proprietor. All he really wanted to do was surf.

In that era, Skip told me, traveling surfers would just shack up in the back room of his shop for weeks at a time. One of those surfers was the Pensacola teenager Yancy Spencer. Skip spent one blissful winter down in Pensacola, running a surf shop there and enjoying the warm water, before returning to his Delaware shop for the summer high season.

As I learned about Skip's ties to Florida, I thought about all of the connections between the southern surfers I interviewed. They had all surfed and lived around the region, building a network of friends. If I mapped these connections with pins and strings, it would look like the work of a conspiracy theorist, a web of lines from Texas to Alabama, Maryland to Florida, Virginia to North Carolina, South Carolina to California. It's a cliché to talk about surfers as a global tribe of wave hunters, but real ties bound southern surfers to one another and to their peers around the world.

Skip closed down the Delaware shop in 1971, moving through a series of odd jobs over the next quarter century to support his growing family. He sought a balance between surfing, work, and family, but the scales often tipped toward wave-riding. "If I had a job and I had to be there at nine and on the way to the job took me across the Indian River Inlet Bridge, the car would just turn into the parking lot and wouldn't turn up [at work] till midday or something," Skip explained, blaming these transgressions on his vehicle. That damn thing was always stocked with a board, wetsuit, fishing rods, and hunting equipment just in case it decided to take a detour before, during, or after work. "I'd come home sometimes and my wife would say, 'You've been surfing, haven't you?' I'd say, 'No, hon, I haven't been surfing!' And I'd have wax on my arm from carrying my board."

In the 1990s, Delmarva surfers of a certain age congregated a few miles north of the Ocean City boardwalk in the 62nd Street Longboarders' Club. They surfed, played music, ate barbecue, and drank together. Skip met Will Lucas and Karen Robbins in the club, swapping stories while they bobbed in the frigid mid-Atlantic beach break. Skip was the first of the crew to ditch Delmarva for the warmer waters of Florida's Space Coast in 1997. Will and Karen followed a few years later.

I asked Skip about how aging affected his surfing life. First, he explained that it inspired the move to Florida. Wearing wetsuits more than half of the year in Delaware and Maryland became a real grind as he got into his fifties. As he entered his sixties and seventies, Skip moved progressively farther from the beach. When I interviewed him, he lived in Cocoa on the mainland across the inlet from Cocoa Beach. "I think the last couple times I did surf," he admitted, "I had trouble getting up quick enough. When I go back out, I won't be able to surf like I used to be able to surf—just won't feel right." Skip didn't have any serious ailments like other folks his age, and he had every intention to continue surfing. "I wash my board off, clean it up, re-wax it and all that. I've got all the wetsuits in the world if I need one. I've got everything," he concluded with resignation. "I just don't have the gumption to get over there."

"Alright, Skip," I said, starting to wrap things up. "I don't have any other questions, so I appreciate you talking to me." Surfing Yoda stroked his Van-dyke disapprovingly and shot me a scolding look through a cloud of exhaled smoke. "Yeah, I don't know if I'm done." Chastened, I encouraged him to continue. "You probably saw my social life walk by here a few minutes ago," he joked, motioning with his cigarette toward one of the squirrels in his yard. "That's who I talk to." We laughed and kept chatting.

The interview turned into a Jedi training session. I half expected him to beat my recorder with a stick or force me to carry him on my back and levitate rocks in his yard. Skip schooled me on longboard techniques. He'd been riding longer boards much of his life, and I'd only just started. He had lots of wisdom to share about how to cross-step, which boards went with various types of waves, how to start with cheater-fives and work up to hanging ten. My mind wandered, as often happens to students when masters' lectures run long.

As Skip talked, I had an epiphany in the form of a musical analogy. What if shortboards were like guitars and longboards more closely resem-bled basses? I had started out playing guitar. When I shifted to bass, I still played it like a guitar. I noodled all over the fret board as if playing a low-end solo. Look at me, I thought, I'm Jaco Pastorius or Bootsy Collins. I'd shred through tunes, ripping as fast as I could up and down the scale. That was riding shortboards in a nutshell. Speed and radical maneuvers were the goal. Sure, you might throw a long power turn to reposition yourself on the wave, but speed remained the paramount objective. One day, I was playing bass in a band, and the drummer told me to quit noodling. "Listen to the kick drum," he ordered. "Play with it and around it." I learned to stop fight-ing the rhythm and start riding it. Skip's insights about riding longboards amounted to pretty much the same idea. Staying in the pocket on bass or a longboard was the key to stylish playing and surfing.

At the conclusion of the interview, Skip followed me out to my truck. He drew my attention to a personal mantra in gothic script on his calf, inked in the very place where one would attach a longboard leash. The tattoo read "Carpe Wavem."

~~~~~~~~~~~~~~~~~~~~~~

On trips to Ocean City, I often rode rentals from Chauncey's Surf Shop near the Dunes Manor Hotel. Chauncey Rhodes, the shop proprietor, comes from a family that has run surf shops in Ocean City for decades. Even though Ocean City has never produced a Kelly Slater, the waves on the Eastern Shore can get good, particularly when hurricanes or other storms approach the coast. I've ridden it overhead, woefully outgunned on egg-shaped rental boards.

No storms brewed anywhere near the Eastern Shore when we arrived for the final leg of our southern surf trip. The report actually called it flat, with a forecast of zero to one feet the entire time we were in town. My daughter found the castles, aliens, and windmills on the mini-golf courses along Philadelphia Avenue more enticing than the tiny surf. Zinnia had reached the end of her patience with the father-daughter surf trip. It was once again payback time. Payment came in the form of boardwalk junk food followed by nausea-inducing carnival rides and mind-numbing Skee-Ball games.

Unwilling to admit defeat, I picked up a board the night before our final day in Ocean City. At Zinnia's request and Chauncey's wise counsel, we rented an eight-foot soft-top. A lesser surfcraft than even the Bingo Board, the soft-top punctuated the kookish nature of our southern surf quest. It felt like Don Quixote's lance. Based on the surf forecast, I would have had just as much luck joisting at the mini-golf windmills as paddling out for one last session, but maybe the forecast was wrong.

Dawn dashed my hopes once more. Onshore wind continued to howl at first light. Our thin rash guards offered little protection from bracing water temps and the early morning chill. The tide drained almost to dead low by the time we hit the beach, leaving only a few inches of water on the closest sandbar where ripples were breaking. We endured a few raspberry-inducing wipeouts as the waves pitched nine to ten inches above the inner bar. Other than shell scratches and sand burns, we escaped the session relatively unharmed. The soft-top proved indestructible as Zinnia and I took turns beaching the thing. Finally, Zinnia had had enough. She demanded to get out of the water after forty-five teeth-chattering minutes.

As we walked back to Chauncey's with the rental board, a local guy came out of his apartment to walk his dog. I could see a quiver of boards in the window of his place. The guy had the look of a lifelong surfer. "Any waves today?" he asked, just making conversation. Standing there with a soft-top, I immediately started to worry about looking like a kook. "Nah," I grumbled, an octave lower than my regular speaking voice in a manly tone reserved for guitar stores and sports bars, "it was flat." "I'm sorry to hear it," he said.

Then, as he turned to walk away, I realized that wasn't the right answer to his question. Maybe it wasn't even the question that really mattered. "It's okay," I told him in my normal voice. "I pushed my daughter into some ripples, so we had fun." He smiled and said, "Cool." I realized, for the first time, that "cool" didn't sound all that different from "kook."

# By the Waters of Babylon

After the surf trip, I took time off from teaching to write. I walked Zinnia to school most days and picked her up in the afternoons. She told me about the rebellions large and small of the popular kids. I inoculated her against such rebellions with hours of *Star Trek*. Any kid who can tell you about Spock, Data, Worf, Dax, Quark, and the Borg has to be at low risk of a teen pregnancy, right? On the way to school one day, Zinnia said, "No offense, Dad, but we've been spending too much time together. I want to walk home from school by myself." It almost made me cry. It more than almost broke my heart.

Ever since Zinnia was young, my wife and I would sing her a lullaby before bed. When Zinnia was a baby, we sang "Rainbow Connection." As she got older, we started to sing a reggae tune called "Rivers of Babylon." I'm sure that my wife started this. She's much better versed in reggae than I am. I always sang the chorus wrong, referring to the "waters" of Babylon. Although I hadn't heard the reggae version before, the words sounded familiar. The song, it turned out, was based on the 137th psalm from the Bible.

In the scripture, the Hebrews have been captured and taken to Babylon, where their captors demand that they sing songs about Zion, their home. The Jewish people wept by the Babylonian rivers, unwilling to sing songs of their homeland while in captivity. In the reggae version by the Melodians, descendants of African slaves face a similar dilemma, having been ripped from their homes and brought forcibly to the New World in the Middle Passage. Adapting the song to Rastafarianism, the Melodians sing, "How can we sing King Alpha's song in a strange land?"

I sang this song to Zinnia hundreds of times. It became such a ritual that our dog, Django, would lie down in our daughter's room as soon as he

heard the first few bars. Sometimes, I'd play it on my guitar or Zinnia's uku-
lele, but most nights, I just sang it a cappella. Often, these performances
were less than inspired. Weak strains of the melody croaked from my
throat. The lyrics, once so passionate, devolved into a rote monotone. Still,
rituals sneak into your consciousness gradually altering your worldview.

One evening, the words of the song washed a sense of enlightenment
over me. Maybe I had gone surfing that morning and so the water became
the Pacific and Babylon became California. California had always been my
Promised Land, because of its bountiful surf, but it did bear some resemblance to Babylon. I sensed the strangeness of this new land—a strangeness measured in distance from my South Carolina home, my family and
friends, the magical places and myriad problems of the South that shaped
me. Much had been gained in moving to California, but these gains had
blinded me to what I had lost. I feared that this loss, this disconnectedness,
had kept Zinnia from understanding her southern heritage.

How could I sing this song in a strange land? A chorus of southern
surfers from Houston, Texas through Ocean City, Maryland helped, but
it would be fair to ask if they had the keys to the kingdom. In writing
about surfers from southern coastal towns, had I gone about this project
all wrong? After all, I had skimmed along the margins of the South rather
than investigating its interior. I had focused on a relatively marginal sport
instead of something more central to southern identity. Well, I'd argue that
you can't map a region without exploring its edges. You can't always see a
thing when you look directly at it. To sing of the South—in the words of
"Dixie"—you have to look away.

The Melodians counseled that the best way to sing in a strange land
was with "the words of my mouth, and the meditation of my heart." This
book contains those words and meditations. Surfing and writing became
my ways of articulating what it meant to be southern—of singing that song,
as best I could.

A few months after Zinnia asked me to stop walking with her to school,
she said, "Hey, Dad, are we going to go on another southern surf trip?" Yes,
I think we just might.

# Acknowledgments

I should have been writing about the history of the peanut butter and jelly sandwich. That was supposed to be my next book. Everyone said so. Maybe, someday, I'll write that book. But that book would have meant hours more in the archives away from my daughter who was growing up fast. So I wrote this book instead. Still, I want to start by thanking everyone who encouraged me to write PB&J history. That far-fetched idea made a history of southern surfing look downright sane.

Once I got the hairbrained idea to surf my way across the South, the first people I turned to were surf shop owners in the various places that I planned to go. Scott Busbey, Boog Cram, Sean Fell, Bill Frierson, James Fulbright, Tim McKevlin, and Lynn Shell answered all my questions and connected me to many of the other legendary local surfers in this book. If you are reading this book in Galveston, Pensacola, Charleston, the Outer Banks, or Virginia Beach, put the book down and go buy something at one of their shops—a bar of wax is good, a T-shirt is better, and a new board is better still!

As for the other people I interviewed for this book, I owe each and every one a huge debt of gratitude, whether their stories are featured in the book or not. Every surfer I spoke with helped me better understand our sport and the South. May the biggest set waves come directly to each of you in your next session and may the kooks gracefully give way as you style down the line.

I have to throw shakas to my surf buddies: Matt Walker, Chris Wyrick, Rene Hayden, Philip Estes, Alexander Krings, and of course, Randy Dodgen, who have surfed with me on quite a few big, beautiful days and a whole lot more small, terrible ones. The folks at the City Surf Project in San

Francisco and Big Dog Surf Camp in Marin get special shoutouts for doing great work in their respective communities and for letting me and Zinnia help teach the next generation of surfers. I want to give a very subtle nod of the head to all of the other Ocean Beach locals who've kept me company for the last twenty years. Thanks for the parking lot pep talks, hoots, hollers, and almost imperceptible head nods after good rides.

In the academic world, I found support from old friends and new ones. Chris Myers Asch and Jason Sokol read a rough draft of this manuscript that was much longer than the final version. They helped me refocus on the stories. For transcription and research support, I turned to Amanda Kreklau-Pipken and Lea Grgich. Thanks to the surf scholars (David Kamper, Jess Ponting, Mike Roberts, Angel Bucci, David Cline, Anne-Marie Debbané, Bill Nericcio, and Paul Wentura) for gathering smart and stoked wave riders from around the globe for the Impact Zones and Liminal Spaces conference at San Diego State University in 2019. Everyone I met at that conference inspired me to write this book, but I want to thank especially: Krista Comer, Kevin Dawson, Maia Dery, Scott Laderman, Todd LeVasseur, Michael Brown Parlor, Keith Plocek, and Lindsey Usher. For help with archiving the interviews, I want to thank all of the amazing folks at the Southern Historical Collection and Southern Oral History Program at the University of North Carolina.

My colleagues and friends at Sonoma State University tolerated my incoherent ramblings about this book for far too long, enduring annual slide shows about my summer vacations thinly veiled as academic talks. Although SSU couldn't (and shouldn't) have paid for the trips themselves, the School of Social Sciences Summer Stipends and the Social Science Undergraduate Research Initiative provided support for the research and writing of the book. A rare (and much appreciated) sabbatical gave me time to finish the first draft of the manuscript.

When I started to think about publishing this work, I immediately thought of the *Journal of Southern History* and UNC Press. At the *JSH*, Bethany Johnson and Randal L. Hall were excellent editors. At UNC Press, Lucas Church proved to be a kind advocate and thoughtful critic of this project, helping to shape the book in innumerable ways even as he wrestled with the professional and personal challenges facing many of us during a global pandemic. Doug Powell and Scott Laderman served as the peer reviewers for the book, giving me support and guidance at just the right time to finish the last round of revisions. Elizabeth Orange, Dylan White, and all of the other hardworking staff at UNC Press made the publication process run smoother than I could have hoped.

Finally, I turn to home. My wife, Carol Spector, gave me the love and support, time and freedom to take our daughter away from our San Francisco home for this surfing odyssey. To make matters worse, I did it during the foggiest, coldest, and windiest part of the year—summertime, when the living is decidedly not easy. Sure, our dog, Django, kept her company. But she could have easily told me "No, you're crazy" when I first broached the idea for these summer trips. Instead, she simply said, "Go have fun!" (She was definitely thinking "You're crazy," but true love is knowing when not to verbalize such thoughts.) Carol may not be a big character in this book, but she is the most important character in my life. There's so much more I could say about Zinnia Spector Estes. Anything that I write at this moment would only embarrass her, so I'll just say thanks for being the best daughter a father could ever have.

# Note on Sources

As a historian, writing without footnotes felt like performing acrobatics without a net or surfing without a leash. Of course, this was an illusion. *Surfing the South* is based on numerous sources about surfing, the American South, and oral history. These works inspired and informed *Surfing the South* in more ways than I can count.

I have a library full of books and magazines on surfing, which I mostly thumb through for pictures. Yet the words are just as powerful and evocative. William Finnegan's Pulitzer Prize–winning memoir *Barbarian Days* (2015) captures the experience of wave-riding like no other. The most comprehensive popular history of surfing is Matt Warshaw's 500-page magnum opus *The History of Surfing* (2010). Eminent scholars have written insightful and rigorous analyses of the sport. They include Krista Comer, *Surfer Girls in the New World Order* (2010), Kevin Dawson, *Undercurrents of Power* (2018), Scott Laderman, *Empire in Waves* (2014), Isaiah Helekunihi Walker, *Waves of Resistance* (2011), Peter Westwick and Peter Neushul, *The World in the Curl*, and Dexter Zavalza Hough-Snee and Alexander Sotelo Eastman, eds., *The Critical Surf Studies Reader* (2017).

I also benefited (that is, borrowed) from impressive state and local histories of surfing. These include Paul Aho, *Surfing Florida* (2014); Joseph "Skipper" Funderberg, *Surfing on the Cape Fear Coast* (2008); and John Hairr and Ben Wunderly, *Surfing NC* (2015). Exhibits, films, and interviews by John Hughes, Will Lucas, Sean O'Hare, Tony Sasso, and many others also informed this project.

Beyond surf histories, over a century of surf journalism, memoir, and fiction writing guided this project and kept me stoked on flat days. You can find vivid descriptions of the sport in Daniel Duane's *Caught Inside* (1997),

Kelly Slater and Jason Borte's *Pipe Dreams* (2003), Mark Twain's *Roughing It* (1872), and Allan Wiesbecker's *In Search of Captain Zero* (2002). Kem Nunn created his own genre of surf noir fiction, and I'd recommend all of his books, especially *Tapping the Source* (1984), *Dogs of Winter* (1997), and *Tijuana Straits* (2004). Perhaps it's not surf noir, but Paul Beatty's *The Sellout* (2015) casts a Black surfer from Southern California as its protagonist in a blistering satire of American racism. Finally, I throw a shaka to all of the photographers and writers for surf magazines and websites, including *Surfer, Surfer's Journal, The Inertia, Surfline,* and *Magic Seaweed,* as well as the now defunct *Surfing, Eastern Surf Magazine,* and Swell.com (RIP).

I've been reading southern history since my first class on the subject at Rice University in the early 1990s. For innovative general histories of the modern South, I relied on Jim Cobb's *The South and America Since World War II* (2011) and three excellent essay collections: Matthew Lassiter and Joseph Crespino, eds., *The Myth of Southern Exceptionalism* (2009); Byron Shafer and Richard Johnston, eds., *The End of Southern Exceptionalism* (2009); and Michelle Nickerson and Darren Dochuk, eds., *Sunbelt Rising: The Politics of Space, Place and Region* (2011). On southern sports, see Patrick B. Miller, ed., *The Sporting World of the Modern South* (2002); Charles Ross, ed., *Race and Sport: The Struggle for Equality on and Off the Field* (2006); and H. G. Bissinger, *Friday Night Lights* (2015). There is no better single work of southern environmental history than Jack E. Davis's brilliant and lyrical book *The Gulf* (2017). Finally, near the end of this project, my editor suggested that I read a cool book completely unrelated to surfing that might serve as a model for my own. Doug Reichert Powell's *Endless Caverns* (2018) explored very different southern spaces beneath the Appalachian Mountains with humor, thoughtfulness, and creativity that helped shape this book.

Oral history is as much a "natural art" as riding waves or shaping surfboards. It's also a lot harder than it looks. The best guide to interviewing is Don Ritchie's *Doing Oral History* (2003). For theoretical discussions of oral history, see Michael Frisch, *A Shared Authority* (1990); Alessandro Portelli, *The Death of Luigi Trastulli and Other Stories* (1991); and Robert Perks and Alistair Thompson, eds., *The Oral History Reader* (2015). Since this was my first foray into interviewing about sports, I relied on two insightful articles to guide me: Susan K. Cahn, "Sports Talk: Oral History and Its Uses, Problems, and Possibilities for Sports," in the *Journal of American History* (1994); and Fiona Skillen and Carol Osborne, "It's Good to Talk:

Oral History, Sports History and Heritage," *International Journal of the History of Sport* (2015).

Even more than reading, I found listening vital to the success of *Surfing the South*. For this project, I formally interviewed forty-three surfers—thirty-seven men and six women. The majority of the narrators were white, but I also interviewed African American, Latino, and Native Hawaiian surfers who hail from the South or call the region home. You can find transcripts and audio for these interviews in the collections of the Southern Oral History Program at the University of North Carolina. Not all of the people I interviewed are mentioned by name in the book, but they *all* influenced my thinking and writing about southern surfing. I can't thank them enough for sharing their stories with me. Without them, there would be no book.

# Interviewees

| | |
|---|---|
| Will Allison | Linda Grover |
| Mike Barton | Tom Grow |
| Jason Borte | Billy Hingle |
| Scott Busbey | Todd Holland |
| Scott Bush | John Hughes |
| Bobo Conde | Will Lucas |
| Hal Coste | Larry Martin |
| Mike Cotton | Tim McKevlin |
| Boog Cram | Lisa Muir |
| Melody DeCarlo | Dewayne Munoz |
| Clif Dodd | Michael B. Parlor |
| Randy Dodgen | Tom Proctor |
| Renee Eissler | Kaipo Robello |
| Sean Fell | Skip Savage |
| Walker Fischer | Lynn Shell |
| Foster Folsom | Stone Singleton |
| Lilla Folsom | Glenn Tanner |
| Bill Frierson | BJ Williamson |
| James Fulbright | Sharon Wolfe |
| Skipper Funderburg | Ben Wunderly |
| Gene Gabel | Mike "Tank" Young |
| Dave Grover | |

# Index

Italic page numbers refer to illustrations.